52 Ways to Protect *your* Teen

by

SUSIE VANDERLIP, CSP

INTUITIVE WISDOM PUBLICATIONS
3128 E. Chapman Avenue #112, Orange, CA 92869

52 Ways to Protect Your Teen

ISBN: 0-9744624-9-7

Senior editor Diane Armitage
Cover design by G.Go Creative, Gary Gomez
Inside layout/design by Patti Knoles

First Edition
10 9 8 7 6 5 4 3 2 1

Printed in the United States of America

"This is excellent reading for adults and teenagers."

"52 Ways *is trustworthy information, sound advice, and an excellent resource that parents and teenagers can use to make a great success out of this challenging stage of life.*"

– Dr. Art Ulene
Former NBC Today Medical Expert

"In my career as an educator and counselor, I've never seen a more valuable resource for parents."

"Susie Vanderlip's personal experiences and conversations with thousands of teens after her 'Legacy of Hope®' presentations have led to her keen insight into the hearts and minds of adolescents. As parents read this book, they will better understand the world from the eyes and emotions of teens and will learn down-to-earth strategies to build strong relationships with them – such relationships are the best protection parents can give their teens. In my career as an educator and counselor, I've never seen a more valuable, user-friendly resource for parents."

– Janice Christopher, Ed.D.
Assistant Superintendent of Pupil Services
Monongalia County School District; Morgantown, WV

"This book shows parents and teens how to meet their needs."

"In the book, 52 Ways, *Susie Vanderlip cleverly demonstrates how teens can meet their needs and how parents can meet their needs while keeping the lines of communication open between them. This eventually leads to young adults who take effective control of their lives and function as responsible citizens in the real world."*

– Corinne Pridham
President, National Association of Peer Helpers
President, Massachusetts Peer Helpers Association
Reality Therapy Certified, Faculty Member, William Glasser Institute

"She provided a roadmap for understanding the difficult challenges of adolescence."

"Susie provided a comprehensive and concise format for teens and their families to follow. She really left no stone uncovered. She succeeded in capturing the essential components of adolescent development and provided a roadmap for understanding their difficult challenges. She demonstrated broad insight into the mind of the adolescent allowing for a unique understanding of teenagers during their difficult times. She was able to address both the emotional and spiritual needs of the adolescent and family."

– Gary Ruelas, D.O., Ph.D.
Psychosomatic Medicine
Clinical Neuropsychology
Pediatric Adolescent Health Services

"Susie believes in those who have been left for lost."

"Susie Vanderlip is a beautifully refined and talented storyteller, caregiver and believer in those who have been left for lost. She will leave a lasting impact in the heart and soul of any and every community that invites her to share her stories."

– Alexandra Lopez, MA, CADC, SAC
Coordinator of Community Relations
District Substance Awareness Coordinator, Carteret Public Schools, Carteret, NJ

"Susie captivates both teens and adults."

"Susie captivates her audience of counselors, administrators, parents and teens with her practical suggestions on helping young people grow and realize their full potential. Dynamic, engaging and animated, Susie delivers a powerful message of the value of each and every individual. Regardless of one's background, past history or personal tragedy, each person is capable of great things and making healthy and positive choices in their lives."

– Joanne Silberman, Director
Nassau Counselors' Association, Inc., Nassau, NY

"You've served as a catalyst to mobilize our community at large."

"Susie, you not only help people better understand human struggles and how they happen, but you also help many know there are others who share their difficult issues. And then, in such a convincing, genuine manner, you convey hope – not only to those needing support to deal with their struggles, but also hope for staff who sometimes think the problems are too pervasive to address. You've served as an absolute catalyst to mobilize our community at large."

– Janice B. Christopher, Ed.D
Assistant Superintendent of Pupil Services
Monongalia County School District, Morgantown, WV

"Susie's contagious energy impacts today's youth on a whole new level."

"Susie's contagious energy and elevating humor impacts today's youth on a whole new level. Her inspirational stories leave them with a powerful message that motivates them to continue leading healthy, productive, drug-free lives."

– Jessica Czapleski
Special Events Coordinator
Drug Free Youth in Town, Miami, FL

"Your message is one the students want to hear."

"Your message arms teens with tools to help evaluate their choices and reach out for help."

– Lisa M. Silver
Elementary Principal
Chazy Central Rural School, Chazy, NY

"Now I know how to broach my teens on difficult subjects."

"As a mother of a 12- and a 14-year old, I couldn't put this book down. 52 Ways *gave me so many insights into raising my teens and offered me the tools I needed to bring up key subjects that I'd previously found difficult to broach with my teens."*

– Carol Stone
Lead Security Specialist, TCA, Orange County Airport
Working mother of two teenage children

"Susie's message goes beyond the simple recognition of pain."

"Susie's message goes beyond recognition of the varieties of pain our teens experience to a clear vision of the hope that comes with recovery. She makes a difference."

– Riley Regan
Executive Director, State of New Hampshire Department of Health & Human Services
Division of Alcohol & Drug Abuse Prevention and Recovery, Concord, NH

"Susie is extremely sincere and concerned for our young people."

"Not only is Susie an amazing performer who captivates teen audiences with her characters, but she is amazingly warm and giving. She is extremely sincere in her concern for young people dealing with the pressures related to alcohol and drug abuse and the resulting problems of neglect, abuse, teen pregnancies, and sexually transmitted diseases, to name a few."

– Anne Winters
Advisor/Teacher
Family, Career and Community Leaders of America
Fredericksburg, TX

"You give us hope."

"Susie, you touched the lives of so many kids at my school and you gave a lot of them hope because you gave them the chance to see that when things fall apart, you can put the pieces back together. You might not have what you began with, but you can make it be the best you want it to be, and you may end up with something better."

– A high school teen

About Legacy Performances

"Your visit accomplished a feat seldom seen."

"As professionals in the field of education, addictions or just taking care of others, we do yearly searches for a presenter that is going to actually make a difference in the minds of our delicate future; a speaker that truly defines the goals of preventative education.

"To do so an individual must be real ... have some true stories ... live by example. They also have to be loud and assertive ... they need to talk the talk ... and they need to look each member of the audience directly in the eye and not be afraid. They must interact individually with a thousand-member audience ... they must make the children feel truly special and they must engage the audience in a believable journey. You – Susie – were able to provide all of the above; a feat very seldom seen."

– Alexandra Lopez, MA, CADC, SAC,
Coordinator of Community Relations
District Substance Awareness Coordinator
Carteret Public Schools , Carteret, NJ

"There has never been a keynoter who moved the audience more."

"In the 11 years I have attended our state conference, there has never been a keynoter who received better evaluations, moved the audience more, or who received a standing ovation. Susie Vanderlip was truly awesome!

"Susie speaks directly to what is troubling America's kids and families today. She dances, acts and shares personal stories. She understands and cares deeply for people, for youth AND for the counseling professional. She communicates that understanding with clarity, conviction and an amazing repertoire of characters."

– Dr. Dan Windisch, President
Washington Counseling Association
Dupont, WA

"This was a life-changing, life-clarifying experience for us."

"On rare occasions, meaningful opportunities present themselves to high school principals whereby they are able to have a profound impact on the lives of their students. From my first exposure to the message and the messenger – Susie Vanderlip of Legacy of Hope® – I knew that I had happened upon one of these opportunities.

"The Legacy of Hope® was not an assembly we asked high school students to endure as is too often the case. It was not a performance we hoped they would enjoy. It was a life-changing and life-clarifying experience and, for some, a picture of what life yet can be."

– L. Paul Couture, Principal
Stevens High School, Claremont, NH

"In one afternoon, you gained the trust of two diverse generations."

Over the past 10 years, I've had the opportunity and responsibility to book many different speakers for various MADD programs. But without hesitation, I can assure you that you made an impact that is very difficult for me to put into words. Simply put, you touched every life at this year's TeamSpirit conference, both adults and youth.

"Your sincere nature and your ability to gain the trust of two diverse generations speak highly of the effort you put into life. Thank you for bringing your total being to a program that represents the essence of hope to so many families."

– Gabrielle M. Abbate
Assistant Executive Director
MADD, Rhode Island, Providence, RI

"Susie Vanderlip's presentation is worth more than 1,000 business meetings."

"Legacy of Hope® brought the focus of our group to one very fine point and gave us the energy to go about the business at hand – helping teens. Susie's presentation was worth more than 1,000 business meetings – it could not have been any better."

– Carol A. Neiman
Associate Executive Director for Professional Affairs
American Counseling Association, Alexandria, VA

"We're a stronger and better community because of you."

"Susie, I can still hear the echoes around our halls about how much the students enjoyed and benefited from your presentation. They were deeply touched and we have moved forward to provide support services to those who need them in the area of peer pressure and parent alcohol and substance abuse. You gave the students permission to speak about the difficulties and pain in their lives in a way that we always strive to accomplish."

"We are a stronger and better community because you were here."

– Gwen Cote
Principal
Seton Catholic Central
Plattsburgh, NY

"More people need to hear this message."

"Our goal was to bring something to our students that would build them up and give them hope in the midst of taking a look at their emotions and the behaviors that cause problems in their lives.

"We have had an overwhelming response from our students and the community.

I've had personal thank-you's and phone calls from parents, many of whom are asking how they might bring Susie back to our community so that even more people have the opportunity to hear her message."

– Mary Cumming MS LMHP
High School Counselor
Ogallala Public Schools
Ogallala, NE

"I no longer need to hide."

"As a parent, I went to hear your presentation in the evening and could see how well the kids in the audience were relating to you. You were so inspirational to me personally when you told your own story. If you can face audience after audience candidly revealing your life, it shows me that I no longer need to hide my secrets and my shame."

– A parent from Lake Placid, NY

"You touched the hearts and souls of all our men. Your performance transcended gender, race and language barriers."

"Your original dance and drama performance touched that which must be touched and examined in all addictions, be they chemical or behavioral. Your performance transcended gender, race and language barriers, which can be formidable in recovery. Many men here were given the confidence to understand others when they correctly identified the feeling you portrayed. You touched the hearts and souls of all our men and the undersigned is no exception."

– William S. Porter
Director, Rehabilitation Services
The Salvation Army
Long Beach, CA

"Susie scored a '10'!"

"To say we are a tough crowd to impress is not an understatement. Susie scored a "10" for grabbing the audience, holding their attention and sharing a heartfelt message. Indeed, her community performance earned a standing ovation from the large crowd. The number of parents and students present at her additional night performance was reflective of the impression she left on the students at the school assemblies that day."

– David Z. Messner, Ph.D.
Middle/High School Principal
Lake Placid Middle/High School
Lake Placid, NY

"This is not your typical drug awareness presentation."

"Our student-athletes were impressed with Susie's ability to touch on a number of relevant issues in a manner that they could relate to. With Susie's openness and honesty about the people she has had and does have in her life, our student-athletes were comfortable sharing many parts of their personal lives as well. It's a rarity to have college age students feel that they can discuss their private lives with "a complete stranger," but Susie's personality puts you right at ease.

"To a person, our student-athletes said that Legacy of Hope® was the best

program they had ever been to that touched on these social issues – it's nowhere close to your typical drug awareness presentation."

– Scott Shaw
Head Athletic Trainer
Cal State Northridge
Northridge, CA

"Students returned with their parents ... Other communities sent their students to hear you!"

"Susie, thank you for connecting with our students and staff and sharing your message. The fact that so many students returned with their parents at night, and that other communities sent students to hear your message, certainly speaks to the power you unleashed in a very short time."

– Susan Chandler
Assistant Principal
Stevens High School
Claremont, NH

"Our students' responsiveness testifies to the fact that this is an extremely relevant program for youth."

"While Susie's particular combination of dance and drama was new to our students, they were completely captivated. Susie got their attention, drew them into the story, and made her points with directness and poignancy.

"The strength of her unique presentation continued in her follow-up discussions with the students. Our youth had a lot of questions and Susie's personal warmth, moral strength and honesty really came through in these sessions. Their responsiveness to Susie is all testimony to the fact that her presentation communicates some extremely relevant concerns to our youth."

– Dr. John R. Heidel
Chaplain
Punahou School
Honolulu, HI

52 Ways to Protect Your Teen

Guiding Teens to Good Choices and Success

nearly verbatim, that I recorded after a day at their schools. Their stories shocked, startled, appalled and saddened me. Their stories desperately need to be told. It is a tough reality many teens cope with – alone – on a daily basis because most adults do not know how much they are needed.

Chapters

Programs for kids on the edge to programs for over-achievers. Police officers, judges, counselors and teachers are vital contributors. Add a dose of parental support. Teens thrive through the admirable efforts of adults who care.

Chapters

Note: Throughout this book, identities have been protected by using fictitious names and/or altering other identifying information.

Acknowledgements

To every one of the 20,000 teens who shared their stories with me. This book would not exist without the thousands of teens who came up to talk after Legacy of Hope® assemblies and presentations, inspiring and impassioning me to share their cries for help.

Ken Vanderlip, Ph.D. – Dearest husband and business partner, thanks for your mantra, "This book is the number one priority." I am forever grateful for your amazing patience, kindness and nurturing spirit, the precious love between us, and your encouragement to me to take whatever time and space was necessary for the birth of this book!

Frieda & Bernie Baskin – Mom and Dad, thanks for the DNA that made my dreams possible and the great love that makes them worth it!

Bessie Baskin, Beverly Bimson and Barbara Enochian – My three sisters, each with a potent and powerful personality. You consistently ignite the "Baskin" can-do spirit in me and helped inspire this book!

Jean Vanderlip, David Vanderlip and Kathy Smith – Thanks for being patient, kind and caring in-laws. Special thanks to Jean (Mom) for your feedback on early book chapters.

Toni Nelson – Soul sister for 17 years, I treasure you as the fierce advocate for Legacy of Hope®, for kids and for integrity in parenting. Thanks to you and husband **Garry**, for sharing your most precious treasures: brilliant daughter, **Barbara**, and life-enthusiast son, **David**. Many of your parenting skills, ethics and responsible values are the very models I have drawn from, and from which many other parents will glean in the book.

Barbara Nelson – Thank you for reading the first draft of the book. At only 19, your intelligence, integrity and mature discernment made your feedback invaluable.

David Nelson – You reminded me why I was writing this book – because teens are vibrant beings and parents need support to properly nurture the precious vitality of teens!

Carol Stone – As a single, busy working Mom of three, including two teenage boys, you were the perfect reader for the latter version of the book.

Heather Lambert – As a teacher of Advanced Placement high school teens and mother of three grown children, your conviction that even Advanced Placement parents need this book erased any doubts during lengthy rewrites.

Will Nagel & Robyn Quinones – Thank you! Wise and faithful friends.

Loie Boero – Thank you for sharing your passion to help kids and your encouragement of this book.

Victoria Gomez-Vidrio and daughter, Yzreel – The faith we share in God's guidance often gave me strength to believe I could finish this book.

Diane Armitage – Huge thanks for your writing talents, creating a workable structure from my 71 newspaper columns and for months of dedicated editing, publishing and marketing support. This book would not exist without your expert help.

Kukla Vera – Your marketing support and publishing expertise has been invaluable! Thanks for abundant wisdom, kindness and passion for quality.

Patti Knoles – Naturally, your expert skills at layout have been essential. Even more than these, your devotion to your pre-teen daughter and hunger to apply the messages in this book have given me great joy, encouragement and hope for teens!

Veronica Garcia and Lauren Kopit – As high school interns for me over the summer of 2004, your help was invaluable in finishing the book. You remind me that teens are incredible human beings and why I dedicate this book and my mission to teens!

Tustin Monday Night Meeting — My love and thanks, dear spiritual friends, for your limitless unconditional love, experience, strength and hope. You see me through the bumps in the road of life and celebrate my joys! Special hugs and heartfelt thanks to sponsors **Jill** and **Jo C.**

Stan Smith, Minister of Teaching, School of Actualism Meditation — Your inner stillness amidst worldly chaos has been a guidepost along my own inner journey and cleared away many fears. Many heartfelt thanks!

Mike Rounds, Nancy Miller, Eric Chester & Fran Berman – You have been the most supportive and cherished colleagues, offering insights and support whenever needed in writing this book. As professional speakers, I have enormous admiration for each of you. As friends, you are priceless!

Megan McIntosh – I greatly appreciate having your poetry in the book and the honest expression of feelings you shared. Your wisdom, love, and fortitude continually inspire me; and I treasure our friendship!

Janice Christopher, Assistant Superintendent, Monongalia County School District; **Wanda Fisher,** Head Counselor, Atlee High School; **Pat Kvam,** Chairperson, Shenendehowa PTA Council Substance Abuse Prevention Committee; **Yvonne Lott,** Network Director, Eastern Adirondack Health Care Network; **Corinne Pridham,** President, National Peer Helpers Association and School Psychologist, Dighton-Rehoboth Regional High School; **Gayle Smith,** Teacher and PAL Advisor, La Vista High School – I so appreciate each and every one of you for the depth of your humility, sincerity, and commitment to helping youth throughout your careers and within your families. I am deeply grateful for the projects and programs we have collaborated on. I have gleaned much wisdom from working side by side with you. I have gained the joy of great friendship by knowing you. Each of you has imparted a unique, soulful wisdom and encouragement to me that is priceless. If I were to gather you all into one room, no doubt, you would recognize one another as fellow angels!

Sallie Coltrin & Terry Quinlan – The first two people to believe in me and my performance-art recovery outreach in 1991! Nurturing my dream from its infancy, you both were instrumental in this program that has brought hope and recovery to hundreds of thousands.

Wellington Daily News and Tracy McCue, past Editor – You gave me, a complete newcomer, generous weekly space for my column, *"It's Not Easy Being a Teen."*

The Legacy of Hope® cast of characters – THANK YOU, God, for introducing me to the people who inspired the poignant and thought-provoking characters in Legacy of Hope® and for using these characters to continually motivate tens-of-thousands of teens to talk with me about personal concerns.

FOREWORD
Do Adults Fear Teens?

Julio hung out in the hallway of the Holiday Inn Mart Plaza Conference Center in Chicago. Waiting, as he had hundreds of times before, he scanned the conference attendees to see if his menacing appearance was causing discomfort. Were women taking double takes at his baggy pants, black skullcap, dark sunglasses and gang swagger? He saw several pull their purses closer as they attempted to nonchalantly move a good distance away.

Julio was sure the men had taken notice. Several men now stood more erect, puffing out their chests, subconsciously if not consciously responding to him with territorial threat postures.

And then I, Susie Vanderlip, made my entrance as keynote speaker for the event. Well, not exactly me, rather it was "Julio," my alter ego and startling opening character in Legacy of Hope®. My theatrical one-woman show has carried me to 46 states, Canada and Guam since its inception in October, 1991, reaching out to nearly a million teens and adults.

"Julio" is one of eight characters I portray for teens, parents, and other adults who care about the emotional well-being of teens and their families. Julio is a 14-year-old male gang member who skulks about in his gang 'colors.'

I pull off a rather convincing charade as a young Hispanic "homey" from the hood, becoming the son my mother never had! In reality, I am one of four daughters and an Anglo 'baby boomer' brought up in the suburban middle-class community of Long Beach, California. I've come a long way from that simplistic perspective of the world, having now worked with teens and families of nearly every race, creed, color and class in America.

Imagine with me now, that you are entering the ballroom of that conference facility and are a professional in a field such as crime prevention, counseling, school administration, nursing, maybe even insurance. You are expecting to hear a specialist in your field on education or counseling, maybe crime prevention, substance abuse or parenting. You anticipate a dry presentation filled with facts, figures and measured outcomes. When, out of the corner of your eye, you catch a glimpse of a teenage boy in gang garb lurking in the shadows, making every effort to intimidate. You expected to be at a safe convention facility. What would your first thoughts be?

On a number of occasions, conference attendees have alerted hotel securities who then accost me in the halls right before my speeches!

"Sorry to create concern. But, really I'm a lady and the keynote speaker," I swiftly divulge to them in secrecy.

To my relief, security guards, policeman, and hotel management all respond amused AND astonished.

"I thought you were some kid who wandered in off the street to make trouble! You really had me fooled! Real sorry to bother you," a recent hotel manager mused.

One particular conference stands out in my memory. I was speaking to the California Crime Prevention Officers Association annual conference. Everyone was a uniformed police officer or community crime prevention officer.

Prior to my entrance, I (as Julio) was hanging outside in the hall as usual. I leaned against the wall projecting my best recalcitrant, anti-social "tude," when a six-foot-four-inch muscled police officer sidled up to a bank of pay phones 15 feet across from me/Julio. The officer began to place a phone call when he abruptly whirled around and verbally accosted me, "I don't like nobody watching over my shoulder when I'm making a phone call. You get out of here!" he blasted at me.

Without breaking character, Julio (and I) offered him a wayward glance over the shoulder and ambled off to another wall to lean and taunt him with my 'street' attitude.

Most adults *do* fear teens. In fact, it doesn't even take offensive or anti-social appearances for adults to fear and avoid them. Many of my peers from a range of lifestyles and cultures think teens today are TROUBLE waiting to happen.

Is some quick-thinking teen going to attack the lifestyle they are entrenched in? Is some snot-nosed teenager going to make us question our choices and look back with regrets or, worse, with shame? Maybe teens pose a threat because they have the distinct ability to read beneath our manicured facades and upset our comfort zones.

Many American adults admit that they fear teens. Why?

According to *Kids These Days: What Americans Really Think About the Next Generation*, a report published by Public Agenda, a nonprofit research organization in New York: *"Most adults look at today's teenagers with misgiving and trepidation, viewing them as undisciplined, disrespectful, and unfriendly."*

At some level, teens are looking for much the same things as adults.

My experience across America with gang members and wanna-bes, Goths, skaters, druggies, foster-care kids, cheerleaders, athletes and high-achievers has revealed that teens have the same basic need as adults: the need to be loved.

In the 1998 Summer edition of *Assets Magazine*, published by Search Institute in Minneapolis, teens are found to be just like adults in their need and response to "praising them, taking time for them, being interested in them, working to understand them."

I believe *Assets Magazine* has it right: "Adults may simply be taking caution too far." It results in feeding alienation and misunderstanding between adults and teens.

Appearances can be deceiving. True, the average adult cannot tell if a kid in sagging, baggy pants is armed and dangerous, but statistically, only 6.2 percent of all people arrested in the nation are under the age of 15 according to the FBI. Only one-half of 1 percent of teens is arrested for a violent crime in any given year. The vast majority of teens are not hoodlums or dangerous, nor aspire to be. They simply want to be heard, have their opinions and feelings respected, and be given supportive and caring guidance from adults.

According to *Assets Magazine*, "Adults who've pushed past their discomfort with teens are often startled at how rewarding interactions with them can actually be, even very simple ones like greeting a teen neighbor by name or smiling at a young person cruising the shopping mall."

Perhaps it is simply a matter of adults overcoming their own basic fears – fear of the unknown, fear of being harmed, and fear of not being loved!

How I started talking to teens ... and what I've learned since.
I first stepped into the arena of the 'teenage unknown' in 1991. It started innocently when I went into a dance studio to choreograph a piece about relationships and came out with a powerful, angst-filled interpretive solo that reflected a deep well of pain and suffering I'd experienced some years prior.

In 1991, I was eight years past the end of an 18-year relationship with my first husband – my high school sweetheart, best friend throughout my adolescent and young adult life. We married after college and moved to San Francisco where he completed his dental degree and I got my PHT – "Putting Hubby Through." Life was rosy, wonderful and financially abundant ... and so were drugs and alcohol – his choice for weekend entertainment and managing a stressful career.

His problem with alcohol and drugs was not evident to me in the first eight or so years of our 13-year marriage. Maybe I didn't see alcoholism and addiction coming because I had no experience with them then, or maybe I was in complete denial and never thought high achievers could lose control of life. In any case, I watched my beloved husband deteriorate from a fun-loving, affectionate, respected medical professional into a drug and alcohol-addicted, sullen, irritable man.

I, too, became someone I didn't know. My very best friend – my husband – was becoming my worst enemy and telling me I was his problem. "I don't have a problem with drugs and alcohol; the only problem I have is YOU!" he'd scream, then throw shoes at me from across the room, or punch a hole in the wall with his fist.

I emotionally went down with him. I thought that it was something I was or wasn't doing that was causing him to stop loving me. I worked two jobs and managed a rental property we owned to make enough money so he could work only three days a week. It was the stress of the work, he said, that kept him so depressed. So I worked to solve that problem.

But limiting his work to three days a week didn't change the chaos and disintegration in our home. I found myself engulfed in a daily dance with gut-wrenching despair, wild unrelenting fear, disillusionment, hurt, rage, shame, guilt, and anxiety that kept me bouncing from a victim of paralysis to an obsessively determined "fixer."

One Saturday night, while he sat in our bedroom playing video games for twelve hours straight, stoned and loaded, I begged him, "Please, just stop playing for a second. Just look at me. Talk to me! Just put your arm around me. You used to be my best friend."

He said nothing.

I remember racing through the house, out of control, ready to jump into my car and drive as fast as I could toward the cliff near our home, and not turn the wheel...and I wouldn't have to hurt that bad ANYMORE! Here I was, the student voted "Most Likely to Succeed" of my high school class, and, on that night, was most likely to commit suicide on the feelings of living with and loving an alcoholic/addict.

Somewhere deep inside a voice said, "You just want him to feel really sorry he ignored you so he'll quit drinking and using drugs. You just want him to go back to being the loving best friend you married so many years ago." The sensible side of my nature stepped in.

So, I held on through that night. And the next day, I was driving to work, sobbing my eyes out but telling no one how much our "perfect" loving relationship had deteriorated. I turned on the radio, and the first of many miracles happened. The National Council on Alcoholism and Drug Dependence (NCADD) had a radio spot.

They asked, "Do you listen for the sound of opening cans, like someone drinking beer?" (The hair on the back of my neck always stood up when I came into the house and saw the cans and the slouch in his body.)

"Do you think if you could just be more perfect, you'd get everything under control?" (Oh, I'd tried EVERYTHING to make him happy and attentive again.)

"Do you feel lonely, unwanted and alone?" (No doubt, I felt all three.) The light went on in my head! **It wasn't that he didn't love me anymore; it was that he couldn't! He was an alcoholic and an addict.** I called the NCADD for help, which wisely guided me to support programs for the families of alcoholics. There, I began to separate my hatred for the disease and his behaviors from my love of the man as a person.

Over the next year and a half I learned ways to shift my attitude from self-pity to gratitude for the small but true gifts of my life: hot showers to flowers; serendipitous phone calls from unconditionally loving friends at just the right moment; and unexpected moments when my husband would be lucid and caring. I also learned to take responsibility for my own happiness and accept that he was losing a grip on his life and our marriage.

I saw the light in his eyes – and in our relationship – flicker and finally go out. I filed for divorce and moved out. Six months later, I got a phone call. The previous evening, he had mixed alcohol, cocaine and the prescription painkiller Percodan. By morning, his heart had stopped.

At the age of 35 my beloved was dead.

When you live with an alcoholic/addict, or when you lose someone to the disease of alcoholism and drug addiction, it has a lifelong impact. On top of the emotional trauma, the chaos of the disease led to the foreclosure of our home. With the divorce, I lost the life insurance and much of my savings and financial security. My self-esteem plummeted. I struggled for several years with grieving. I attended support groups for families of alcoholics and sought therapy to address my grief. Through the years with the help of the experience, strength and hope of others, I have found the courage to take responsibility for my part in our problems and found the compassion, not only for him but for myself, to let go of the guilt, shame, blame and resentments.

Over time, I learned that not only did I have the necessity, but also the responsibility to learn how to identify my painful, angry and hurt feelings and to share them in safe and supportive places where I could heal. This spiritual process has repeatedly brought me peace beyond all understanding.

I also found a language through which to express my feelings in the world of DANCE. In college at UCLA, I had minored in modern dance. Even in my very first dance class, I found that dance completely absorbed my mind and fed me emotionally and spiritually.

In 1975, a few years after graduation from college, I auditioned and was accepted into a local modern and jazz dance company, Dance Kaleidoscope of Orange County. It was within this unique ensemble of dancers that I blossomed artistically – choreographing, performing and directing for the company for more than 20 years. Eventually, my experience led to opportunities to share my love of dance as a teacher at the Daria Bearden Dance Studio in Tustin, California, and at Coastline Community College as an Associate Professor in Dance.

In Dance Kaleidoscope, I found friends that remain some of my closest and most treasured to this day. Thanks to my involvement in Dance Kaleidoscope, I had a supportive and expressive world in which to deal with the overwhelming pain of my first husband's addictions and death.

Though I danced every spare moment I could, I simultaneously pursued a career in the computer industry. Programming and analysis, project management and computer services sales filled my financial needs. I also had the support of a Higher Power, whom I choose to call God, in the form of a miracle.

It came just at that point when I was finally able to accept that my happiness could no longer depend upon my addicted husband and I surrendered my crippled marriage over to God. I distinctly remember praying, "God, what I really want in my life is a marriage the way you have designed it to be: a true partnership emotionally, mentally, spiritually, physically, financially, intellectually, in all ways. If that can be with my current husband, then so be it. If not, let it be with whomever YOU choose."

And thus, I let go and let God.

Within two weeks of that prayer, I met an exceptionally patient, compassionate, kind and healthy man – in the dance studio no less! I began a friendship with that man who is now my current husband of 20 years. Though many months, if not years, of grief work remained for me, I have found in my marriage to Ken Vanderlip the reliable love, partnership and emotional sanity I had prayed for.

In addition, Ken introduced me to Actualism meditation on our second date – a profound practice of meditating with God's light into deep layers of consciousness to reveal the true purpose and design for our lives – service and joy. I folded that practice into the spiritual lessons I gained from support groups for the families of alcoholics.

I learned to keep life simple and to use the most humble and effective of prayers on a daily basis: "God, I pray to know your will for me and for the power to carry that out."

Time passed; and in 1991, eight years after my first husband's death, I entered the dance studio to choreograph something on "relationships." What I thought would be a strong statement became a profound expression of the intense desire and simultaneous repulsion I'd felt while married to a man with addictions. The dance became known as Legacy of Obsession, depicting not only his obsessions with substances but also my obsessive need for his unavailable affection.

I performed Legacy of Obsession at a local arts festival and was amazed at the response. Following the performance, Karen Shanley, now retired Chair of the Orange Coast College Dance Department, asked me to expand the piece for the college's touring dance ensemble. In the middle of the night, I'd wake up and remember the pleas and painful stories of others I'd met at support groups and open Alcoholics Anonymous/Narcotics Anonymous meetings which I attended in an effort to understand my first husband's disease.

The memories of these suffering adults and children around addiction compelled me to create monologues of their struggles, which I accentuated with dance. I had no idea where I was going with this creative flood of material. I simply felt God pushing this creativity through me.

One night, I shared at my spiritual support meeting that I felt God was pushing this material through me. And it scared me! What did God want of me?

At the end of the support meeting, a woman came to me and said, "I'm a counselor at a high school, and I think God is talking to you. I'm going to hire you to present what you are creating for Red Ribbon Week. So, you have to finish it; and it has to be GOOD."

Knowing schools as I do today, I now realize that what happened that night was a legitimate miracle. First and foremost, I'd been asked to do something by God in a spiritual setting. There is no other viable answer to that than to say, "YES." But the depth of the miracle goes further. Today I know that schools do not hire speakers lightly. Principals, committees and PTOs scrutinize speakers' credentials and their ability to hold the attention of a mass audience of antsy teenagers in an auditorium or gymnasium.

The fact that this counselor put her job on the line and her principal agreed to risk his reputation for an unseen, unfinished assembly program is completely unfathomable to me today!

Legacy of Hope®, my one-hour theatrical one-woman show and school assembly, premiered in October of 1991 to 800 high school students in southern California.

That day, my eyes, my mind and my heart were changed as dozens of quietly tormented, hurting and grieving teens came up after the assembly to share about their tortured lives around alcoholic, drug addicted fathers, mothers, siblings, boyfriends, girlfriends, and loved ones. A blaze of compassion and empathy was ignited in me.

I realized that teenagers are not to be feared but to be encouraged.

They are just like me. They hurt when life disappoints and overwhelms them. They grieve for lost security and love in their lives. They, too, are sensitive, kind and compassionate, especially when they realize that even in their own troubled lives, they have much to give away that will help others.

Since that remarkable day, God has inspired me to create several more characters whose monologues and dance segues have entertained and enlightened nearly one million teens and adults in 46 states, Canada and Guam. It is a completely unforeseen and life-changing miracle in my life.

The characters I portray, as well as the conversations I have interspersed in this book, are ruthlessly honest and based on real conversations with real teens and real parents I have met along the way. Honesty is crucial if teens are to trust my message and to be hungry for healing. Teenagers are incredibly emotionally discerning; they're still young enough to have not denied their feelings.

For adults to respond, my program must depict truths that hit a deep cord, or the well-developed adult denial system will continue unbroken. And, the will to reach out will remain

suppressed from fear of disclosure.
My goal is to make it easier for hurting teens, frightened parents, and those in isolation to reach out and ask for help.

I stay after every performance so teens and adults can reveal what is hidden in their hearts. One on one, they let out the painful secrets of their lives and their families due to the heartless disease of alcoholism and drug addiction. These deep and heart-wrenching confessions have put me in conversation with at least 20,000 teens across nearly every state in America. Teens and an occasional adult regularly e-mail me with precious, as well as desperate, questions:

"My boyfriend keeps pressuring me to have sex. He says if I loved him, I'd do it to make him happy. But I don't want to. What should I tell him?"

"There is NOTHING to do in my town if I don't go to the parties and drink. What can I do if I don't hang out where everybody is drinking and smoking pot?"

"I'm really worried about this guy I like. He says he doesn't do drugs, but at a party last night, all these girls talked him into smoking some marijuana and drinking some beers. How do I get him to stop without getting him into trouble?"

"What do I do about my girlfriend who is sleeping around ever since her parents got a divorce when she was in sixth grade?"

"What do I say to my Mom when she tries to get me to smoke pot with her at home?"

"How do I stop my brother from beating me up and throwing me down the stairs whenever my parents leave the house?"

"I've been cutting on myself every night for a week. I know I'm bad for doing it, but I don't know how to stop. Help"

"After seeing your show, I know I need to tell someone. I think about suicide all the time. What should I do?"

"My Mom and Dad are both addicts, my Dad is in prison, my Mom leaves me at home for days at a time with no food or brings home a different drunk guy every night who stares at me. I don't feel safe and I don't know what to do."

"My Dad died six months ago from an accident on our farm. I don't know why, but I don't wanna do any of the sports and stuff I used to do. I feel like none of my friends are worth hanging around any more. I started drinking a lot a couple months ago and tried some pot at a party last weekend. I never did any of that before. Can you help me?"

The questions go on and on.

Only a small number of teens who e-mail me come from severe circumstances: shelters, foster homes and juvenile probation. The vast majority of the teens that reach out appear quite "normal" to the untrained adult eye.

They can be gang members, good students, failing students, blonds, brunettes, fat or thin, athletes, nerds, valedictorians or drop-outs ... ALL types of teens are desperately hungry for someone to comprehend their fear and their pain. These are America's teens. They may be your teen.

Each day that I am on a school campus, your children are my children.

I thank you! And, I hold myself accountable to you parents. Above and beyond my commitment to parents, I hold myself accountable to the Highest Authority of all to teach from truth. I am rewarded when a struggling teen is willing to reach out for the first time and ask for help. It is quite an honor for any adult to be the lifeline to this remarkable age group, with their still penetrable shells and malleable souls.

Given I am not a school counselor, vice principal, athletic coach, psychotherapist, or nurse, I am a safe resource for a teen that is afraid of being reported, reprimanded, punished, or persecuted. I get to listen with my entire heart, mind and spirit, to HEAR THEM in a way that few adults have, due to lack of time, comfort with teens, deep emotional trauma, or just plain lack of desire to do so.

Still, I know it is not my place to give teens advice or to be their parent. Instead:

- I get to share my own experience of overcoming a serious life challenge that many of them are experiencing as well.
- I provide real life stories that teens as well as adults identify with.
- I help them see the choices in their own lives. The hardest thing in the midst of external chaos or inner turmoil is to see that we have choices, much less figure out what they are!
- I am very grateful that I get to share about the grace of a Higher Power I choose to call God and to bring to others an essential ingredient for change, the gift of HOPE.

Initially, I thought I would help a few kids with these conversations.

I had no idea so many children live with parents who drink or use drugs abusively, then verbally mutilate the self-worth of their kids. Within the first three years of bringing Legacy of Hope® to middle schools and high schools, I was appalled, heartbroken, then angry and even obsessed with reaching as many young people as I could. I see teens so wounded by life's losses and family cruelties that they are running from life into every escape imaginable, unable to focus on an education or even care about a future.

Soon, I realized that I was being given a firsthand exposure to real life as it is for many teens today, and a broader, larger exposure than anyone else I knew.

It was hard to find other adults ready to grasp the extent of the problems that teens were carrying on their shoulders. Most parents hold onto the hope that it won't happen to their kids or their children's classmates.

It is this bird's eye view that is the engine of my passion to keep reaching out to hurting teens and the adults who care about them.

Teens don't often divulge everything to their parents. Parents don't always pay attention to their teens. So my job includes sharing with other adults and parents the insights gleaned from my bird's eye view. As adults overcome their fear of adolescents, they can communicate, guide and emotionally support teens. That is when parents, in particular, can let go of the nagging fear that they will fail and/or damage their kids. Parents then become a major part of the solution!

Naturally, I have spoken to my share of parent's in denial, who have given up in resignation, and even those apathetic and irresponsible about raising their kids:

"It can't happen to my child. My kid's a good kid."

"If their going to use, I want them to do it at home where I can supervise what's going on. So, I provide the keg for the kids so long as they drink at my house."

"My kid doesn't listen to me. He/she has a bad attitude. I don't have any control over him/her anymore."

"I give up. I don't care what they do; just don't drag me into it."

"I sent my kid to a shrink. It's their job to fix them."

The fact is – we can't disbelieve or deny any longer.

Now, it's not all bad. Understand that teens are just trying to cope with daily stressors and emotions, just like us adults. The key is that we accept teens as very much like us – adults – on a feeling level. In that regard, they want what we want.

However, what is different is that a flood of dangerous alternatives is incredibly easy to access and readily available to kids of all ages. Worse yet, we have a world with shredded moral fiber that looks at our youth as nothing more than profits to be manipulated and exploited without conscience. We can no longer naively pretend that this is merely "adolescence" with its normal experimentation, hormones and curiosities, regardless of the way the world has changed. To blindly hope the teens you care about will get through the next six years of adolescence relatively unscathed is to invite danger and loss into both your lives. It is a different world out there and our children are at risk.

From my travels, conversation, and observations, I have come to some strong opinions and fact-based suggestions for living with, parenting, and guiding teens. In 2001 thru early 2003, I shared some of this body of experience for 71 weeks in my own weekly newspaper column *"It's Not Easy Being a Teen"* for the Wellington Daily News, Wellington, KS. The column gave me a forum to speak on the many topics and insights my national outreach has afforded me. Now, this book is an opportunity for me to share with a wider audience.

I have selected from the weekly columns while infusing additional stories and insights that may help you accurately grasp teenage life today. Additionally, I have opened each section with a quote from one of my Legacy of Hope® characters, quotes that ultimately come from the teens I've met across America. Through my inside access to teens, I believe that your kids have told me what it is they really want you to know. My hope is that you will find ideas here for crossing the bridge from fear to fellowship with a teen you love.

SECTION ONE

Talk May be Cheap, But Communicating with Your Teen is Priceless!

We've all heard that we have to keep the lines of communication open with our teens. All well and good, but exactly HOW do we do this? Are we just supposed to know how to talk to teenagers because we've been one or because, as adults and parents, it is expected of us? Of course not. Open, honest, forward-moving communication takes commitment and practice.

In this chapter, I outline just a few pointers of small talk, "barometer" readings, the art of asking, the science of listening and – what might be most surprising – facts behind how committed teens are to trying to hear us.

Middle-class teenage cheerleader from *Legacy of Hope®* presentation:

I love my Dad. He promised me a car at graduation ... if he remembers. Like the other day, he forgot to pick me up from practice. He's under a lot of stress from work ... Yeah, he does drink too much sometimes. But he doesn't throw-up or fall down in the street or anything. He does get real mean though. But then sometimes he says he's sorry and takes me shopping and out for a Starbucks Frappacino ... I'm gonna help my Dad! I'm gonna be so good. I'm gonna get such good grades – get into the college he wants me to; I'm gonna be so skinny. He won't ever be disappointed in me again!

CHAPTER ONE
Just When You Concluded They Weren't Listening to You ...

The great thing about teens, if not a bit annoying at times, is that they are always thinking ... and, believe it or not, not always just about themselves. Teens are some of the most empathetic, listening, and caring people you'll come across. Recognizing and treating them as "peers" on an emotional level can do wonders for both you and the teens in your life.

I encourage adults to empathize with teen angst, insecurity and their need for encouragement and support. Teens, like adults, have a full range of emotions. They simply do not have as much life experience with which to gauge the significance of their feelings. Many adults I know have not yet mastered the art of coping with feelings. Why should we expect teens with less life experience to do better than most adults?

How a teen helped me get through tough times as an adult.

This past year illustrated to me how an investment of patience, tolerance, kindness and encouragement in a troubled teen can pay off on many levels. I met one particular teen, Stacey, following one of my school assemblies at her high school, an "alternative" school for teens that have not succeeded in a regular high school. Since then, Stacey and I have had an active mentor-mentee relationship via e-mail for more than two years. During those two years, she struggled to make sense of a family riddled with alcoholism, drug addiction, and heavy criticism.

I had spent many months listening, empathizing and encouraging Stacey as she dealt with her serious personal issues and confronted her destructive coping mechanisms: self-mutilation/ cutting herself, alcohol and drugs. I was rewarded to find that my many months of encouragement had borne fruit. She was no longer cutting, or drinking and used drugs far less often. I received another reward I never expected. She came to my rescue by giving back encouragement and perspective when I was in a moment of confusion and self-doubt myself. The circle of life repeated itself in her empathetic words. To hear them from a teen who had once had not an ounce of hope was the greatest encouragement of all. If Stacey could go through life optimistically while overcoming the burdens of her life, I certainly could overcome mine!

Stacey came to my support just when I was going through the reverse "change" in a woman's life – the mania of menopause! Having traversed life with an attitude of adventure and a can-do spirit, I presumed I would sail confidently through this experience as though it were but one more curious transition. To my surprise, my apple cart flipped over! Sleep patterns went awry, a lifetime of 'Energizer Bunny' levels fluctuated and sputtered, and I became moody...no, I became emotionally volatile. I found myself intensely nostalgic, bereft over lost dreams, and considering if I should just trash the way I'd lived my entire life (including my precious husband a time or two!) in hopes of leveling a tottering sense of life balance.

With Stacey's loving support, I saw the parallels between adolescent hormonal turmoil and my middle-age mood swings. More importantly, I saw the parallels between teens and adults, our feelings and our needs.

I now go beyond the empathy I preach.

I look on teens as fellow travelers in a journey exhilarating and despairing, knowing and confusing, controllable and helpless, joyful and sorrowful, psyched and forlorn. The emotional roller coaster of low-level menopausal hormones seemed to me at the time to be just as potent as the wild wave of brand new adolescent hormones. By seeing that parallel, I now relate even better to teens. The saving grace for adults is that we have "reference points" from a lifetime of personal experience to guide us; and we hopefully now have the insight to listen to the experiences of others who have gone before us.

I was heartened by the support of peers. There is nothing more reassuring than a friend calling or e-mailing to share her experience from her own journey. For teens, the same can be true, particularly if the peers they turn to have been formally trained Peer Helpers on their school campus.

Peer-helping at all ages provides vital reassurance that we are not alone in traversing life's chaotic shifts. It is more than having a friend share in juicy gossip or listen to us blame the person who did us wrong and commiserate with our justifiable plight (though at moments this kind of friend may seem just what we need). When ready to find solutions, there is nothing like the insights and encouragement of a peer who has learned important lessons from experience, forgiveness and acceptance.

Just because you're an adult doesn't mean you can't be an emotional "peer helper" to a teen.

I have had the opportunity to share many stories with teens through the years about triumph over tragedy and overcoming disappointing circumstances. Some of my stories come from my own childhood, some from the trials of adulthood. What they relate to best in these stories is the honesty about my emotions:

Those moments in my life when I was scared to the core yet the outcome came out just right!

Those moments when I really knew there is a Supreme Being looking out for me; examples of when I've seen the hand of God take care of me.

Teens want examples and reference points from life, that help them believe they are not alone in a world that scares them, and that faith of all kinds is not the path of weakness but of strength.

I also find teens are excited and eager to share their success over life trials with their peers as well. Many teens have had the veils of doubt and apprehension lifted by the personal stories of a caring adult or a respected peer.

On that day when Stacey mentored me, I was touched and encouraged to see this teen so strong and confident when once she had been so broken. I was thrilled to see that my support had borne fruit. AND I was ever so grateful she was now able to encourage me!

Many teachers and school club advisors, parents and mentors have had this unexpected reward of hearing their very words of guidance to a teenager spewed back when they needed to hear them most. These adults agree that a teenager's encouragement has a very special nurturing flavor, a fresh energy that reminds us of the unlimited possibilities in life. I can see those possibilities in every teen. It's quite uplifting when they, too, see them in me!

Pour your experience, strength and hope into a teen. It is well worth the effort; and you, too, may be blessed when he or she returns insights in your time of need!

CHAPTER TWO
Check Your Teen's Weather Report Lately?

Small talk is what makes the world go 'round, especially when it comes to teens. Here's how to create and engage in "small talk," so that you actually end up with a great barometer reading of your teen's activities and attitudes.

Have you ever been at a loss for words to start up a conversation with a teen?

Many adults express a discomfort, even downright FEAR of trying to create conversation with a teen. They sense that teens can see right through the masks and hypocrisy of adulthood we sometimes cover up under the guise of responsibility. Yes, teens do have a knack for detecting adult fear and phony affection, but they are also very responsive to the smallest amount of sincere adult caring and attention.

The key lies in the motives. Are you sincerely unselfish, non-manipulative in your **caring**, or do you have an ulterior motive? Teens have special antenna. They won't react so much to what you say as to how you say it. Tone of voice and body language do reveal our true motives. Do you honestly care about their feelings, ideas, interests, and response to your questions? Do you listen with ALL of you, not just that portion of you left over from your long day at work or the housecleaning, other children's demands, telephone calls, bills, TV, sports and e-mails? Do you listen with your heart or just with an anxious, busy and critical head?

When you don't know where to start – start with *their* weather.

One way to engage a teen when you just don't know where to start is to ask them for their weather report. Not the temperature, humidity or rain forecast; rather, their OWN weather forecast.
I experimented with this conversational exercise with a group of teens at a retreat not long ago. I asked the teenagers to describe to me their state of mind from morning through that afternoon like a weather

report. Taking on the role of a weatherman was a non-threatening approach to sharing about himself or herself. Tweaking a teen's imagination is a great way to overcome his or her distrust and doubt.

A quiet girl shared the following personal weather report: *"I woke up and the skies were overcast, gloomy. I had breakfast and soon it was a sunny day. Then I had a situation with this girl and it was like a stormy day, lots of thunder, lightening. But then I came to this retreat; now it's kind of a cool day, a few small clouds. Overall, pretty sunny skies."*

Her brief personal weather report gave me a quick snapshot of what her day felt like to her and a peek at how she reacts to confrontations with another teen. This exercise also helped her be comfortable letting me know what mood she was in at the moment. In turn, through this simple process, she saw how her moods come and go throughout the day, like the weather. Most importantly, she grasped that, like the weather, feelings don't last forever. Moods may impact us in the moment, and may feel profoundly permanent, but the truth is they come and go and do not have to spoil an entire day.

It helps both teenagers and parents to view teen moods as weather fronts just passing through rather than permanent flaws with which to condemn them.

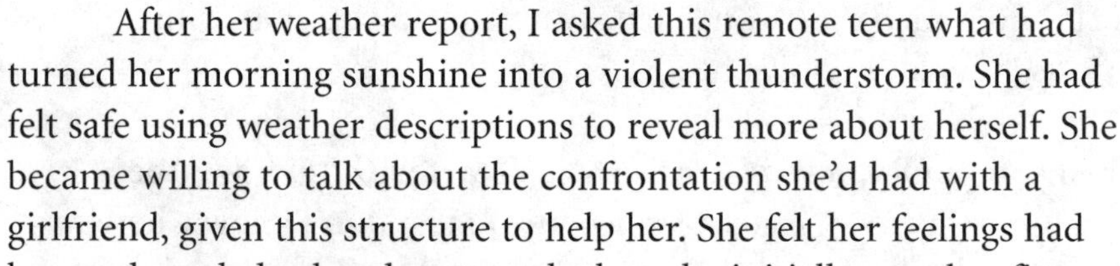

After her weather report, I asked this remote teen what had turned her morning sunshine into a violent thunderstorm. She had felt safe using weather descriptions to reveal more about herself. She became willing to talk about the confrontation she'd had with a girlfriend, given this structure to help her. She felt her feelings had been acknowledged and respected when she initially gave her first weather report. This was a new and hopeful experience for a teen accustomed to hiding in the shadows of life.

Now that this previously reluctant teen no longer feared being ridiculed for her emotions, she admitted that her roller-coaster moods also determined her attitude. It occurred to her that she could change the “emotional” weather of her day and move out of a mood by using this analogy and imagining the sun coming out behind the clouds in her mind, drying up the rain, and evaporating the heavy black clouds that were settling into “a bad attitude.” The visual nature of a personal weather forecast helped her see she had some choice over her moods and attitudes, something every teen (and most adults!) could use.

CHAPTER THREE
Why It Is Important Dinner Time Still Exists

The dinner table can be both the best and the worst place to begin a conversation with a teen. Too much probing can feel manipulative, an effort to control them. Too little attention, and teens feel invisible and ignored. WATCH OUT for serious consequences from ignoring an adolescent! Teens are particularly sensitive to being ignored, not only by their peers, but more so even by their parents.

Many a teen has shared rage, resentment and serious low self-esteem from parents who paid no attention. They seriously act out for years, trying to get back what they never received from those parents. I know many adults who have spent an entire lifetime with such feelings trapped inside, never quite aware of what is troubling them or motivating their many bad life choices.

The dinner table is a great time to pay attention to and acknowledge the progress you see in your teens. I encourage you to use this time wisely, thoughtfully and PATIENTLY! It is some of the most concentrated time you may have with your teenager.

Even the research says your efforts are worth it.

As tricky as dining with teens may be, research shows that teens that eat frequent family dinners are less likely than other teens to have sex at young ages, get into fights or be suspended from school. That's a powerful payoff! These teens are at lower risk for thoughts of suicide because they feel they matter to the family by being present around the evening meal.

Frequent family dining is correlated with doing well in school and developing healthy eating habits. This pattern holds true, says The National Center on Addiction and Substance Abuse (CASA) at Columbia University, regardless of a teen's sex, family structure, or family socioeconomic level.

CASA's Surveys from 1996 to 2000 have consistently found that teens that eat dinner with their parents twice a week or less were four times more likely to smoke cigarettes, three times more likely to smoke marijuana, and nearly twice as likely to drink as those who ate dinner with their parents six or seven times a week.

***CASA's 1999 Survey* found that teens from families that almost never eat dinner together are 72 percent more likely to use illegal drugs, cigarettes and alcohol.**

These statistics make it abundantly clear how important it is for a teen to feel a sense of belonging, family values and accountability that are subtly passed on to children through conversation and attitudes shared at the dinner table. And, certainly, "breaking bread" with your teen is always a mood lifter. Eating is an opportunity to recharge our body chemistry, which creates a more receptive mind and more willing heart in both teens and parents, even if only for a short while!

Think about it: When a parent's mouth is full, he or she is bound to be a better listener. When a teen's mouth is full, he or she is more apt to lend an ear to your stories about "when I was a kid" and the intended moral of the story.

CHAPTER FOUR

Don't Let Outside Forces Shut Down Communication Lines

Teens are sensitive to the impact of global and social concerns on their futures and on their families. Keeping the lines of communication open are important to the well-being of your teen while adults are handling "outside stressors."

The traumatic 9/11 bombing of the World Trade Center certainly has had a major impact on the whole world. I was curious to know what teen thinking would be on such a significant global issue some six months afterwards. I read several articles from *Join Together*, a premiere source for substance abuse and gun violence information (see many website references at my website, **www.legacyofhope.com**).

I found that teens have remained relatively the same as they always have despite the changing world around them. Their lives are definitely absorbed in handling their immediate world – getting to class, doing homework, flirting with the opposite sex, dodging the demands and criticism of their parents, playing sports, hobbies, surfing the Internet, etc. etc. etc! As a 15-year-old boy aptly summarized the impact of 9/11:

> *"It didn't really last very long, unless a teen was personally affected, like lost a family member. Patriotism was kind of trendy. Now it's kind of disappeared."*

Unless it impacts a loved one directly, the most dramatic impact a teen feels from world events is the tension from his or her parents as they struggle to handle their anxiety, fear and economic uncertainty.

What can parents and teens do to improve relations?

Though many parents don't get this impression, they truly are the primary influence on their teen's thinking and feeling. I asked 15-year-old David, what he thought a teen could do to improve his or her relationship with their parents.

> *"Openness," he shared. "Teens need to try to set aside time from their busy schedule to communicate with their parents. Teens can take more notice of their parents. Say, during a morning commute in the car with a parent before school, or after school, rather than just get into the radio, have a real conversation with your parents."*

Sharp advice from a teen! Since David was clearly an astute judge of human nature, I asked for reverse advice from his youthful perspective: What can a parent do to improve communication with their teenager?

Again, forthright and thoughtful, David shared:

> *"Parents really need to make an effort to talk about stuff their teens can relate to. Not just work, or business, or the house or problems. Give kids the chance to talk to them. When in the car in the morning, don't get on the cell phone."*

And as for topics, David suggested:

> *"Make conversation on what kids are enthusiastic about. Like their hobbies."*

How do you query a teen without intruding on or "annoying" them?

According to *Join Together* research: "Many parents say it's hard to be involved in a teen's life. Often, parents find it difficult to draw the line between being involved in their children's lives and being intrusive." So I queried David once more and asked him just what topics should a parent bring up with their teens to encourage them to talk without feeling the parent is intrusive or annoying? David's worthy suggestion:

> *"Ask questions about school like 'What are you thinking about that biology class?' But don't make assumptions," he emphasized. "If you assume or judge a teen about school work or life, it gets annoying."*

Recognize when stress interrupts your communication.

Statistics accrued after the World Trade Center attack indicate that tobacco and alcohol use among adults surged after 9/11, as "fears stemming from Sept. 11 caused people to seek comfort in cigarettes and alcohol," according to British psychologists in a Dec. 30, 2002 *Join Together* News Summary.

> *"A similar trend took place during and after World War II, when smoking quadrupled and alcohol consumption doubled despite food shortages. People are concerned with their anxieties and a feeling of having no control. In such times, tobacco and alcohol offer a crutch," according to Clive Bates, director of the anti-smoking lobby, ASH in Britain.*

As parents succumb to their own anxiety, and especially if they increase their own tobacco and alcohol use, it is common to become more reactive. Parents can become more impatient, get stuck in an attitude of fear, assume the worst, and then transfer those stress reactions onto those closest to them, especially challenged teens.

Trying to control a teen when you are under excess stress may be a reaction to the world at large, which is completely beyond your control. When teens are nearby, they may become the easy outlet for adult anxieties. But this is destined to create more stress and anxiety. **Teens, like most people, resist being controlled rather than reasoned with.**

The key to better relations with your teen and within the home is to refuse to let stress, including terror, and other external events, have control of your home. Teens will still be self-involved, interested in getting attention, and have the same need for consistent, patient guidance from home as they have always had. It is their time in life to be both child and burgeoning adult. Whether we experience a personal event or worldwide trauma, the best job a parent can do in times of turmoil is to help teens understand the ramifications of the situation. Equally important, be sure to tell them that they are neither responsible for the situation nor responsible to fix YOUR feelings. Include them in comprehending life's realities without burdening them with the fears.

Neither national nor local politics, world affairs nor state economics will shock teens out of being teens.

Through thousands of conversations with troubled teens, I have learned that unresolved fear in an adolescent can either be handled through healthy conversation with an adult/parent, or it can drive them to seek unhealthy relief. Today, relief is found in readily accessible drugs, alcohol, dangerous companions, irresponsible sexuality, self-mutilation, depression, eating disorders and/or suicide.

The antidote to FEAR is open communication and a loving dose of encouragement.

CHAPTER FIVE
When Teens Feel Ignored by Their Parents and Parents Feel Ignored by Their Teens ... What To Do?

Teens aren't psychic. They may not know what to ask, how to ask, and will rarely use the right words.

I regularly correspond with teens via e-mail and have learned much about teens from these open and honest exchanges. Recently I received the following e-mail from a middle school teen. Her concerns are typical of those I hear from teenagers everywhere:

"Dear Susie,

You just came to my middle school and after listening to your characters, I know I have some problems. I have the feeling like I can't talk to my parents ... I tend to keep to myself when things are going wrong. I know they love me but I feel ignored. Yeah, I felt like running away but there's nowhere to go, so I skateboard. Skateboarding keeps me inline, and helps my anger and ignorance. I soon hope that one day they will see how really good I am at it. But they ain't never got the time. Should I be more open to them? Should I let them know how I feel or should I wait till that big ball of anger and sorrow bursts? ...What should I do???

Sincerely,
Lonely Thirteen-Year-Old girl (LTYO)"

Hi Lonely Girl,

Thanks for e-mailing! That takes guts, and it's smart to reach out. I know that a LOT of teens feel ignored by their parents. I remember as a teenager I thought my Dad and Mom were too busy to have to worry about me. So in high school, I never told them when I was feeling lonely or overwhelmed or afraid or any other uncomfortable feeling. I thought by 15 I could handle life by myself. That way, I also didn't have to worry about disappointing or burdening them.

As a result, my parents thought I was doing just fine and pretty much left me alone. They figured I didn't need anything from them and they focused their parenting energy on my two younger sisters. I didn't know until a conversation with my Mom when I was over 40 years old that my parents thought I had no problems when I was in high school. I never let them know, so how could they? I finally realized that parents aren't mind readers!

That may sound silly, but the truth is, I believed my parents ought to know what I needed without my asking. They were my parents, weren't they? **As a teen, I made a rather typical assumption that most kids make: Parents should automatically know what their kids need; and, if they fail to know, it's because they don't care.**

Of course, I now know that's a very unrealistic expectation of even the most loving parents.

Most parents don't know what their teens need and that scares parents a lot! They may know what their kids need from them to *physically* grow from birth to 9, but by the teen years, parents are overwhelmed, worried and stressed themselves! If you have brothers and/or sisters, they may be even MORE stressed just worrying about making enough money to feed, clothe, and care for everybody in the family.

Money is a HUGE stress on parents. It does NOT mean they don't love their kids more than anything else in their world, they just get distracted and absorbed in running a family, holding down jobs, paying a mortgage and all the other adult responsibilities.

So, what can you do so you don't feel like "running away or exploding with anger and sorrow?"

First, work on seeing your parents with new eyes and hearing with new ears.

Imagine yourself in their shoes for a little while. Do their lives look stressful? Does being an adult with adult bills look scary? Really open your eyes and notice if they are trying to cope with a serious family problem like an illness or a drinking or drug abuse problem within the family (including your grandparents, one of your brothers or sisters, themselves, their spouse, YOU)? These concerns easily push a parent into overwhelming fear, anger and worry, and soon your parents may look like they are always angry and blaming you or just don't seem to like or care about you any more.

The truth is, a parent may actually be caught up in those same angry and sorrowful feelings YOU have!

What do you do? I encourage you to talk more openly with your parents. You might start by asking one of your parents to go out for a lunch or a snack to your favorite restaurant, a walk at the beach or in the woods, a place where you can both relax and look to enjoy each others company.

Let your parent know that it's just "you and me time."

For example, tell them:

"I would really like to have you come watch me skateboard sometime soon. How about Saturday or Sunday?"

Parents are likely to react more positively, understand your needs and respond with willingness to make some changes when you ask in a non-blaming way.

From the thousands of parents I've met, most harbor the basic fear that they aren't doing a good job, especially when their kids become teens. Teens are independent. They no longer look to their parents as having the right answers. In fact, teens often appear to ignore their parents, telling mom and dad they don't know anything any more. Parents figure they can't do anything right in their teenager's eyes. And yet, parents worry more than ever about what their teens are getting into, who they're hanging out with, if they will make a mistake with drugs, alcohol, sex, gangs, skipping school and ruining their futures. Unfortunately, teens don't come with instruction manuals.

Most parents learn to parent by trial and error. If you, a teenager, blame them for your problems, it triggers your parent's deep fear of failing you as a parent and causes layers of guilt over every real or imagined time he/she may have hurt you as a child. If you judge your parents and verbally accuse them with statements like "YOU hurt my feelings by ignoring me," your parents may feel hurt because they may well have thought that was exactly what you wanted them to do. **Notice, however, that when parents have fear and guilt, it usually comes out as anger!** They may blame you back and act critical of you.

Parents can also feel that their teenager doesn't care about how hard they are trying, and get *their* feelings hurt. A vicious cycle can occur where both sides stop trusting one another and stop believing in the love that is really there.

What if trying to be open with your parent(s) goes badly?

The worst thing that can happen is to have a parent yell, argue, blame you or act like they don't care. Painful as that is, some parents don't have the ability to be there for their kids. If your own parents grew up feeling ignored, verbally or physically abused, etc., they may have a very tough time being thoughtful and compassionate to your needs. It isn't that they don't love you, they might just be what I call "emotionally handicapped" — damaged from a bad childhood of their own. If they never talked to anybody about their own anger and sorrow, it can create an angry attitude about life, even toward their own kids. Obviously, holding painful feelings inside causes emotions to explode outward in time, and, sadly, too often upon the kids.

If the worst does happen, however, there are other options. We never have to go through life alone unless we choose to. There are other capable, responsible adults who you can reach out to. It is OK to ask an aunt or uncle, a teacher, a counselor, a coach, a pastor, the parent of a friend or some other adult who is trustworthy to listen to your feelings; ask them for ideas, too. Many teens ask other adults to help them handle life, to be a mentor and encourager, when their own parent(s) are unable to be compassionate, patient, kind and available for them.

Lonely Girl, I'm glad you are doing something different with your feelings by reaching out and communicating with me. That is healthy and positive. Now you have some choices about what you can change. Try taking one small step and just see what happens. Try to let go of expecting a bad response or none at all. Have the courage to try something healthy and different and miracles can happen!

Your encourager,
Susie Vanderlip

CHAPTER SIX
For Teens: A Lesson in Asking a Parent for What You Need

Lonely Thirteen-Year-Old (LTYO) did tell her mom she felt like her parents didn't care about her because they never seemed to notice her skateboard tricks in front of their home. She told her mom she was feeling very lonely and really wanted to spend time with her. To LTYO's surprise, her mom replied, "Sure, let's go to lunch today."

Off they went to the local Applebee's for lunch. LTYO was amazed how easily her worst fears worked out. And how relieved she felt! At lunch, her mother shared some disturbing news, but it helped this troubled 13-year-old understand why her mother and father had been so distracted. Her parents were getting a divorce.

This news wasn't altogether unexpected by LTYO. Her mother explained how much emotional turmoil she was in and how stressed she had been for weeks. Her mom just hadn't had the energy or emotions left to show her daughter how much she cared about her. Her mother hugged her, reassuring her that they would stick together through the changes. Her mother also reassured LYTO that her father loved her just as much, but that he, too, was emotionally struggling with the painful process of divorce.

LTYO and her mother made an agreement that whenever anything was bothering LTYO, she was to ask her mom out to lunch at Applebee's. That would be their signal not to ignore problems, especially as the future involved new changes, new fears, and lots of emotion.

Though Lonely Thirteen-Year-Old was not thrilled to have her parents separate and divorce, she did find her mother and father willing to talk with her AND take notice of not only her skateboarding, but her schoolwork, her friends, and her need for guidance and attention.

LTYO was a clear example of how sensitive pre-teens and teens can be; **how vulnerable teens are to assuming that parental problems are somehow the teenager's fault, resulting in the teen literally believing that he/she is no longer lovable.** From here, it is an easy step for teenagers to look for ways to escape such a painful self-recrimination.

By LTYO being honest about her feelings with her mother, asking her mother to clarify why she was ignoring her daughter, and then LTYO asking for the time she needed with her mom, a serious, long-term wound to LTYO's self-esteem was avoided. Ultimately, it helped improve relations within the whole family. Her parents actually reached out for counseling and, as of this moment, are working through their problems as they, too, make the effort to learn to communicate with more honesty, clarification and sharing about what they need from one another.

The key to asking for what you need from your parents, or from your teen for that matter, is to use the right words! LTYO's approach to her mother offers an example of excellent communication skills. These include:

- **Avoid starting sentences with the word "YOU."**

YOU sentences are usually "blaming" sentences like:

"YOU made me mad"
"YOU hurt my feelings"
"YOU should have known"
"YOU just don't care about me"
"YOU don't appreciate what I do for you"
"YOU hurt my feelings when you ignore me."

When we start a sentence with the word "YOU," it often means we expected a person, often a parent or child, to read our minds and know what we think and need. We may subconsciously expect others to be perfect, even hold them responsible for our own happiness. Naturally, believing these unrealistic expectations, we are bound to be disappointed!

- **Instead, use descriptive sentences that describe how you feel when someone does something or behaves a certain way. Then ask for**

what you need or ask for more explanation about their true intent.

For example, try sharing with your parents:

"WHEN we go in separate directions a lot of the time, I FEEL ignored. Can we make a date for the two of us to go to lunch at Applebee's and talk?"

Another example you might use when you are having lunch together:

"WHEN you don't notice how good I'm getting in skateboarding, I FEEL like you don't really care about me. Is that how you really feel?"

Then listen. Keep your mouth shut! And hold back your fear. Listen for where your parents may have been overwhelmed, fearful for you or preoccupied by demands and stressors in their own lives.

CHAPTER SEVEN
For Parents: Listen and Ye Shall Receive

When your teen talks, are you *really* listening or do you just *think* you are? When teens aren't allowed to finish their sentences or have an opinion, beware of the reaction! Here are some quick tips to evaluate if you really are hearing your teen.

If a family communication style includes interrupting teens in mid-sentence, criticizing their opinions, calling them stupid, telling a teen what he/she should think and that his/her feelings are "wrong," then expect to create a teen with fear and, eventually, abundant anger. Teens will fear being wrong and, as a result, may develop a powerful need to be right – becoming a bully. This communication style feels to a teen like being emotionally "bullied" at home. Many such teens withdraw into a hopelessness and despair that looks like apathy. Such states of mind can easily lead a teen to gangs, drugs and alcohol, and/or drive them to bully others in an attempt to feel important and garner respect (even through force) in a desperate need to control something in their lives.

High school student body leaders have shared their anxiety with me when a student body leader takes on a dictatorial attitude within the group. Such a teen leader over-controls student government and club projects, unwilling to delegate tasks due to his/her perfectionism and need to be right. They are the kind of leader that takes credit for other teens' efforts. These teen leaders are known to fly into fits of rage when things do not go as planned. Others become over-achievers, never comfortable that they are enough, regardless of many fine accomplishments. These teens exhibit stress-related disorders, anxiety, and share with me how they are plagued with suicidal thoughts despite many achievements.

I observed a perfect example of this need-to-be-right-and-in-control syndrome at a conference for teenage hospital volunteers. The group consisted of approximately 150 bright pre-med teens. Each was planning a career in medicine and was gathering service hours and experience to enhance college applications to the best schools. In our highly competitive society, this focused volunteer effort is common in highly directed, high-achieving teens. What was disturbing, however, was the conversation I had with some of these teens at the conclusion of the day.

I keynoted the conference, addressing emotional awareness, stress management, and the destructive options (alcohol, drugs, violence, and irresponsible sexuality) that even teen leaders adopt to cope with stress and peer and parental pressures. After my closing keynote, I was surrounded by a group of 20 teens. Their faces did not have the determined, analytical expression I observed when they arrived that morning. Now they showed vulnerability and, for some, even desperation.

These high-achieving teens represented a variety of ethnic backgrounds: East Indian, Asian, Caucasian, African-American, and Hispanic. Regardless of their cultural background, they revealed a similar secret: They felt over-stressed and had suicidal thoughts from the parental pressure to achieve. Their parents expected performance from their teens and made every attempt to control their children's futures by critiquing and criticizing their teens' thoughts, actions and feelings. Most certainly, these parents love their teens, but do they know that their controlling communication style may be demoralizing, perhaps even destructive to their kids?

Some of these incredibly talented youth will join a growing college statistic of depression. A few may attempt, if not succeed, at taking their lives. Others will carry a sense of inadequacy and failure with them throughout their lives, leading to marital problems and health issues. Others may attain the high admissions and enviable careers, but lose their sense of joy and compassion for others in the process.

Communicating with your teens with compassion and patience and giving them room to be human, to have opinions and feelings, can be just as powerful and a far safer approach to high-achievement.

Do you have an underachieving teen?

Curiously, some teens from the same family communication style can have a completely different reaction. Rather than high-achievement and stress reactions, teens may become withdrawn and underachieve.

Shelly is a teen that came from a family with a loud, critical, controlling communication style. Her mother felt she was absolutely clear and right about how Shelly should live her life and, as a result, criticized her incessantly. From appearance to life choices, Shelly's mother told her what to do, regularly cutting Shelly off in conversations when the teen's opinions differed from her mother's.

As a young child, Shelly accepted her mother's opinions as right, or at least not worth resisting. She became docile, withdrawn and isolated. As a teen, however, she began to question her mother's dominance and became tired of being "wrong." She tuned her mother out and silently refused to communicate. She rebelled by making mistakes and underachieving; she stopped caring about her future because the future her mother expected had no appeal. Her mother's style of communication had a significant negative impact on Shelly's under-achievement in school, limited her career choices and inhibited her social skills, impacting life possibilities. It no longer mattered how bright she actually was.

Parents, let go of control and grab onto courteous communication. Your peace of mind is worth the effort!

Consider the following pointers:

1. Control your urge to cut others off, even when you disagree or don't like what you are hearing.
2. Make an agreement that you won't interrupt one another while each is expressing their opinion.
3. Avoid statements like "You are wrong." "You shouldn't feel that way." "I can't even talk to you." Instead, try:
   a. "I'm not comfortable with that."
   b. "Let's agree to disagree for now."
   c. "I need a timeout for (10, 15, 20) minutes. Let's set a time

to finish talking about this." Then keep your commitment to each other and the conversation.

4. Discipline your emotions and commit to not losing your tempers. Flared tempers often cause wounding words, create distrust and resentment, and leave deep, permanent scars in teens.
5. Check your motives, parents/adults: "Am I trying to control my teen or am I truly trying to understand what is motivating them?" Set limits and explain consequences rather than dominate, nag, scold or complain.
6. Set healthy boundaries with calm, simple statements. "These are our expectations and these are the consequences. We set these limits to make sure you are safe. When you show us you can meet them, then we can look at lessening them."
7. Check out the website, Tough Love, for more ideas and support in reaching your highly rebellious teen – **www.toughlove.org**.

80 percent of the message we communicate ...
Be conscious of the following messages teens and adults communicate to one another through **body language**:

- **Hands on hips, leaning forward and a tight-lipped facial expression** are a show of power and/or irritation, disgust and a desire to control the situation. No one feels safe responding to someone in this posture.
- **Both arms crossed** implies an effort to resist the other person and protect oneself from a verbal and emotional punch to the gut or the heart. **If either you or your teen folds your arms tightly across your chest during a conversation, take a timeout.** Change your body language for an immediate change in the progress of the conversation: Uncross your arms, let them hang by your sides, stand up straight and look the other person in the eye.
  Then use a descriptive statement: "I feel that I am being attacked and put down. Can we agree to disagree and take a

break to let go of some of the fear and anger, then resume talking when we are calm?"

- **Head cocked away from the other person, averting their gaze.** The body language of our head and our eyes speaks multitudes! Such body language discounts the value of another person and says: "I don't trust you." or "I fear you are going to hurt me."
  Again, adjust your body language by straightening up, standing on both feet, look one another in the eye, then ask for what you need: "How about we agree to disagree and take a break?" When you resume your conversation, maintain an open, straightforward body language for a conversation that will mirror your body's desire to be present, honest and respectful.
- **If your eyes are everywhere else but directly looking at the other person,** your body in Western cultural interpretation says "I am avoiding you," "I don't buy what you are saying," and/or "I'm not willing to trust you or respond to you." Eyes tell it all.

Communication between adults and teens may start this way, but can quickly evolve into a standoff when emotions get activated. If straightforward eye contact is lost, the adult should request a pause in the discussion to re-establish a positive connection:

1. Suggest that each of you stop for a moment and look each other in the eye.
2. Focus your thoughts into your heart for clarity and calm.
3. Ask yourself what you REALLY want from and for your child.
4. Take several slow deep breaths.
5. Start again, and resist the urge to begin sentences with "YOU."
   Instead each of you share, "I need you ...
   - to hear what I'm saying
   - to listen to me
   - to explain to me

- to trust me
- to cooperate/compromise with me
- to care about me
- to understand how I feel
- to hug me

6. Build trust with one another by consciously practicing tolerance, patience and courtesy.
7. Ask for your teen's opinion or weather report to help you begin again.

These practices may sound unrealistic, however better communication starts by changing the things we can, which is ourselves! Small changes in how you physically, vocally and emotionally express yourself have major impact because people are emotional no matter how much they may deny it to themselves. Small changes can create major successes. An attempt to communicate calmly, more patiently and less judgmentally shows that we accept our part in miscommunication, that we are willing to try and that we care.

I recently had a conversation with Sandra, a very intelligent, driven, 20-year-old young woman. She was angrily "dissing" (criticizing) a roommate. She had trusted this friend to be as committed to the friendship as she was, but the friend decided to move out giving Sandra little notice. Sandra felt betrayed. As she shared, I found myself wanting to control her feelings. I wanted her to think more positively, stop blaming someone else for her feelings, and to just feel better. I began telling her "not to feel that way" and imposing my desires on her. Naturally, she got more upset and became more angry and blaming. The urge to cross my arms, assume the defensive power stance, and resist her intensity rushed over me.

Then I realized I was feeding the miscommunication by trying to force my solutions. I consciously uncrossed my arms, willed them to hang by my sides, and looked her in the eye while using every ounce of self-control to keep my mouth shut and my eyes open rather than squinting judgmentally. I resisted the natural instinct to grimace with disapproval.

Instantly, I felt MY attitude change as I committed to a more accepting and open body language. I found myself hearing more in her words than I had before. I got what I know are "new eyes to see and new ears to hear" – rather than judging her. I could see and hear her fears with compassion rather than react to her angry words.

My own body relaxed and I grasped an important key. It didn't matter that I was right, that I was able to fix her or even that she was happy right at the moment. **It was important that I listened and respected her feelings, which demonstrated that I cared.**

As I felt more relaxed, I was able to accept that she was exactly where she needed to be at that moment. She had lessons in relationship, communication and self-love to learn, regardless of her roommates choices. Those lessons would be learned in HER time, not mine. I could offer love no matter what her level of agitation and fear.

Body language can be altered by choice; and a change in body language immediately changes attitude. Non-judgmental body language is the cornerstone of healthy communication. It is also a critical element in positive parent-teen relationships and, therefore, in healthy teen self-esteem.

Patient listening, positive body language and courteous communication are invaluable investments in your teen's future!

CHAPTER EIGHT
Walk Your Talk for Better Communication

Have you ever heard in the midst of a tense conversation, "Go take a hike!" Or, when tensions start to rise, someone suggests you walk away to cool down? Here's a fresh take on "taking a walk" to improve communication between adults and teens, even under stressful conditions.

Old clichés, simple pleasures and wisdom of the ages have one thing in common – a thread of truth. In raising teens, some age-old truths are still the best practices. One of the best methods for initiating conversation with adolescents (or elders, children, spouses, and even clients, according to my husband who has a clinical psychology practice) is to take a walk together.

Walking is easily forgotten in our hustle bustle lives and quick-fix indoctrination. We are taught to keep kids busy so many parents are buried in chauffeuring children from one activity to another: athletic practices, music lessons, dance classes, tennis classes, voice lessons, hospital volunteering, club meetings, service work, church confirmation, and more. Walking helps us unwind, get fresh air (and fresh perspective) and spend time together outside of our usual ground.

Slow down; calm down; still the irritating internal chatter!

Something is missing in both adult and young lives: Simplicity. Consider the powerful slogans from 12-step programs: "Keep it Simple" and "Easy does it" or the biblical phrase, "Be still and know that I am God." Quiet stillness is a potent source of creative inspiration and, most importantly, peace of mind.

Teaching stress management to all types of teens, from youth on probation to teens at the top-of-the-class, has shown me that nearly 100 percent of teens are awed by the indescribable sensation of a quiet mind. Having guided teens across America in a 7-minute guided meditation, I have been touched that teens unanimously express awe and profound gratitude for the experience of a peaceful mind through this experience. They clearly hunger for a few minutes that still the incessant mental chatter and negative self-talk so common in life. They hunger, as do adults, for that profound sense of peace found in prayer and meditation, especially when practiced over time. Alcohol and drug abuse abound in both teens and adults who are desperate to still the self-critical, angry, judgmental inner voice of their minds.

How can we help teens as well as ourselves attain these moments of calm? How can we promote that peace from which come patience, compassion and courtesy towards one another?

One such way is to slow down our pace for a half-hour each day and simply **take a walk!**

Practice the walk-about.

Author Bill Marsano writes in *A Tribute to the Wonders of Walking*, Hemispheres Magazine, May 2002: "Skeptics should know that the link between walking and thinking has been known if not understood since at least the fourth century B.C. In Athens the Peripatetics (from the Greek word "walk about") would listen and learn as their master, Aristotle, walked with them."

You may not be an Aristotle, but every parent, stepparent, aunt, uncle, grandparent and adult mentor has life experience worth sharing that can be conveyed and, perhaps, best received while walking with a teen.

I learned this lesson in my marriage to my husband, Ken. We are blessed to be quite compatible, the benefit, perhaps, of lessons learned from less-than compatible first marriages! However, I think it actually comes from implementing the tools mentioned earlier AND from 20 years of taking walks together ... especially when we haven't felt so very in tune or accepting of one another!

You know, those moments when both you and your spouse are over-worked, exhausted, frustrated, overwhelmed and at an emotional bottom. We want OUR way. I think of it as the "I want what I want and I want it NOW" Syndrome! It's a state of mind called "Self-will run riot" according to AA and Al-Anon self-help/awareness programs. This conflux of stressors will drive patience, courtesy and constructive communication right out the window of a marriage and even more quickly out of sight when communicating with your teen.

Stop the "yuck" before it starts.

In our better moments, Ken and I are wise enough to give each other a wide berth and to take responsibility for our slumps before we take them out on each other. We get some rest; make sure we eat; seek spiritual clarity and acceptance through prayer and meditation; work up endorphins through exercise; or reach out to a friend to vent before bringing our turmoil home. I am grateful that we are willing to give each other time and space to work through a bad attitude and temporary slip from sanity.

But sometimes life hits hard and fast. Disappointments mount with no end in sight. God has us in the hall of life waiting, all the doors of opportunity tightly shut, and then God goes so far as to remove the door knobs! When there seems to be no way out of our struggles, anxiety and frustrations, desperation sets in and "yuck" happens! **"Yuck" is when gratitude for our lives, our spouses and our children evaporates and what is left is disappointment and criticism, judging, blaming, and resenting those we love.** His hair is suddenly too long, his clothes too sloppy, his opinions too small. "YUCK!" and our relationship goes downhill from there.

"Yuck" can happen in the blink of an eye in an adult-teen relationship. Teens are volatile. Their emotions shift for no apparent reason (though hormones are a great contributor). A teen's opinions can be incredibly frightening to a parent since teens LOVE breaking the rules: they're thinking outrageously and testing the boundaries of their power in the world and in your home. And, just as incomprehensible and extreme as a teen can seem to an adult, adults appear rock-solid rigid and out-of-touch to a teen.

So, how do my husband and I handle "Yuck" and how can you and your teen do the same?

Keep the solution simple:

1. Recognize you are at odds by noticing when blaming and/or resenting one another sets in.

2. Choose to take action to stop it. It IS a choice!
3. Request that you take a walk together; then DO IT!

When the mind and spirit are unwilling, you can still get the body to take action! Ken and I grab our tennis shoes and hit the trail.

While walking, you and your teen face the future TOGETHER.

Sitting or standing opposite one another can quickly turn into arguments because we read the defensive, even disgusted body language of one another. Adults and teens hate to feel judged, rejected, disliked, blamed or resented.

Instead, try walking side-by-side and create a totally different body response. As two people walk side-by-side, we intrinsically find ourselves facing a common path. The future becomes something we are sharing and the focus is taken somewhat off of each other and down the road.

When agitated by life or each other, Ken and I may begin walking the trails in our local park, single file and in silence. Ten minutes, maybe 30 minutes, will pass as we each wrestle with our own feelings as well as the exertion on our lungs and legs. Judgmental, frustrated, angry, and agitated thoughts have a way of diminishing as walking engages muscles and the brain releases endorphins. I know that my pent-up angst will diffuse, my mind will begin to relax, and I become more reasonable. Then we begin to talk as we walk and find we are far more willing to compromise and listen to one another.

Other times we walk side-by-side around the neighborhood. If feelings and frustrations are running high, we may walk in silence until, again, endorphins begin to release the stress, calm the mind. Words take on the calmer rhythms of the body. At this point, we are often more patient and more tolerant, both critical ingredients to communication with you and your teen. When we walk and talk side-by-side, the energy of an angry word is not directed physically at one or the other of us. Instead, the actual energy is directed outward. Someone else's angst is not "taken to heart" because it physically is not aiming directly at us as it is when face-to-face.

In his article on the wonders of walking, author Marsano says, "The slow, insistent rhythm of ambulation stimulates the mind, encourages it to roam and speculate, gives it wings."

Albert Einstein walked to unravel the mysteries of the universe; many religious sects encourage walking pilgrimages to give us the time and physical doorway into our spiritual natures and connection with the divine. My husband even takes walks to conduct psychotherapy, especially with depressed and lethargic clients. When walking along a quiet tree-lined avenue, many troubled clients find that difficult, long-silenced feelings surface more easily and with less fear.

Research shows that 30-minutes of walking daily can help lift depressive feelings. So imagine what it can do for the attitude of an emotionally volatile teen? Imagine what it can do for a stressed out parent!

Walk and talk for better communication with your teen.

- Allow yourself and your teen time for both your minds to wander without pressuring one another for answers.
- Give your brain at least 10 minutes for self-righteous, judgmental, angry and/or fearful chatter to slow down.
- Start talking in short sentences rather than tirades or lectures. Instead, keep up the pace, engage your hearts, and take in full inhales for inspiration.
- Spend 30 to 45 minutes in this walk-about with your teen. It takes time for the body and mind to get in sync with your spirit, when body language takes on more harmonious tones, and we are more open, more willing and more able to trust.
- Keep on walking together, no matter how heated either of you becomes. Trust will build in your relationship when both of you continue walking together rather than walking away/giving up.
- If the conversation gets dicey, just shut up and walk! Allow the silence and the rhythm of your body to calm your mind. Ask yourself, both teen and adult,
  "How important is it to be right?"
  "Do we HAVE to have an answer this very minute?"

Amazingly, another half mile may bring the very answers you need, even if it is to "decide not to decide" on the matter for now or to just to "agree to disagree."

Walk-about communication can be a great starting point with a quiet, withdrawn and isolating teen that is not prone to share. It can also be a great way to find some common ground between two headstrong family members!

The biblical statement, "Be still and know that I am God" is often borne out on a quiet walk by oneself. When we walk with our teens we may find it equally true: Walk to know yourself and to commune with your children.

Two undeniable facts corroborated by prevention research:

1. Parents are the most influential factor on teenagers' choices.
2. How parents communicate with their teens, starting in infancy, determines what that influence will be.

It is never too late or too early to learn and practice the four actions of healthy communication and expressions of love with your teen:

1. Compassion
2. Patience
3. Kindness
4. Courtesy

Your teen, even your spouse, may not be ready to give up efforts to be in control rather than to cooperate. Try out the suggestions in this chapter; and teach them to your children.

Seek progress, not perfection.

The difference when even one parent practices courtesy and respectful communication can be the gift of harmony for the whole family.

SECTION TWO

Healing your Kids, By Healing Yourself

There are no perfect people in my world, doubtless in yours either. As a result, there are no perfect parents. That let's you off the hook! It's about PROGRESS IN PARENTING, NOT PERFECTION.

We adults carry our own imperfect childhoods inside. Some of us have wonderful memories; plenty do not. Some of us have grown up stating that:

"I will NEVER treat my own child the way I was treated."

"I hope I can be half as good a mother as my Mom was."

"I promise myself I'll never hit my children."

"I won't let my kids get away with some of the stuff I got away with!"

We have convictions galore until, of course, we hear our own parents coming out our mouths in a moment of anger or fear over our own teen's choices.

It's important that we explore the impact of our own childhood triumphs and defeats as well as our parents' successes and failures to uncover some of our motivators today.

As children, we all made assumptions about parents and about ourselves as we naturally sought to get our physical and emotional needs met and to feel safe. Around a habitually angry or harshly critical parent, we may have sought to get control in this uncomfortable situation. Others of us might have responded by overachieving, while still others melted into the background of mediocrity. Some of us might have acted wildly rebellious in a counter-attack.

Though we acted out in different ways, our common basic assumption was likely that our parents didn't love us, thus we were somehow not loveable enough. We blamed them or blamed ourselves, adopting behaviors that supported our belief.

Those assumptions and reactive behaviors are likely to color our parenting in the present. And today's teens WILL let us know about it through similar assumptions and reactions as we re-enact the childhood battle of wills!

As intimidating as the process may seem, raising a teen is a great opportunity to find out what motivates you, what assumptions and behaviors you want to hang onto, and which you don't. Through self-exploration, support groups and/or professional therapy, our own childhood anger and resentments can be put to rest. As we heal our past and find forgiveness, our parenting is raised to a new plane of compassion, fairness, patience, clarity and appropriate consequences. As we heal ourselves, we have the opportunity to heal our kids, and even minimize the false assumptions they may make in the first place!

Julio, the gangbanger from *Legacy of Hope*® presentation:

And then I heard like it's OK to pray, man. I mean, like I always pray, man, like, "Hey, God, get me outta this class, man!" Or, "Make that babe look at me, huh?" But like there's a whole 'nother way to pray, man. It's like: "Hey God – Hey dude, what do you want me to do with my life today ... You WHAT?" He's tougher than my old homeys! He wants me to tell you, like, I found somebody to love at these support meetings, man. It's cool, man, it's ME I'm supposed to love! ... He told me to tell you that the real somebody to love ... the real somebody to love, man, that's YOU. That's you!

CHAPTER NINE
Your Own Priorities Rub Off

One of the tough responsibilities of parenting is to guide your teen in establishing healthy and meaningful values and priorities. How else will they know what is and isn't important and have the wisdom to make good choices?

Parenting includes paying attention to how and where your teens spend their time so you'll know when to step in and help. Prioritizing and setting values in life are learned behaviors. How we live our adult lives are the critical models upon which our kids learn values and priorities in their lives.

For the past 10 years, my dear friend, Toni, and I have gotten together for two solid days of marathon cookie baking at the holidays.

What we love best about this tradition, of course, is the rare opportunity to spend 6-hour stretches at a time chatting, laughing, babbling and problem solving one another's lives. Toni is a full-time mom of two secure and well-adjusted children – David, a teenager, and Barbara, a young adult. Toni made the choice over 12 years ago to leave a prestigious position as controller with a major financial corporation to focus her talents and energy on raising her kids.

She recognized the significance of the choice and did so in order to be the key influence in David and Barbara's lives. Toni has been a clear example of the value of a parent's presence to supervise such things as what and how much TV children watch; what friends they keep; what supervision is present when children are at a friend's house; assuring good nutrition by providing home-cooked family dinners every night (which research has shown is a significant deterrent to teen alcohol and drug use); and just being there to guide, encourage, discipline, listen and love them through the good and the tough times.

Like the vast majority of parents, Toni believes her children come first. When her children were three and five years old, she felt compelled to take action on that belief.

While working, she came home from her demanding job exhausted, stressed, and lacking the mental, emotional and physical resources to be fully present with her kids – to play, supervise and enjoy them. As in most two-career parent households, it became impossible to be the parent she wanted to be. So, she walked away from her career and made it clear that her family's well being was the top priority in her life.

In the months after she quit her job and was home full time, Toni's children showed marked changes. They became less agitated, more secure, and, as a result, their behaviors more mature.

Of course, Toni's choice to be a full-time mom may be beyond financial reach for most families today where both parents must work to survive, if not thrive. Nevertheless, her home has been a very interesting laboratory in which I have observed the powerful and positive impact of parents actively demonstrating to their children that they are more important to them than more money, property or prestige.

So how do you translate this into YOUR life, when you are bogged down by house payments or rent, and the other costly stuff of raising your kids?

Allow yourself the courage to make small choices that favor your family and children when you can.

Being present at a teenager's athletic event or school play – even if it means an afternoon off work at no pay – is worth its weight in gold. Make a point of attending those evening functions at the school designed to get you acquainted with your children's teachers.

The vast majority of parents think by high school it's no longer important to show up at a school open house or other youth event. But teens tell me different. **Many teenagers yearn for their parent to care enough to show up and pay attention to who they are now.**

Numerous conversations with teen and college athletes, in particular, has proven to me time and again the critical importance of parents showing up at a child's/teenager's events. I remember the brawny, six-foot, 200-pound baseball player who asked to talk after I presented a program for the athletes at a major NCAA university.

He sat through Legacy of Hope® with his teammates as they watched, laughed, and played slightly macho and aloof to the program's dramatics. Yet, afterwards he had a very personal story to tell:

> *"I've played ball since I was six. I'd come home from school and my granddad would demand I threw balls and had batting practice in the backyard with him every day. Not a day went by. He was tough, kind of mean, but he was gonna get me a college scholarship playing ball. It was all about that. I also remember how my Dad never came to a single game. He went to jail when I was a little kid for drugs, so I lived with my grandparents. Even after he got out, he never came to a single game. Here I am on a baseball scholarship; and he says he'll come, but never shows." At this point he had tears running down his face. "I'll never be good enough for him will I? Sometimes I think I should just quit; what's it all for anyway?"*

No matter his level of accomplishment as an athlete, the deep wound of a neglectful father will likely have a negative and esteem-draining impact on this young man for life unless he seeks psychotherapeutic and spiritual healing.

The priorities of a parent leave a lasting legacy on the esteem and well-being of every child.

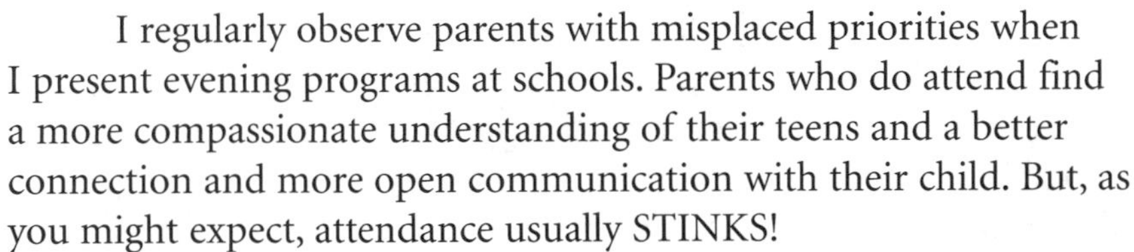

I regularly observe parents with misplaced priorities when I present evening programs at schools. Parents who do attend find a more compassionate understanding of their teens and a better connection and more open communication with their child. But, as you might expect, attendance usually STINKS!

Granted, parents are extraordinarily busy, but by the time their children are teens in high school, even middle school, a vast majority of parents appear to have rearranged their priorities. Perhaps parents assume it's not as important to be involved in a teenager's education. Some may presume that their teenager's are too old to need their parent at school events. Some parents see their teen as too rebellious, self-absorbed, or strong-willed for it to make a difference for them to show up at a school program. But teens are still just kids inside and still highly sensitive to the attentions and involvement of their parents.

Pre-teens and teens need parents involved in their lives as much if not more than young children.

It is critical to teens to know they are important in their parents' lives. And parents' priorities tell it all to a teen. Bottom line, teens feel loved by their parents when mom and dad are present at school events. Conversely, teens feel neglected, at fault, angry, even unworthy of being loved when parents do not show up, whether it is a baseball game or a Legacy of Hope® program that helps parents understand their teen's real-life concerns.

This time spent is a huge investment in your teenager's self-esteem and will reap great dividends in their future life choices.

What do we teach our kids about money?

Using Toni and Garry's parenting practices as a working laboratory once again, I observed how they taught their children a healthy approach to money. They could have given their children most everything they desired; instead they conscientiously decided to give their children allowances as youngsters and imposed certain requirements. Ten percent of the weekly allowance had to be put into savings and another ten percent was donated to a charity of each child's choice. They were required to save their money to buy the things they wanted, learning to budget toward multiple wants.

By the time David and Barbara were in their teens, they learned the priorities of giving to the less privileged, being of service through the gift of their time and money and saving toward the things they want. These teens have a healthy relationship with money that will serve them well throughout their lives. Certainly they see money as a privilege and a responsibility, and both are already eager for careers that will be of service to the world.

What do we teach our kids about prestige?

Once more, I observed Toni and Garry make a difficult decision that illustrated yet another personal priority they wanted to pass on to their son, David. At 15, David was attending a school for gifted students. Clearly blessed with a sharp, engineering mind, he is also an avid guitarist, scuba diver, and volunteer at a local hospital. He shows a great sense of community service, thanks again to the positive priorities his parents have instilled in him. However, a tough choice faced Toni, Garry and David in his sophomore year.

David's high school is rigorous, with nearly every student competing for entrance to prestigious colleges. Like all high-achieving teens today, David came home with four to six hours of homework every night. He was on track to compete for admission to prized universities, especially if he sacrificed his personal interests for a full complement of demanding Advanced Placement (AP) classes. However, as Toni put it, the AP classes were "sucking the life out of him!" Toni and Garry did some serious soul-searching as they sought to set the right priorities for their teenage son.

Following their value system, these two parents decided it was more important to have David opt out of one or two AP classes to allow him time for some hobbies and the expression of joy in his life. To make this decision, they had to consciously observe their son without judging him. They had to set aside their own expectations, fears and egos to recognize and nurture what brought out the best in their child.

As I've heard from many a teen high-achiever, parents do get caught up in fear that their teenagers won't be accepted into premiere colleges.

A teen feels intense pressure when parents put their own ego and expectations above their teen's emotional, spiritual and physical well-being.

Like many accomplished parents, Toni and Garry could have pushed their son into excessive over-achievement. Instead they stuck to their priority of loving their child for who he is including all his unique interests and talents, strengths and weaknesses, setting healthy and productive limits that worked for him.

Too much stress in a teen's life leads to a dangerous legacy.

David's parents were able to see the reality of excessive stress on a teenager's life. They knew that many of David's high-achieving peers were abusing alcohol and marijuana, some even used ecstasy and methamphetamines to cope with the performance anxiety they lived with every day. Was this a price worth risking?

A disturbingly large number of high-achieving teens across the country have admitted to me that they feel overwhelmed by the intense competition, demands of teachers, and unyielding expectations of their parents. They also have shared how this unrelenting stress drives them to reach for drugs and alcohol for relief.

In Chapter Seven, I mentioned my experience when speaking at a conference for teenage hospital volunteers. Three hundred high-achieving teens attended. Sadly, the majority admitted to having had thoughts of suicide because of intense pressure to achieve. Many admitted to abusing drugs. A large number admitted they would consider cheating on exams to meet their parents' expectations.

I met in a circle with two dozen of these ethnically diverse teens (East Indian, Caucasian and Asian) during their lunch break. As we chatted, every one of them shared having had suicidal thoughts on multiple occasions. Though many did enjoy their experiences volunteering at their respective hospitals, they nonetheless were straining under intense anxiety. They literally felt that they would be nothing if they did not please their parents and achieve prestigious careers with substantial incomes. **They had clearly translated their parents' priorities into a dangerous assumption: Achievement is necessary to be loved.**

Remember, parents are in the driver's seat.

In the long run, Toni and Garry agreed that if their son does not get into top East Coast colleges because they opted out of a few Advanced Placement classes, his life would not be ruined and they would love him no less. Together, this family established a healthy work ethic for their son, laced with personal growth that has ripened into playing guitar at church, enjoying community service, and living a more manageable, stress-less lifestyle. David appears to be headed toward discovering many true talents and succeeding at a fulfilling life with healthy priorities.

Now, more than ever, it is time for working adults to revisit their choices and recognize that we are teaching life priorities to our children with every choice we make. It is also important that we recognize the debilitating impact of too much stress on high-achieving teens. Instead, choose a healthy balance of priorities that do not overload your teen and endanger his or her life. The respect and value you show them will build their self-worth and release their greater enthusiasm and creativity. It is from this positive exuberance about life that we all contribute more to our families and the fabric of society.

Parents have the power and the responsibility to promote peace-of-mind to their children. Help your teenager balance personal well-being with the ever-present pressure to attain a greater piece of the American pie!

CHAPTER TEN
Teens Hunger for Spiritual Relationships

Many teens, from troubled to triumphant, have shared with me their hunger to believe in and experience a loving Higher Power/God as the protective and guiding light in their lives. We adults become that "God with skin on" to youth. Parents are our children's initial authority figures and, by default, the earthly role model for their relationship with the Higher Being in their lives. Should that Supreme Being be trusted or disdained? Often for a teen, it depends upon the degree of compassionate parenting they have received throughout childhood.

We can help teens find a fulfilling spirituality and peace they seek by making a conscious effort to communicate with them from a place of compassion.

◆

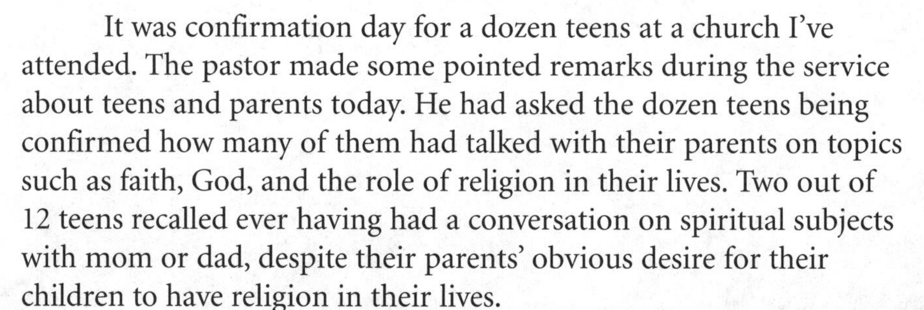

It was confirmation day for a dozen teens at a church I've attended. The pastor made some pointed remarks during the service about teens and parents today. He had asked the dozen teens being confirmed how many of them had talked with their parents on topics such as faith, God, and the role of religion in their lives. Two out of 12 teens recalled ever having had a conversation on spiritual subjects with mom or dad, despite their parents' obvious desire for their children to have religion in their lives.

The pastor also polled the teens to find out if any had ever discussed character, ethics, right and wrong with their parents. Only one out of 12 remembered any such family conversation. In fact, according to a study the pastor had read, 90 percent of teens at a U.S. high school graduation had never discussed the subject of right and wrong with their parents. They did believe, however, that it was right not to get caught doing something wrong!

The point of the pastor's sermon was to motivate the congregation to question why parents, grandparents, aunts, uncles, and other adults in a community do not properly educate our young in values, character and spiritual matters.

Teens hunger for meaning in life including a relationship with a higher being/God that is REAL, that helps them find the purpose to their lives, the love and the joy.

Teens would like to know that the God of their understanding really does respond to their everyday needs. For a teen, this can include regular bouts of being overwhelmed and insecure. They admit they need help sifting through the barrage of media and peer messages that promote instant gratification, over-indulgence as a virtue, extreme-living as nirvana, and a self-serving approach to relationships in every area of their lives. They want their lives to "work" and to feel that they matter, but many haven't the slightest idea what that looks like or trust that a Supreme Being influences the outcome. For those who do not have involved, compassionate parents, all they have to model their lives after are the stars of sports, music, TV and film.

This natural spiritual seeking is evident everywhere I've spoken, from grade school children through young adults in college. When I share about the need to nurture the physical, emotional, mental AND spiritual aspects of our lives, youth listen. I have also mentioned in my presentations that the only way I am able to share my most personal tragedies is because I have found a caring, miracle-making power in my life that I choose to call God. I tell teens in secular schools as well as parochial settings that I felt called to the Legacy of Hope® outreach by the God of my understanding, and that He gives me the passion and vitality to continue through some very trying moments. Teens and young adults enthusiastically applaud the message of an involved and caring God. They are encouraged by the hope that they, too, might be helped and guided by that power.

On countless assembly days, teens as well as faculty have come out of the crowd to say, "Thank you for mentioning God!"

Oddly, many have approached me cautiously, as though sharing a dangerous secret. Though we have legislated God from public schools, I have observed that many teachers and teens continue to express a hunger for a relationship with a power higher than themselves, especially a relationship that is present in their everyday lives. To the schools' credit, in all my years touring nationwide to secular as well as parochial schools, I have never been censured for speaking of spirituality and the God of my understanding.

Because I am not a teacher, I am not restricted by state or federal mandates. Rather, I am governed by the wishes of my client schools. And they continue to appreciate a message that does not promote a specific religion but that does include encouragement to consider that:

- A Higher Power is in charge
- We don't have to be perfect to be loved
- Divine Spirit can provide the Hope to overcome adversity and challenge no matter how old or young we are.

Teens hunger to be understood, to be loved just the way they are, and to be forgiven in spite of painful mistakes and some very devastating pasts.

In thousands of conversations, teens have painfully admitted that they have lost faith in everything and everyone, including God. Many a high achiever has admitted to me that he/she does not put his/her life in the hands of a Power, rather choosing to rely on intense determination, instead. High achievers have been pushed, trained and rewarded for being 'the best,' for 'winning,' for being most in control.

Many achievers come to believe that they are supposed to be able to control the outcome of their efforts. They often feel deep inside that they earn their love through achievements. This illusion about self-worth has resulted in an epidemic of overly-stressed, anxious, worried and even suicidal achievers.

Such teens share that they would like to believe there is a God that really can help them out of the utter sense of loneliness and hopelessness their lack of spirituality produces. They want relief from their fears:

- fear of failure;
- fear of not being perfect;
- fear of not being loved by parents;

- fear of being unlovable and losers;
- fear of making wrong decisions;
- fear of being alone;
- fear of the future.

Excessive stress levels and suicidal thoughts are the manifestation of an achiever's spiritual emptiness.

Teens immersed in overwhelm and stress, whether from family problems, abuse or excess pressures of high achievement, feel that God has forgotten or given up on them. Or maybe God just decided they weren't worthy of His love and miracles. Teens from broken homes, or abandoned or abused by a parent, can have an even harder time with the concept of a compassionate, forgiving God. They equate God's love with the traumatic rejections they have experienced from their real world parents.

However, I have been surprised by how quickly tormented teens to high-achievers will open themselves to the concept of a loving God in their lives. Their hunger is great for something reliable and forgiving in this world that won't let them down or condemn them as losers.

A Supreme Being only becomes REAL when at least one adult in their lives expresses genuine loving kindness, acceptance, and compassion toward them.

When adults use phrases that show an appreciation for a teenagers' feelings in addition to encouraging sound decision-making, they experience more dignity and self-respect, more lovability. Rather than putting blame on your teens, scolding or telling them what they 'should' do, consider trying more neutral statements like:

- "That teacher does sound difficult to talk to. What other ways could you try to get him to understand?"
- "I can appreciate how you feel. I remember when I was 15

and had a similar experience ...
- "I'm sorry your break-up with your boyfriend hurts so much. How can I help to make it better?"

Adults who remain calm, open and listen to teens rather than react with anger, criticism and immediate punishment are examples of a loving Supreme Being accepting and loving us even as we make mistakes and struggle for answers to painful situations.

◆

I have had long-term e-mail exchanges with quite a few 'lost-cause' teens, alienated from parents and their God. I have also been amazed at how they have turned away from destructive habits and suicidal thoughts once they experience the unwavering support of one counselor, teacher, mentor, parent, foster guardian or grandparent that took them kindly yet firmly under their wing. And with a God who cares, a teen's life begins to matter. They believe they count!

Of course, we adults have little to give to a teen unless we invest in ourselves as well. The capacity to be that healthy parent, mentor, counselor or teacher begins when we devote time to our own emotional, mental, physical and, certainly, our spiritual well-being. As our spiritual life grows, so grows our self-worth, hope and healing. Then we can truly be a guide to teens who need and are spiritually hungry.

CHAPTER ELEVEN
The Serious Impact of Abandonment: When a Teen's 'Attitude' is Actually Grief

In all my travels, perhaps the greatest emotional trauma I see in teens is GRIEF. The primary grief is over a parent they do not see or cannot connect with, whether due to abandonment or a parent who is just not emotionally there for them. Many such parents misinterpret a teen's grief as "an attitude." A stepparent can quickly become the logical target, the outsider that can be blamed when a teen's sense of loss for a missing biological parent creates a pain they do not understand or know how to deal with.

Many teens speak of loving stepparents who treat them well. Yet these very same teens are angry and critical of these caring stepparents. Why does a teen perceive their stepparent, whom they trusted and loved as a younger child, with distrust and disregard once they reach adolescence? A pattern emerged that I think ALL parents deserve to know about.

I see this projection of pain quite often in teens that cannot stand their stepmom or stepdad. Many times when teens complain to me about a stepparent, their biological parent is no longer present in their lives. Maybe 'bio dad' left when they were an infant, or before they were born or when they were a child. Maybe they know where 'bio mom' is, but she's engulfed in alcoholism, addictions, prison or her own life priorities and makes no attempt to connect with her offspring. Regardless of the reasons, teens in these situations share similar sentiments with me:

- "I don't like my Stepdad. He says I'm the problem in the house."
- "I haven't seen real my Dad since he left. I want to be with him, not my Mom and Stepdad."
- "My Mom says I'm the reason they fight (are breaking up, getting a divorce). I hate my Stepdad!"
- Or an emphatic, "She's not my real mom, why should I care about her?!"

Both biological fathers and mothers have abandoned children today. Many children are not allowed to see 'bio dad' or 'bio mom' while growing up. OK, so he was an addict or an abuser; she was violent, irresponsible, uncaring. A child entering adolescence asks lots of questions that beg to know more about both parents:

- Who am I? What have I inherited from my family – brains? Good looks? Sense of humor? Hot temper? Rebelliousness? Addictions?
- Do I fit in with other teens? Which ones?
- What am I going to look like, act like, be capable of?
- Am I lovable?

This is when abandoned teens may reject stepdad or stepmom. The stepparent is in the way of answers from the real 'bio-parent' who is missing from the picture. If 'bio-parent' has been in and out of a teen's life, perhaps due to addictions and rotating companions, a preteen/teen can still have a powerful urge to be with them. As teens struggle to fit in with ruthlessly critical peers, it becomes especially important to know that they can be loved by their biological parents. If they do find that love, they are bolstered and stabilized. If they do not, they are crushed. Why should friends love them when their own flesh and blood does not?

In this situation, a stepparent is now irrelevant if not down right irritating, reminding abandoned adolescents that they have a missing piece from their identity puzzle. As a result, friction occurs with stepdad/stepmom. Irrational arguments break out as a teen vents their anxiety, anger, hurt and confusion over the nagging possibility that somehow they were not enough for missing dad or mom to want them. At home, their remaining biological parent may try to maintain the peace or find themselves blaming their teen for what appears to be an inexplicably bad attitude!

Truth is, your teen may well be experiencing grief and loss that no one is willing to validate, understand, or acknowledge as real, much less help to heal. Adults themselves often have repressed their own grief or vent in ways they are not even aware of. Parents and stepparents may feel helpless, often attacking one another because the underlying issue is misunderstood. Mom may demand of a moody teen:

"Why don't you love your Stepdad anymore? He has always been good to you. He doesn't deserve your attitude. Now, you go to him and tell him you're sorry!"

Or Stepmom may cry to her husband:
"She just doesn't like me anymore. I've tried to be a good stepmother to her, but this isn't worth it any more. I just can't take the way she looks at me with so much hatred. She says she doesn't have to do what I tell her anymore; I'm NOT her mother, you know!"

Help lies in understanding the teen years.

The field of neurological psychology has found that the human brain undergoes a growth spurt in teen years similar to that from birth to the age of four. This huge growth (of the cerebral cortex) gives teens the mental capacity to analyze and question everything! From this new capacity to question who they are comes the hunger to connect with their biological roots. Simple answers or attempts to distract their attention no longer suffice to satisfy a growing mind.

Losses from a teen's earlier childhood float up as part of this self-exploration. Old griefs that your child seemed to get over years ago or never even seemed to notice, may now loom large in a teenager's thoughts and feelings. All a teen recognizes of an old grief is that he or she feels confused and angry, rejecting the very people once loved. Stepdad or stepmom, so easily accepted as a child, is now seen through this expanded awareness and refreshed pain. Teens can become acutely aware of what they will never have – two loving biological parents who treasure, respect and adore them.

Grief is a profoundly powerful emotion that re-surfaces when we least expect it.

The loss of a dream is especially intense. For a teen to lose the dream of an intact nuclear family can create grief that lingers for a lifetime.

Adults rarely give themselves time or proper support to process loss. A teen with no concept of how to handle such feelings can get stuck and buried in the anger, denial and rage of grief. Teenagers are naturally self-conscious and self-absorbed, which complicates grief. They will often hide their grief, embarrassed over their thoughts and feelings, and change this already-painful loss into shame. **They often believe that they were somehow at fault for whatever grieves them, especially abandonment.** The loss of a parent, even in a child's infancy, often creates a recurring loss throughout their lifetime.

Enter stepdad or stepmom in the midst of this identity crisis and you find what I call 're-grieving.' Though part of the family for years, a stepparent is now irrelevant to a searching teen. Stepdad is now an irritating disciplinarian who does not really love them the way their "real dad" would if he were around. Stepmom wants to know too much, and it's none of her business to a teen who actually just wants to talk to bio-mom and hear her say, "I love you."

They do not recognize that their anger at stepdad or stepmom is actually displaced grief and loss for a missing biological parent.

Because most adults have either processed or successfully suppressed their own past grief, they may not recognize or want to deal with the grief of their teen. Instead, mom may tell her teen not to bring HIM up any more. She may refuse to let her teen seek out "the jerk" that beat her when her teen was an infant. Thus, the teenager becomes the family "problem" when grief and loss may be the actual issue.

These grieving feelings often fester into tales of depression, suicidal thoughts, alcohol and drug abuse and/or meaningless sexual encounters.

Unprocessed grief can motivate dangerous teen choices.

In 2002, a 15-year-old girl at a high school shared with me that in her early adolescence she began to drink, do drugs and "hook up with a lot of boys" to escape the pain of being rejected by her dad. He had abandoned her and her mother at birth. She had never met him. Now as a teen with increasing awareness and sensitivity, she was plagued by thoughts of being unloved and a loser.

"Why not party in a big way?" she asked, "I'm worthless anyway."

She desperately wanted to find her 'real' dad and believed he would love her if she could only be with him. However, her mother forbade her to seek him out.

"My mom would go ballistic if she thought I was secretly searching for him," she told me.

She saw her mother as an insensitive tyrant when, in fact, her mother did not grasp the severity and the power of her daughter's grief.

Many grieving teens admit to me that they contemplate suicide and act out on themselves (self-mutilate) to cope with feelings they don't know are stages of unfinished grief. I received an e-mail in the Fall of 2003 from a girl who expressed sentiments similar to those of thousands of teens who have shared about grief with me over the years:

> *"My parents got divorced when I was in the 3rd grade and I didn't want to talk about it to anyone. I began to block people out and I really felt no one cared anyway. I thought no one would care if I weren't even here. My own Dad turned his back on me and moved away to be with another person. He cares more for them than me. I figure he hates me. Why should I care about myself? No one else does.*
>
> *"They may say they care but I don't trust anyone enough to believe because they will leave me one of these days as well, so why get close? I now do things to myself to try to get rid of this worry and guilt. I feel it is my fault and I wonder if it is worth it to be here.*
>
> *"I don't want to talk to my Mom because she will hate me as well."*

In serious emotional trauma, this teenage girl hid her grief from her mother, her father and her friends. She is confused and ashamed over what she is feeling. As a result, she has closed herself off from others and her emotional isolation is distorting her perception of how others feel about her. She interpreted her parents' distraction and grief during their divorce as her fault and a sign that they no longer loved her. Suicidal thoughts now plagued her as she continued to interpret her parents' every behavior through a dark curtain of grief and as a sign that no one loves her.

Naturally, I e-mailed back with a good deal of explanation about adult grief in a divorce and teen re-grieving. I commended her for the courage it took to reach out to me and coached her on opening up to her mom. She took the risk to talk to mom and found out her mother understood her loneliness and fear of rejection.

I am always amazed and encouraged at the healing power of one open and honest conversation between a parent and a teen.

How the death of a significant person impacts a teen.

I had yet another conversation with a teen impacted by a different grief, the death of a boyfriend:

"I haven't told anyone, my boyfriend died a year ago from drugs," an attractive, together-looking teenage girl shared with me in the auditorium of her school.

She had a very believable smile on her face, and appeared quite composed and confident.

"I am sorry," I shared. "Is that painful?"

She shrugged, "Maybe."

I continued, "I know when my husband died from drugs and alcohol, I grieved very hard. I felt sadness like a heavy weight on my heart that felt like it would never go away, and I cried a lot. I felt angry. Sometimes I wanted the world to just stop and to run away from everything. Do you feel like that at all?"

She nodded "yes," in spite of continuing to hold the smile on her face. The excruciating grief she held inside was in extreme contrast to how normal she appeared on the outside.

"I remember," I told her, "feeling like I didn't want to live anymore when my missing him was so painful, no one seemed to understand or want to talk about him anymore, and life felt too overwhelming and lonely." And I looked deep into her eyes as she nodded a big nod in agreement.

So I went on to describe my grief to give her something to

compare her experiences to. "On his birthday, or on our wedding anniversary, or when I was at a restaurant that used to be our favorite, or I found myself at a special place that reminded me of him, it hurt – it hurt really badly."

One more time, she nodded as she related to the feelings then started to cry.

"I've thought about killing myself, sometimes," she murmured.

I reached out; and she hugged onto me tightly as she sobbed for several minutes, and then gently pulled away. As I placed a supportive hand on her back, she said, "Thank you...thank you."

She continued to listen intently with open eyes and a hungry heart as I shared openly and honestly about my own grief experience: "It is normal to feel deep sadness and loneliness when someone we love dies. It is normal to cry at unexpected moments after someone we dearly love dies. It's important to get the pain out, to cry and let someone be there with you when you need the support, to hold and reassure you that you are not alone in such agonizing sadness.

"I even wrote letters to my dead husband," I continued, "telling him how deep my sorrow and sadness were. A therapist suggested I do this to uncover all my feelings. And, guess what? Under my deep sorrow, I also found anger, a ton of anger!

"I was furious that he killed himself with drugs! Once I got out my deep hurt and rage at him for killing himself with drugs, I felt some relief and was then able to get back into my day. So, I encourage you to write when sadness wells up in you during the day. Let the anger come out. You may find yourself swearing, even ripping the paper as you write. That's OK. A big part of grieving is anger with the person who has died and maybe anger with God as well for letting it happen. You may feel angry at everyone else around you; they can just seem so superficial for awhile. That is just plain old powerful, bite-you-in-the-rear GRIEF!

"Get it out of your head and onto paper. Then find an adult to share your feelings with. Your counselor can be great person to share your writing with. It's called processing your grief, and, believe it or not, school counselors are trained to understand this process and help you get through it. You may want to share with your mother or a teacher you trust, or a pastor at your church.

"Reach out to someone you know who understands grief and knows how to listen without trying to fix you or tell you to "get over it." I encourage you to read your letter to this trusted person. When people listened to how I felt and let me get it out, I no longer felt crazy, alone or wrong about having these feelings. I found out they are a pretty normal reaction to losing someone you love. And get hugs. We all can use physical comforting and reassurance. It helps when someone is there to help us walk through the pain, the past and back into living in today."

She had calmed down by then, let out a big sigh and hugged me once more. She was able to put words to her feelings and let out her depression and thoughts of suicide.

"Now I think I can stop hating my Mom and my Stepdad," she realized. "I've given them a really bad time since my boyfriend died. They didn't even know about him. I hated them for thinking I'm so perfect, I'd never hang around somebody who does drugs. But I LOVED him, and I couldn't even tell them or say why I was so angry. I just shut myself in my room. My Mom thought it was my Stepdad, because I refused to talk to him any more. He thinks I'm so perfect. I couldn't stand to see him look at me like I'm so sweet when my life is so screwed up right now."

She agreed to go to the counselor with me, share her story, and bring her mom and stepdad in to share the real truth of her love and her loss.

A week later, she e-mailed,

"It's all OK again! THANK YOU for listening. I never knew what it meant to lose someone you love so much. But now I have my Mom and Stepdad back! I love them, too. I'm so glad you came to my school or I might never have had the courage to tell them. And they were fine and hugged me, too."

Watch for the sign of "re-grieving" in your teens. Don't underestimate the power of past loss to trigger adolescent "re-grieving" in your teens.

If your pre-teens or teens begin to reject stepdad or stepmom, I encourage mothers to broach the subject of 'biological dad.' And, dads, broach the subject of 'biological mom.' Ask them about any other disappointments or sadness in their lives right now.

As you help your teen uncover, talk out and accept loss in their lives, you give them strong layers of trust and security. You teach them resilience to life's inevitable pain. AND you can heal current rifts with stepmom or stepdad. Bring peace back into your home!

Suggestions:

- Answer your teen's questions about a missing parent, no matter what your opinion of them may be. Help your teen explore his/her heritage with physical and personality descriptions and a family history of both parents. Try not to color your answers with your own anger, grief and loss. Be factual and as helpful as possible.
- Consider reconnecting with missing grandparents so your teen can reclaim their missing half.
- Suggest your teen journal about their questions and feelings about 'real Dad' and stepdad, 'real Mom' and stepmom.
- Stepdad or stepmom may find it helpful to spend private time with your teen. Don't push for closeness or expect a chummy relationship. It is your investment of time and your willingness to endure the distance that proves your love to a teen. Remember, this is only a stage, not a permanent condition!
- If a teen's anger persists and is intensely focused at stepdad\stepmom, get help! Seek professional counseling. Plan on you – the parent, the stepparent and teen to all participate in therapy. It is not realistic to take a teen to a professional and say, "Fix him/her." It takes an entire family to heal grief and loss and to rebuild trusting relationships.

Be forewarned, a teen's loss will not just go away. It will remain an open wound in heart and mind if forced to hide or repress it.

All pasts return to haunt us until we make our peace. Perhaps in helping your teen come to terms with grief, you may heal your own.

CHAPTER TWELVE
Turn Gripes into Gratitude

You won't believe the positive attitude shifts your family can make in a single week by keeping a Gratitude Journal!

Parents gripe about their teen:
"He's a slob!"
"She's lazy."
"I have to nag at them over and over."
"I resent their attitude. This is MY house. They don't appreciate a thing I do for them."
And teens gripe about their parents:
"They're always on my case. I'm never good enough."
"They nag at me all the time."
"They never let me be with my friends."
"They blame me for everything!"

Is griping a necessary rite of passage between parents and teens?

Perhaps, yet the process of teens finding their unique identities and destinies, individuating, can be less painful for both teens and parents by a simple change in perspective. Adults and teens often get stuck in a pattern of judging and criticizing one another. Each becomes set on being right and believing the other is wrong. This mindset can appear as permanent as the hardwiring of your computer. Truth is, thinking patterns are more akin to computer software. They can be modified.

Turn gripes into gratitude through a daily Gratitude Journal.

By recording small successes and positive moments in relationships, you can convert a tough day into a meaningful one and a troubled relationship into a hopeful one.

It is an invitation for parents to deepen their appreciation for their teen and for a teen to be appreciative of their parents! When either teen or parent keep a Gratitude Journal, the relationship will improve. When both practice gratitude, the relationship will flourish!

Hanging onto blaming one another destroys family unity and leads to arguments, sarcasm, nagging, scolding and complaining. Diffuse stuffy old resentments and judgments with gratitude.

Regardless of how unrealistic and uncomfortable it may seem at first, I encourage parents to write in a Gratitude Journal every day for an entire week. Write a minimum of three things you are grateful for in your teen. At bedtime, you might record what you are grateful for from the day. Start with small things, as minimal as a good meal, a hot shower, a roof over your head to an unexpected phone call from a friend, a kind word from a family member, even angry words you kept from saying to the kids. Whenever you want to judge, degrade, or lose your temper at your teen, your spouse, other family or friends, take the time to list everything you can think of to be grateful for instead.

Al-Anon, the self-help recovery program for family and friends of alcoholics, provides the following truth, "Take the action, and the feelings will follow."

Amazingly, we can get relief from built-up resentments and anger when we continue to exercise 'gratitude muscles' on a daily basis. By taking the action of trying to find things to be grateful for even in a person, place or situation we resent, feelings begin to change; a deeper understanding and acceptance seeps in. Disappointments, judgments and criticisms begin to fade away, even when it comes to a volatile teen!

Teens – It's your turn!

It also works wonders when teens write a Gratitude Journal on their parents! It is easy to take parents for granted: their financial support, the meals, all those material needs AND WANTS (!) of life that parents regularly provide for their kids. It is also easy to read a parent's actions as insensitive, thoughtless, even selfish, and miss the moments when parents are doing all they can for their teen. Gratitude reminds us to look beyond our own self and self-interest to the spark of goodness in one another!

Try one week at keeping a Gratitude Journal.

The key is to consciously practice gratitude even when you don't feel like it! Yes, it will feel uncomfortable, probably forced, even irritating if not revolting at first.

"Why should I be grateful for that kid?" a parent's mind may say, or "My Mom and Dad won't let me go to parties. They ground me. What do I have to be grateful for?" an angry teen may protest.

Take a deep breath and open your mind for just a moment. Would you like to be free of the anger and angst or has it become so familiar, it is almost comfortable? Looking for reasons to be grateful may not change a situation immediately, but it will change the possibilities. As our attitudes toward one another become more positive, especially between parent and teen, amazing changes can occur in the relationship.

"Ok," a parent may concede, "I'm grateful for my son's sense of humor. He makes me laugh. And, yes, he is healthy. He's old enough that I have some freedom now."

"My daughter is doing well in school. I'm grateful she'll be in college in two more years."

"He/she noticed I had a hard day at work."

Teens may recognize:

"My parents leave me alone in my room when I ask them to. They're trying to know who I am, even if they try too hard!"

"My Mom listens when I'm mad at my friends."

"Dad always gives me money to go to the movies."

"Mom makes sure my jersey is washed for every game."

I encourage parents and teens, JUST JOURNAL IT! If you make the effort to find things to be grateful for, your heart will feel more accepting and you will listen with more compassion and understanding. A subtle forgiveness toward your kids and your spouse will appear. If you are consistent about writing on gratitude, your sense of humor will return! And laughter builds a bridge across the greatest divides in our relationships.

Even at the second week, things begin to change.

Teens and parents gain a greater awareness of the underlying pressures, fears and hopes in each other's lives. It's what is biblically referred to as being given "new eyes to see and new ears to hear" – the compassion and patience we long for with our children. Here is when parents and teens can let go of unrealistic expectations of one another.

"Live and Let Live" from the Twelve Step programs embodies this effort. A Gratitude Journal can bring us serenity and joy as it helps us let go of a need to be right and a need to hold onto pesky resentments that make us judge and separate us from the ones we love. This holds as true for teens as it does for parents!

Over time a Gratitude Journal will enrich your relationship with yourself as well.

- As you write daily, become aware of moments in the day when you got answers to a need or to the smallest of prayers. Record the joy when long-held hopes and dreams are finally realized!
- Notice moments of progress:

Parents: Note when your teen remembers to take out the trash, does their homework without being nagged, brings home improved grades, and is courteous even when you said "No, you can't have the car tonight."

Teens: Note when a parent kept an important promise to you, how your parents really are not too self-absorbed to care. Notice when your Mom makes a special meal because it's something you like, or when stepdad listens without criticizing.

Noticing small miracles can increase our faith in life, and trust in a Supreme Being, which reduces our need to expect too much from others. With that reality check, we all gain more patience and trust in one another.

◆

Gratitude worked wonders in my life!

I started a Gratitude Journal on January 1, 2001 to increase my patience and my faith during some significant health challenges my husband was experiencing. He was suddenly hit with severe environmental allergies. Cleaning products to perfumes, smoke to colognes, formaldehyde to flowers all triggered a severe tightening in his chest, breathing issues, and an angst that would last for hours. Let's just say, he was not a happy camper nor was I as we became prisoners in our own home to avoid daily allergic episodes.

As his anxiety, anger and angst increased, I found myself wanting to fix his problem and improve HIS attitude! Gratitude Journaling helped me to see what was still good in my life: a safe home during this time of reactivity; a hopeful referral to an acupuncturist who was treating environmental allergies with a protocol called NAET; dear friends and family who listened when I was fearful; a sunny day, the delight of my garden; walks in the nature park which we could still take together; a nice hot shower; and a friendly lick from my kitty, Alafia.

Gratitude for the simpler things each day would stop my head from fearful projection into the future and enhance my faith in a power greater than I. When my fear of the future was quieted, I no longer felt that nagging urge to control my husband's condition and his attitude. I was surprised and pleased when he, too, began a Gratitude Journal all on his own.

As I wrote in my journal, I was often amused how something in the day might seem so terribly significant but by bedtime would be resolved. I often laughed at the simple things my husband would be grateful for including entries he liked to share with me that said how grateful he was for *me* that day ... which helped on days when *I* wasn't particularly grateful for me! Our journaling set a helpful and healing tone for us both over many challenging months.

As I look back at entries over the next two years of journaling, I saw how both of our perceptions changed. There were moments when we found gratitude even for those people, places and things we once griped and moaned about, perhaps even resented.

With gratitude, we began to see the necessary role people and situations played in our lives, how they became the catalysts to important choices we might otherwise never have made.

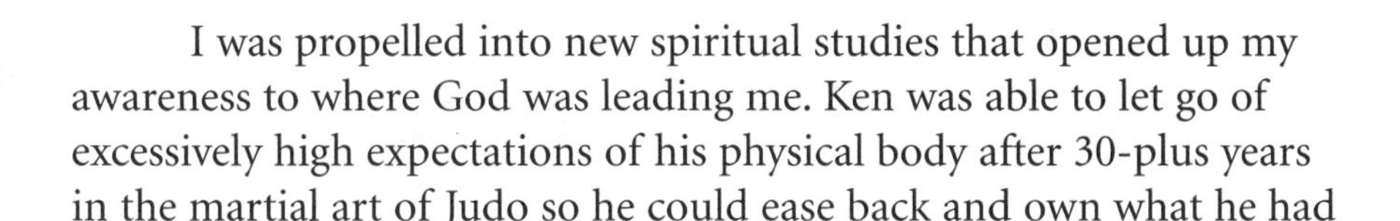

I was propelled into new spiritual studies that opened up my awareness to where God was leading me. Ken was able to let go of excessively high expectations of his physical body after 30-plus years in the martial art of Judo so he could ease back and own what he had become: the wise and venerable Sensei, and leave the painful rest to the young!

I also got important personal insights and a greatly deepened faith. Keeping a daily Gratitude Journal helped me grow in compassion, prayer and patience for both of us.

We found gratitude for one another in spite of the challenges and fears. Throughout this trying year, the daily Gratitude Journal helped me remember that "This too shall pass" and "All things are possible with God!"

Today, Ken is 90 percent less reactive. We feel God gave us a miracle which was possible because of our willingness to release resentment and find gratitude in a tough situation.

Start a Gratitude Journal to rekindle the attitude of gratitude you had for your teen when he or she was an adorable toddler. Use a journal to remind you that adolescence, too, shall pass! Make a commitment to expressing loving kindness and respect in your relationships, even with your teens! They definitely need a communicative and loving relationship with parents to make it through the complex stressors of the middle and high school years.

All it takes is a blank journal from your local bookstore and 10 to 15 minutes of quiet time each night. If even one member of a family commits to gratitude as an attitude, it has an impact on the whole family. Remember, as Nike says, "Just Do It" — *especially* when you don't feel like doing it!

Though the circumstances of your life may not change immediately, your attitude and communication with one another will. And THAT changes everything!

CHAPTER THIRTEEN
Sowing Seeds of Teen Self-Esteem

Interestingly, many of the same factors that impact an adult's self-esteem and subsequent choices also govern the self-esteem of your teen. Self-worth from another point-of-view:

Last Christmas, I was caught up in my annual frenzy to buy just the right presents and find all the best sales. Even as I felt the spirit of the season swell in my heart, I was unsuspectingly blind-sided by materialism. The advertisers weaseled in with one too many appealing offers that increased my appetite for more stuff, more material success in my life. This time it took the appearance of a kitchen remodel, new carpeting ... maybe a new home altogether!

On the tail of this "frenzy" crept the fear of not being enough. I felt it invade my brain and take over my attitude, creating a bout of misery as I lost self-acceptance. Soon, my gratitude for the season was sapped. I felt one of life's most dismal experiences – losing the joy of Christmas!

In the midst of all this, I received an e-mail from a 16-year-old girl I'll call Sarah. From her sharing, it was clear that her entire childhood was riddled with torment, harsh verbal abuse, neglect and molestation. I knew I needed to pull myself out of my own self-absorption to respond to her attempt for help. As I tried to "lighten up" and focus on her, I came across a book in my office, *The Freedom Writers Diary*. This book was compiled from diaries written by 150 teens from Erin Gruwell's classes at Wilson High School, Long Beach, California. One teen wrote:

> *"I needed designer clothes to make me feel accepted by others in school. While everyone was wearing Nike and Cross Colors, I was wearing Pro Wings and swap-meet specials. Wearing them made me feel that I wasn't accepted by anyone. Not even myself!... Since my father wasn't making me feel wanted at home, I really needed to feel accepted by my peers at school. But in order for me to feel accepted by them I felt like I had to have the same things they did.*
>
> *Now that I am a part of something like the Freedom Writers,*

I don't have to try to fit in or to buy my way into acceptance... Now as a young adult I've realized that love is more important than material things. Material things can't love you like a father can!"

A teenager helped me understand the adult me.

This teenage girl's writings reminded me that the material things do not have the power to give or receive love. Through her words, I saw how I, too, needed to focus on taking action to bring hope and encouragement to others. As the teen in *The Freedom Writers Diary* expressed, some adolescents transfer the need to be loved into an adamant desire for a the newest MP3 player, name brand jeans, a red cell-phone cover, or the hottest piece of sports equipment. But the key remains the same – the need to give and to receive love.

I was now ready to respond to Sarah's e-mail. The best salve for my own sinking self-esteem and poor-me's was to reach out and help someone else, encouraging Sarah in her far more desperate place.

Adults and teens alike need to reach out to one another. We all are helped by moments of unconditional love, encouraged by the care and kindness of another. Kindness reminds us that the material world's solutions don't hold the answer to really loving ourselves or making our lives better. Acceptance does. Loving communication does. Service to others does.

Bear this in mind as you deal with your teen and the incredible amount of counter-acceptance messages he or she hears. The world of corporate marketing does everything in its power to disturb your teen's sense of self-acceptance and create a need for their products. The result is often a battered sense of self-esteem. Teens are over-indoctrinated and over-exposed to marketing messages and peer pressure, which are truly one and the same!

Offer your teen unconditional love, listen without criticizing, accept them and their warts, tongue studs, streaked hair and all! Create, encourage, even require participation by your teen in service to those less fortunate, those who are younger and less experienced, older and frail. Guide them into service experience where over time, they are likely to feel true self-worth, gratitude and the self-esteem they deserve.

SECTION THREE

Resources for Everyday Teen Torments

Even with the best of communication, raising a teen is daunting. The world is filled with distractions and dangerous yet exciting escapes for adolescents. Ideally, we all might feel more secure parenting teens with the support that comes from an intact "nuclear" family within a supportive community "village." Wouldn't life be great if every teen had two well-adjusted and available parents plus grandparents, close peers and caring, involved neighbors to guide and encourage them?

Today's real world, however, works quite differently. You might be a single parent with no family and no help from an 'ex' to care for the kids. Take heart. You don't have to handle the challenges of parenting a teen all alone.

As I've traveled, I have found an amazing array of remarkable people and programs devoted to helping single parents (as well as couples) rear healthy teens. You can find help to substantially reduce the hand-wringing and hair-graying associated with the troubling teen years!

Angela, drunk grandmother from *Legacy of Hope®* presentation:

Why didn't she just say NO? Huh? You know what she says to me? "Well, Mom, I wanted him to like me." She wanted him to like her? Now isn't that stupid? Isn't that just like a stupid girl. Doesn't she know they never do, not for long anyway ... So why didn't she think? You know what she says to me? "Well, Mom, we were so wasted by then, it's not like we even really thought about it." My daughter is only 14; at least I waited until I was 16 (to have a baby).

CHAPTER FOURTEEN
Who Told You That You Had to Have All the Answers?

My work puts me in contact with a wide variety of teenagers and their parents. Some of the descriptions given by teens make it abundantly clear that the parents are dysfunctional with a capital 'D.' However, the vast majority of parents I meet care deeply about their kids regardless of their own capabilities at parenting. Many are willing and eager for input on how to do it better.

I keep my eyes open for resources to help parents understand and better guide adolescents. And, I have run across programs that have great promise to ease the journey.

One such resource is **Al-Anon** for parents coping with teens already caught in the crossfire of alcoholism and drug addiction.

How Al-Anon Family Groups can help.

Al-Anon provides safe and sane meetings for families to face the reality of an addicted child, and to learn about the healthy choices rather than go it alone.

I observed a meeting at a rehab facility where a woman shared about her 20-year-old alcoholic son who has been in and out of rehab three and four times, drinking heavily since the age of 12. She shared how she has learned with support to release both her worry and her guilt, one day at a time. She may have the feelings, but also found tools in **Al-Anon** to dispel them and move forward courageously, if not optimistically. She talked of how she maintains a loving relationship with her troubled son by refusing to enable his problems, yet give him compassion and patience, of which she had little before practicing the **Al-Anon** suggestions.

No, he can no longer live at home if he is drinking or using. No, she does not give him money for food or shelter any more. No, she does not take on the responsibility for his getting clean and sober. But she never neglects to say, "I love you" no strings attached. She shows him respect by staying conscious of his right to learn his lessons in his own way and own time. She practices an active spirituality that gives her the courage to turn her fear over to a power greater than herself, a power she calls God. She continues to find her peace-of-mind and sanity in Al-Anon self-help meetings for the family and friends of loved ones with a drinking problem.

I saw the faces of parents at this event change as they began to see the hope of relief; hope for the survival of their young; hope even for their teens' recovery. The teenagers in attendance (all in rehab) also began to grasp the pain their addictive behaviors put their parents through and the devastating possible outcomes of their use.

I saw the expression on one 17-year-old boy's face, garnished with lip and eyebrow piercing, transform from haughty disdain to remorseful tears. He morphed from uncouth rebel to sorrowful son as the gut-level awareness hit him. He realized how very much pain his addiction had wrought on his mom.

Ongoing programs offer real skills – and hope!

Group support in programs like **Al-Anon Family Groups** provides parents with support minus judgment, shame or blame.

Al-Anon Family Groups offer continuous, confidential support meetings for a lifetime if one desires. Depending on where you live, meetings may be held as often as every day or, in smaller communities, once a week. They are usually held in rented rooms at churches or other easily accessible and safe places. A one or two dollar optional contribution is the only cost.

Parents learn skills to communicate in constructive ways with their drinking/drug-using teen; how to stop enabling a recalcitrant child; and how to significantly reduce the tremendous worry, anxiety, fear, and anger they have when a teen has a substance abuse problem. Al-Anon offers a deeply supportive spiritual component as well as practical behavior skills.

Consider the following tips and see your teen through new eyes:

1. **For a moment, set aside all your assumptions and expectations of them.**
2. **See them fresh and with loving detachment by taking the time to observe your teen from afar when he or she is not aware you are watching.**

3. **Suspend judgment and interpretation when observing.**
4. **Look at your teenager as a kid you don't know and seek out qualities you can appreciate, complement, and even enjoy!**

I, too, ask you to observe your teens, being open to their beauty, amazing strengths, precious frailties, needs and fears while you remain strong in what is and isn't acceptable in your home. Your heart will find a renewed compassion, courage, patience, and firmness.

- Contact Al-Anon Family Groups about support meetings in your area at **www.al-anon.alateen.org** or call 800-344-2666 for a World Directory of meetings

CHAPTER FIFTEEN

Pay Special Attention to Your Teen, Especially a Middle-Child

Studies have conclusively found that middle children feel more "invisible" to their parents. What may seem as calm or self-sufficiency in children may lead to resentment and life problems for your teens. Here's how to focus a warm spotlight on your middle child.

When on the Internet, I resist the barrage of pop-up screens. With a deluge of spam, important e-mails, and long to-do lists, we all have more than a keyboard full each day. But I could not resist an AOL (America Online) parenting banner that flashed across my computer screen in recent weeks that stated "Middle Children: Finding Their Own Pride of Place."

I am a middle child, with one older sister and two younger. The article intrigued me, and much of it rang true. If you have a teen who is a middle child, or a middle child soon to be a teen, I encourage you to take note.

The article by Robert Needlman, M.D., F.A.A.P. states that "Oldest and youngest children can usually find reason to be glad about their place in the family. Not so for middle children. They often aren't the biggest and strongest, they aren't the babies who get away with murder; they aren't really anything special, at least in their own minds. Sometimes they feel invisible."

Middle child may build resentment for "second-hand learning."

I remember that very feeling growing up, especially in the early teen years when my older sister was maturing much faster than I was, attracting boys and parental attention as my parents learned to cope with their eldest daughter. In turn, my parents appeared to assume I had learned everything I needed to learn by watching my older sister learn to date, handle curfews, etc. My mother taught my older sister how to put on nylons, shave her legs, and cope with menstruation. I, in turn, got the second edition version from my older sister's coaching.

It wasn't that my parents cared less for me, though I may have misconstrued it at the time. It's just that by the time my turn came round for these rites of passage, Mom had her hands full with two more younger children. If my older sister could mentor me, that was all the better.

Problem is, says Dr. Needlman, "The sense of being less understood makes some middle children feel unloved. In terms of sibling rivalry, the firstborn may be struggling to maintain her position on the top, but the middle children seemingly struggle just to be noticed at all."

You may see your middle-child teen reach outside the family for significant relationships more than your oldest or youngest.

Feeling less important in the family, they may seek a close circle of friends to fill the need. "During adolescence, in particular," says Needlman, "they may be especially influenced by their peer groups, often to their parents' dismay."

In my case, I chose a peer group of high-achievers. My parents lucked out! But my younger "middle-child" sibling chose a more rebellious crop of teens. Her adolescence was smattered with acts of willfulness, rebellion, less achievement in school and more party time. Thank goodness it was an era of few drugs on the teen scene. Today, a middle-child teen may be more susceptible to drug and alcohol use and an active sexuality as he or she seeks a sense of importance to defuse the painful impression that they are invisible to their parents.

Don't be surprised if the middle teen veers to a completely different track than the older child.

Dr. Needlman makes another accurate observation, "Often, rather than competing head-on with that older sibling, the middle child chooses to go in a different direction. If the older sibling is a great student, for example, the middle child may become a musician or an athlete. Some research suggests that middle children are more likely to engage in dangerous sports, perhaps because they are used to taking risks. By choosing a niche that isn't already occupied, a middle child increases his (her) chances of standing out and being noticed, and decreases the risk of negative comparisons."

I certainly can see how several of my life choices were made in order to be different than my older sister. I remember in high school how my parents raved about her drawing and painting talents. Today she is a distinguished artist, of which I am quite proud. But rather than compete with her as a teen, I pursued cheerleading, dance and math. I chose a career in computer science and semi-professional modern/jazz dance while my older sister became a wife and mother.

My sister and I made different but productive choices. But it could have been very different. Today, many teens I speak with tell tales of attention-seeking behaviors that are far more dangerous. They describe anger, resentment and intense feelings when they feel invisible, especially in a world that worships stardom.

So when teens ask to share their problems with me, I often ask about where they fit in the birth order as well. Perhaps some of their risk-taking behaviors can be averted by better understanding the unintentional "stigmas" of birth order.

Uncovering the motives beneath their choices gives a teen power to be more responsible – 'able to respond' rather than programmed to react.

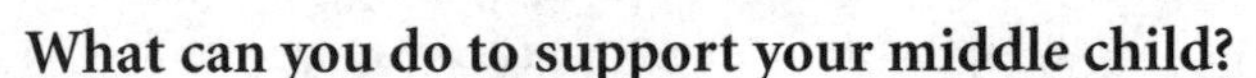

What can you do to support your middle child?

1. **"Take the time to look – really look – at your middle child,"** says Dr. Needlman. "What is it that he (she) does best and makes him (her) unique within your family? Offer him (her) genuine praise based on his (her) good qualities."

As a middle-child, by the time I was a teen I learned to be cooperative and avoid drawing negative attention. Later, as an adult talking with my mother, I discovered that when I was a teenager, she always thought I had no problems growing up. I appeared so self-sufficient. Instead, she focused her attention on raising my younger siblings, leaving me "well-enough alone." She never knew that I was actually hungry for a greater share of attention. I did not know how to ask for attention, I simply over-achieved my way through high school and garnered the attention I needed from school.

That strategy worked well then but, as an adult when I ran into my first husband's addiction problems, it was once again impossible to get attention. It was a painful time, but I finally did learn the critical skill of recognizing my needs and asking for what I needed from those around me.

Learning to ask for what we need is a powerful tool for a middle child, equally so for every child of any age!

2. **Consciously respect your middle-child teen's need to be different.** "Don't insist on measuring him (her) by the same yardstick that you use with your firstborn. Let him (her) know that it's OK to seek his (her) own path."

3. **Always make special time for your middle-child teen, particularly says Needlman, "if he (she) doesn't seem to need it.** Middle children are often quiet about their needs; they may be more likely to withdraw than to make a fuss."

When you can, make a date with your middle-child teen, just the two of you – mom and teen, dad and teen. Get to know your middle child and let him or her experience just how really special he or she is to you.

CHAPTER SIXTEEN
Music – Salve for a Growing and Expanding Soul

A teen's music is an important part of identity. Rather than take offense to their choices, better to understand their musical tastes.

I learned a thing or two about teens and their music while sitting on a sold-out flight from Philadelphia to my home town in southern California.

I had been traveling for two weeks to schools and conferences across five states and, needless to say, I was excited to be heading for the "barn" and thoroughly exhausted.

To soothe my "savage traveler," I opted to listen to music and channel surfed the airplane offerings until I came across a station of easy listening tunes. Ahhhh ... My mind was transported to a new reality – one without burdens, woes, responsibilities, fears or foibles. Music is such a gift with its power to transform our moods and evoke emotions in an instant.

That moment reminded me of a time when I became aware of how music can transport a teen to a whole new place in a way I'd never suspected. I was on a Southwest flight and sitting in what I think of as "the conversation pit." These are the front bulkhead seats where three passengers sit facing backward knee-to-knee and eye-to-eye with three other travelers facing forward.

I was sitting across from a 16-year-old boy, a big kid about 6'3", 250-plus pounds. He was wearing his own headset and listening to music he had brought with him. His mind, like mine under the influence of easy listening music, was being transported to a reality far and away from the actual airplane we sat in.

I intruded: "Excuse me, mind shifting your feet a little?"

He reacted politely enough, so I continued, "You look like you are really into your music. What are you listening to?"

"Heavy metal," he replied, "and some rap."

I paused, then asked, "May I listen a little?"

He looked very surprised that I'd be interested in his music. He'd have been right if he'd said he didn't think that would be my favorite music. Nevertheless, I was curious to know just what loud, screaming guitars he was so captivated by.

"Why do you like to listen to heavy metal music?" I asked. His response surprised me:

"It calms me down," he said.

It calms me down. Now THAT was a mind-altering awareness! It had never occurred to me that loud, sensory overload was exactly what would calm a teenage boy.

Like every generation of adolescents, teens have such a natural state of energetic frenzy, sensory awareness and emotional overwhelm from hormones and the world around them, it takes their own brand of music to sooth the savage mental static.

Not so very different than we adults!

I finally understood why so many teens wander about life with headsets glued to their ears. They – like you and me – are eager to disengage from the demands of the world they live in. When we adults are bummed, we seek music that soothes, uplifts, encourages and opens our hearts and minds, too.

Teens not only listen to music, they *worship* it and the singers who give them the freedom to feel, express and release the barrage of feelings they are experiencing and have difficulty controlling. My concern is that some teens become so attached to their headsets that it becomes dependence, an habitual escape from communicating about feelings and seeking solutions. Music is a remarkable gift to augment but is not designed to replace the skills of handling uncomfortable situations and positively engaging the world.

And that, my friends, is our job as adults: to kindly monitor the quantity and quality of sensory and mental input that reaches the eyes, ears and minds of our kids. It is critical we pay attention to what we allow our toddlers and children to watch and listen to. Too much TV – they do not develop an imagination. Too much angry, hopeless music – teens will exhibit attitudes and feelings congruent with what they've been listening to. The mind is a sponge and becomes what it absorbs.

Use music as a bridge to communicate to teens about concerns and feelings.

Don't know how to start the conversation? Ask them who their favorite musical group or artist is right now. Ask if you can listen with them. Listen for the emotions in the music. Sure, a lot may be songs that express strong sexual energy (teens are certain to have a lot of that!). You may also hear angst, anger, control, hopelessness, vengeance, jealousy, rage, depression, desperation, anxiety or dejection in the lyrics and beat as well.

WARNING: Avoid being critical or judgmental of their favorite music if you really want to know them!

◆

Instead, use their musical preferences as a key to open the door of communication, to better appreciate the reality of your teen. Try sharing how the music makes *you* feel. "That song makes me feel (happy, sad, angry, depressed). How does it make you feel?"

Eventually, they may understand that you, too, appreciate music.

Music brings feelings to the surface, helps us disengage from the demands of everyday life, even empowers us. We all use music to find parts of ourselves, sometimes peace of mind, sometimes excitement or arousal, sometimes to simply be at one with the world. Teens also use music to find that "self" they can call their own, to feel safe, to feel and vent strong emotions. They may be amazed to realize that you care to understand what their music does for them.

CHAPTER SEVENTEEN
"Like" What?

In case you can't remember the phrases you used as a teen that drove YOUR parents nuts, here is a reflection on dealing with your teens' common phraseology in a more, "like," caring manner!

"It was, like, AWESOME!"

"Like, no way!"

"OK, Mom, I'll pick up my room already. Like, what's the big deal anyway?"

"Like" is a communication pause that allows teens to express naive, unconscious enthusiasm as well as anger, strong opinions, scorn for opposing points of view, and often acceptance of peer attitudes vs. parents and society.

"Like" is the great qualifier. It is used for emphasis and for caution.

"Like ... it was just so ... !" says I'm taking a nanosecond to calibrate just how excited to act in order to fit in.

"Like, no way..." says I'm taking that nanosecond to express my complete disdain to the objectionable idea and/or person it represents.

Here's how to get in the way of "like."

I would encourage an involved and conscientious parent to discourage his or her teen from consistently using "like" in conversations with them. Sure, it may be their lingo with friends, but to gloss over the word completely denies your teen the practice of stopping and thinking before speaking. Rather than use "like" to express a whole variety of emotion and thoughts, encourage your teens to try to be clear about what they think and what opinions they hold. Occasionally stop them in conversation and ask for more clarification of what they think and are really saying.

Of course, teens may be more willing to reveal information about themselves with an adult besides their parents. I find when I ask teens what they mean when they use a slang phrase, they actually can identify clearly what emotions they are feeling and even what triggered them. They are capable of being emotionally intelligent, but need the incentive to do so. In my conversations with teens, that incentive is that they know I'm sincerely interested in who they are, and not determined or attempting to change them. I will not make them feel wrong for who they are, so they open up and "like" becomes a full conversation.

If your own teen rejects your attempts to get to know him or her better, I encourage you not to overreact. Don't lose your temper; don't insist on answers every time. Choose your battles! How important is it anyway? But do keep on trying! Only then can you get a window into true attitudes and possible actions.

To help your teen get out of the "like" habit, try reflective listening.

For example:

"It sounds as if you really (like/want/dislike) that (person/place/situation).

"What is it that bothers you about them? What is it that turns you on about that?"

Then offer:

"Thanks for sharing your opinion. I like it when I learn more about you. You're a neat person."

This encourages openness and sharing by a teen in the future.

CHAPTER EIGHTEEN
What's "Whatever!" Supposed to Mean?!

"Whatever!" I hear teens say to teachers, friends, and definitely to parents. Just plain, "Whatever!"

Teenagers use this term and other throw-away phrases when they do not want to respond. The underlying attitude can irritate an adult's nerves like fingernails on a chalkboard. A simple "whatever" can be worse than an outright "no." It leaves the recipient dangling with no resolution, no knowledge of what to expect. To a parent, educator and even a peer, "whatever" can sound like: "I give up" or "I don't care enough about you to explain myself!" or "I don't trust you and refuse to risk explaining myself." **Simple words with powerful messages!**

From tens of thousands of conversations with teens, I think their use of "whatever" is their attempt to defend themselves when they feel overwhelmed or inadequate to fix, change or be enough for the people around them.

For example, repeated criticism and nagging by a parent makes a teen feel like a failure. They feel inadequate to change their parents' negative opinion of them. In e-mail from preteens and younger teens who are upset about parents ignoring them or criticizing them, teens often get to a point in their stories where they just wrap it up with a "Whatever..."

They are saying that they don't believe anything will ever change. **It is an expression of hopelessness.** It is true, to a teen, today's trauma feels like forever. This is when a teen needs help seeing choices. Being able to identify choices is a big part of maturity, and a worthwhile lesson to work on with your teen. Otherwise, the only choice they may feel is to resign themselves to "whatever!"

"Whatever!" may be:

- An attempt to deflect a teen's feelings of failure or inability to please an adult, friend, or handle a situation.
- A teen has stopped caring because he/she never seems to satisfy the critical parent, friend or teacher no

matter how hard they try.

- An expression of annoyed acceptance when there is a lack of communication on both sides.
- An expression of frustration when a teen can't get what he or she wants – simple self-centeredness, which we all have at times.
- A statement of rebellion, "I write you off, you don't even matter."
- A learned disrespect. If a parent has not respected a youth's privacy, boundaries, and personal opinions throughout childhood, then disrespect cultivates disrespect.
- A mirrored attitude of what a teen has observed in a friend, imitation of a peer.

Do not allow a word to become a wall between you and your teen. Look for and consider what is *behind* each "whatever."

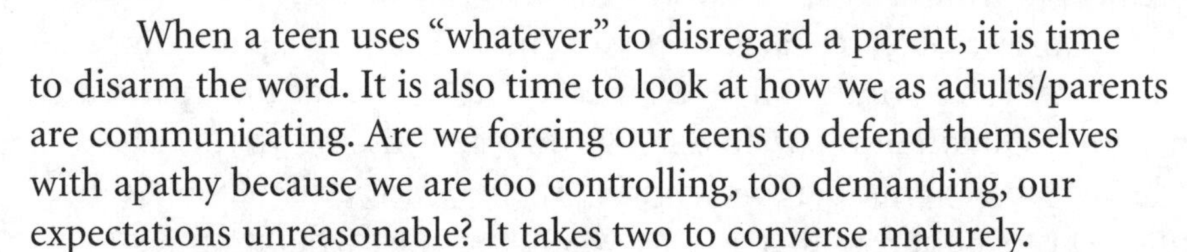

When a teen uses "whatever" to disregard a parent, it is time to disarm the word. It is also time to look at how we as adults/parents are communicating. Are we forcing our teens to defend themselves with apathy because we are too controlling, too demanding, our expectations unreasonable? It takes two to converse maturely.

Every teen and every adult feels the desire to have power over others at times. Some have more need to dominate than others. When a boss is overbearing, when we are gossiped about, or when a friend ignores us at a party, adults as well as teens may have the urge to respond with "Whatever." We rebel, resist and avoid response rather than let our anger, hurt and vulnerability show or face a painful confrontation. But avoidance, resistance, and rebellion do not teach our teens how to handle disappointments and the uncomfortable situations in life.

Don't let "whatever" put you off or shut you down.

In *The Power of a Praying Parent*, author Stormie Omartian shares how she and her husband helped their teenage son move from an attitude of rebellion to one of honor, respect and obedience without losing his self-respect and creative self-expression. They related how their son, Christopher, put posters of musicians he admired on the walls of his bedroom. The problem: The musicians' attire and music they represented were morally and spiritually offensive to the parents. Certainly, their son balked when asked to take them down, but they stood firm. "Oh, whatever," he remarked and belligerently removed the posters from his walls.

"A short time later, however" says Stormie, "he replaced them with new ones which were just as bad." Many a parent might judge, criticize and scold, saying something such as, "How can you like such garbage? Those posters are disgusting! You shouldn't listen to that music. It's sick. What is WRONG with you?!?"

Teens translate such reactions into "I am stupid, disgusting, and a big mistake." And/or "My parents are JERKS!"

Instead, they spoke to their son with tempers under control, stating clearly that his posters were unacceptable. They let him know his rebellious behavior – rather than he and his personality – was inappropriate. And finally they asked that the posters be removed, once and for all.

They stated their rules and expectations based on their beliefs; but they did not criticize his taste or his personality. As a result, he was upset due to his disappointment, but not because he felt unloved or unworthy.

Disappointment doesn't last; low self-esteem does.

Christopher came around. He got over his disappointment by finding acceptable musicians' posters to display on his wall. He recognized that his parents were disciplining his choices not controlling his tastes and that, because of their calm, this was an expression of love and respect. In the process, a potential debilitating "Whatever" (hopeless and resentful) attitude was nipped in the bud!

CHAPTER NINETEEN
Specific Parent and Grandparent Role Issues

Certain relationships in a teen's life have extra special influence and impact. For a girl, it is usually her dad. For both boys and girls, a grandparent can have an incredibly positive if not life-saving impact.

How dads raise daughters is critical.

Dad, the research says it's true: Your teen daughter's decisions and relationships now and into the future really <u>do</u> rely on <u>you</u>. Whether she's choosing values, peers, team activities, boyfriends or eventually a husband, it's your bond that lights her way.

Some 20 years ago, I heard a marriage and family counselor, well known in the world of recovery for alcoholics and their families, speak about what it takes to raise healthy sons and daughters.

"For a boy to grow up with healthy self-esteem," therapist Pat Allen said, "he must be respected by his mother. For a girl to grow up with healthy self-esteem, she must be adored by her father."

This quote is simple, but its impact on teen behavior is profound.

"Dad's either too busy or too critical ... "

Many pre-teen/teen girls share that they feel a deep hurt and sadness because their fathers ignored them as they grew up and now verbally criticize them as teens. I am amazed at how many fathers have accused their 14 and 15-year-old daughters of sexual activity they have not had. Some fathers find it difficult not to project their knowledge of teenage male sexuality onto their daughters. Maybe it is shame over their own sexuality, maybe it is fear for their daughter's well being. Regardless, relatively innocent daughters can become the scapegoat for a father's feelings.

Some fathers restrict teen daughters from talking on the phone to boys and do so with harsh words and thoughtless accusations. Their daughters say they feel horribly insulted, disrespected and unloved when treated with inappropriate distrust by a man they want to accept and appreciate them.

One teen's explanation came through loud and clear, "Why try to be good when my father already thinks I'm sleeping around anyway? It's like nothing I say or do pleases him. He doesn't really care about me. He just cares about controlling me!"

Most dads are simply repeating what they grew up with themselves.

In talking with some of these irritable, angry dads, they share how they were disrespected, if not abused, as children as well. Many of these teen girls have fathers who were severely criticized by fathers and/or mothers. Many a teen's grandparent was, or is still, a heavy drinker, quite probably alcoholic. Verbal abuse and the more serious physical and sexual abuse patterns all go hand-in-hand with alcoholism and/or drug addiction in families.

Dad then grows up with low levels of trust, self-respect and compassion, which seriously impact his self-esteem *and* his parenting. In his anger, hopelessness, hurt and shame, a dad may have acted out as a teen himself including sex without respect for the girls who gave it. His anger becomes disdain for "easy" girls. As his own daughter matures, he may well project those memories onto his daughter. Without experience in respect, trust, adoration, and the development of positive self-esteem, such a dad repeats the treatment he knew as a child and proceeds to shred his daughter's self-esteem.

Sadly, this is when innumerable teen girls have said they seek relief from their own worthlessness, hopelessness, and feelings of not being lovable. Why not allow boys to make them feel loved at this point, even if but for a brief moment?

Dads have the power to shift their daughters' lives.

A father has a powerful opportunity to prepare his teenage daughter for what it takes to resist the pitfalls, including sexual exploitation. That preparation begins at the daughter's birth and is consistently played out through her teens. A father demonstrates to his daughter just how other men should treat her. A father teaches his daughter not to accept selfish manipulation, mistreatment or abuse when dad is patient with her from the time she is a toddler and through her teen years.

When dad takes time to know his daughter's likes and dislikes; when he listens to her chatter as though it were profound and important to him, she will grow up expecting men to treat her as an equal, not as chattel. She will expect respect, equality, compassion, patience.

When dad listens to her feelings from childhood on, he prepares her to listen in return to his fears and concerns when she is teenager. If Dad discusses with her that he feels a party is safe or unsafe to attend; when he sets a workable curfew; when he broaches what he feels are the family's morals and expectations; and then gently, though firmly, tells her that she deserves only the best treatment, a teenage daughter is going to be more receptive. By now, she feels adored and will be much more willing to comply.

Don't get me wrong, teenage daughters will ALWAYS have their moments of rebellion, disagreement, even disillusionment in dad, but these will be temporary. And her love can be re-won in small moments of honesty and caring.

Though fathers may presume a mother's influence is more significant than their own, both the psychological professionals and my own experience with thousands of teenage girls prove otherwise. Dads may find it easiest to get involved in soccer or Indian Princesses, but they must not forget to share in her love of dance lessons, her pets, her teachers and friends, and be there for her hurts, her hairdos, her party dresses, and her embarrassment over boys. Most of all, dad should value her for her preciousness, and tell her as often as he can so that she never doubts she is, indeed, precious. As she matures, dad will see that she allows no one else to treat her as anything less!

Remember the powerful role grandparents play.

There's more to a grandparent's input than "when we were young" stories or what kind of birthday gift he or she gives. Grandparents do matter greatly and can get more actively involved in raising healthy, high-esteem teens.

More and more grandparents today are raising their grandchildren. A few years ago I spoke at a conference called "Grandparents Raising Grandkids." I was incredibly touched by the total commitment many grandparents are making to their grandkids. I heard heart-wrenching stories from seniors whose own children were rendered incompetent due to alcoholism, drug addiction and jail-sentences. Then I heard the dilemma of many grandparents who had stepped up to the plate to raise a third generation of family.

There were many senior citizens whose retirement and social security did not cover the cost of raising their grandkids. Many had second mortgaged their homes. Some had even lost their homes in the process and were moving to rentals to make ends meet for their grandkids. To my amazement, few of the grandparents obsessed on blaming their own children's inadequacies as parents. Instead, they were simply at the conference to help their grandkids, looking to learn and to share tips, hints, and network with other grandparents for support and ideas.

It was at this conference that I became acutely aware of two points:

1. Many grandparents raising grandchildren get no support from the state or federal government as foster parents can, and seriously struggle financially on their own.
2. Grandparents are significant contributors to the self-esteem of grandchildren.

Grandparents are the primary source of consistent love that many a grandchild ever knows.

I am amazed at how many teens have expressed to me the enormous grief they feel because of a grandparent's death. When teens come up to talk with me following an assembly, however, they don't come right out and tell me they are grieving. Teens rarely know they are grieving. It is unfamiliar territory and it is rarely talked about sufficiently at home. Our society is uncomfortable with aging and even more uncomfortable with death. So a teen with a great sense of loss over a grandparent may just become lethargic or irritable and ready to blow at family and friends, or start with drugs and alcohol. Some teens retreat from friends, suddenly finding the normal gossipy conversations annoying and irrelevant. They often just begin with a simple statement, "I don't seem to care about anything any more."

I probe and ask, "What's changed in your life lately?"

"Nothin ... " and after a brief pause and a shrug of a shoulder, "My Nana," "Grandma," "Grandpa," or "Pops" died 6 months/one month/a week ago and she/he was the only one who cared about me."

Such a grandparent treated them as though they mattered, and these teens are shattered.

They are greatly relieved to find out they are in the midst of grieving and that they are not wrong for these feelings. They lighten up when they hear that it is all part of the grieving process and that they won't feel like this forever. Then they get refocused in today and and can go about living in the moment. Of course, I also warn them that these feelings will come and go for some time, that it is important to talk to a knowing adult when the anger, sadness, or despair returns.

Bottom line, thank goodness for grandparents! So many teens would not have made it into or through adolescence without the memorable love and support of a grandparent.

We have 60 million grandparents in the United States. Grandparents can have a significant impact on teenager's choices including preventing substance abuse, teen pregnancy, gang involvement, self-mutilation and suicide.

Message to Grandparents:
Don't let the teens in your life convince you that you're out of touch. That's nonsense!

◆

"According to AARP," says the Campaign, "Grandparents cite drugs, alcohol and sex as the most difficult topics to discuss with their grandkids. With this in mind, the National Youth Anti-Drug Media Campaign website has much to help grandparents. Go to **www.theantidrug.com** and search on 'grandparents.' This site offers information specifically for grandparents about drug use and the effects of drugs, plus tips to discuss substance abuse with their grandchildren.

Consider these strategies offered by the Campaign for Grandparents:

1. **START:** It is never too early to prevent your grandchildren from trying drugs. Simple gestures, such as letting your grandchild know you care, serve as protective factors and play an important role in deterring them from drugs. State your position clearly and often. One of the major reasons teens decide not to use drugs is the fear that their parents or other family members will lose respect for them. Teens do not want to let down their families.
2. **CONNECT:** Take the opportunity to build lines of communication and do things regularly with your grandkids. Spend time together – eat dinner with them, read together, play a game, go shopping, go to the movies, attend a baseball game or go sightseeing together. Use opportunities like family gatherings or inviting your grandchildren to stay overnight to show that fun doesn't require drugs.
3. **LISTEN:** Take a more active interest in what is going on in your grandchild's life. Listen to his or her cares and concerns by fostering family openness and communication. In this way, youngsters will feel more comfortable to open up to you when they need your advice.
4. **EDUCATE:** In honor of Grandparent's Day, spend at least 30 minutes discussing the dangers of using drugs with your grandkids. Continue the discussion on a regular basis.
5. **CARE:** Make sure your grandchildren know you care that they are drug-free.
6. **SUPPORT:** Explain to your grandchild that you are always there for them no matter what happens. Make sure that they know to come to you for help or information.
7. **LEARN:** Children today are sophisticated. In order to educate your grandchild about the dangers of drugs, you need to educate yourself first. Sit down and learn about what messages kids are bombarded with everyday through peers, school and the media. It is up to grandparents to help teens sift through those messages and decipher right from

wrong. Grandparents should also be aware of all of the risks drugs pose.

8. **LEAD:** Young people are as aware of what you do, as much as what you say. Don't just say the right things, do the right things. Set a good example. If you, yourself, have a substance abuse problem, get help."

The Anti-Drug Campaign suggests, for more information on communicating with your grandchild, visit **www.theantidrug.com**. The site offers a brochure titled *Parenting Skills: 21 Tips and Ideas to Help You Make a Difference,* which may also be ordered by calling (800) 788-2800. For additional grandparenting information and excellent resources, visit **www.aarp.org/grandparents.**

One last well-respected resource that will give you ideas to guide your way comes from The Search Institute. The Search Institute was founded in 1958 by Dr. Merton P. Strommen as an applied social science research organization focused on the healthy development of young people. Over many years of research, they identified a framework of **40 Developmental Assets** for raising successful adolescents as well as a second set of assets for young children (ages 6-11), all based on healthy child development.

> *"In an effort to identify the elements of a strength-based approach to healthy development," says the Institute, "Search Institute developed the framework of developmental assets. This framework identifies 40 critical factors for young people's growth and development. When drawn together, the assets offer a set of benchmarks for positive child and adolescent development. The assets clearly show important roles that families, schools, congregations, neighborhoods, youth organizations, and others in communities play in shaping young people's lives."*

The 40 Developmental Assets (**www.search-institute.org/assets/**) recognizes the essential assets teens need to resist the dangerous distractions. All 40 assets are best established in early childhood and include family members who value and appreciate them, parents and other adults that model positive responsible behavior, and support from adults other than their parents. Grandparents certainly can fill the bill!

For more information and insightful direction on parenting, visit their website at: www.search-institute.org/assets.

◆

Parenting and grandparenting is not for the faint of heart, indeed! While raising the teenagers in your life, there will be times when you need help to understand, to cope, to endure the "schizophrenia" of adolescence. I have heard some parents say, a teenager is just like an alcoholic – unpredictable, self-centered, and crazy-making!

Truth is, teens are also joyous, energetic, unfiltered creativity on the run!

◆

Hold onto the hands of those who have succeeded before you and who will support your every effort to lovingly guide your teenager into adulthood where they thrive on their own two feet – and not under your roof!

Give special thanks to grandparents and stepparents, for they often unwittingly end up with your kids living under *their* roofs, instead.

◆

SECTION FOUR

Misunderstood and Overlooked Trouble Spots for Teens

Each day in America, hundreds of thousands of teens in school hallways appear perfectly normal, yet harbor serious secret emotional and psychological pain. The feelings that plague them and what they do to cope with this pain are often hidden from their parents, other caring adults, and even from their best friends and peers.

Perhaps you have noticed significant withdrawal in your teen. You may even be embroiled in some of the serious consequences of a teen's effort to self-anesthetize his or her emotional discomfort with drugs and alcohol, self-mutilation or gangs. Whether these issues are present in a teen you love, or you just wish to be alert and conscious of how difficult adolescence can be, I encourage you to enrich your base of knowledge on the challenges of being a teen.

Disturbing and heartbreaking teen issues can come from rather innocent, seemingly unrelated beginnings. Of utmost importance is that you read on and educate yourself about the possibilities rather than live with the false sense of security that comes from believing, "not MY child!"

The more you know, the faster you can act. The faster you can intercede, the more hope for getting your teens back on track.

Christalisa, 16-year-old soccer player from *Legacy of Hope®* presentation:

You know my friend, Josh? He's that guy everyone makes fun of, say bad things about him on the Internet, call him gay. Well, he's been like my best friend since I was four; he always knows how I feel and stuff. He committed suicide two days ago ... Yeah, I cut on my arm last night. I only do it when I can't stand it anymore. But don't tell my Mom, OK? 'Cause she gets really mad when she finds out I've been cutting on myself. I gotta go.

CHAPTER TWENTY
Communicating With Teens on the Tough Stuff

Since I began speaking to teens in 1991, I have broached the tough subjects of alcohol and drugs with tens of thousands of youth. We adults have a responsibility to mentor the youth around us at every possible opportunity. However, we adults can easily feel stuck and at a loss for words when broaching serious and significant issues with a teen.

None of us are genetically engineered to know how to talk to a teen about drugs and alcohol. As Barry McCaffrey, past Director of the Office of National Drug Control Policy, states, "Anti-drug parenting strategies rarely are instinctive, even for the best of parents." Many parents question if there really is anything they can say or do to influence their teens.

One valuable approach is to learn to communicate with your teens by following some simple tips:

- Be absolutely clear with your kids that you do not want them drinking or using. Ever! Anywhere!
- Be a better listener. Ask questions. Ask for his or her input. Give honest answers.

Here are more suggestions from my own experience in talking to hundreds of thousands of teens:

Don't beat around the bush. Watch your voice and expressions.

- I suggest asking teens straight out: "How much drinking and drugs do your friends do? How do you feel about that?" Teens will share honestly on this question when an adult's tone is non-judgmental and they appear open to accepting without shock or criticism whatever the feedback may be.
- "How much do you drink or use? What do you think about that?" puts teens more on the spot, but I've found them equally willing to answer the question if they feel they will not be scolded and shamed for an honest answer. Teens will usually respond carefully at first, while evaluating your motives. They will accept adult concern in response, but shut down on adult scolding, complaining, ranting and raving.

When asking a teen a touchy question – I encourage you to remember, **it is not what you say, but how you say it that can make a significant difference in how a teen reacts.**

I suggest you consider your goal before opening your mouth. Set your goal on listening and learning about your teen and on building their trust.

◆

Let your teen say whatever he or she wants and express whatever opinion he or she may have at this moment. Let the first and foremost goal of the conversation be to lay the groundwork of trust and respect. Bite your tongue when you feel the uncontrollable urge to tell teens they are wrong, stupid, and absolutely out of their minds! I encourage you to avoid responding, "You don't know what you're talking about!" Fear for a child's safety and fear of consequences on our lives quickly unleashes the URGE to control those uncontrollable teens! **Instead, practice the powerful Don'ts and Do's of Communication:**

If you want a teen to talk to you and share what he/she is really thinking, consider the following **DON'T's of Teen Communication:**

1. **Don't dominate, nag, scold or complain.**

   When we adults get caught up in fear over a teen's beliefs or behaviors, we instantly project into the future and envision the worst of actions and trouble our teens will get into as a result of what we see as "faulty thinking." Our minds become inflamed with imaginings of what a teen may have already done.

   Fear quickly transforms into anger, and anger produces an even more profound impulse to control. We become *incensed* rather than *sensible*!

   Teens naturally do not trust enraged, controlling adults. How can teens be honest with parents and feel understood if parents jump down their throats motivated by fear and uncontrollable rage? From that moment on, credibility with a teen is caput!

2. **Don't lose your temper.**

   As I've mentioned, fear quickly escalates into anger and control. Lost tempers destroy credibility and safety. Any chance to share your experience and insights that might influence a change in their thinking is lost in the bonfire of emotions.

3. **Don't tell them their feelings are wrong.**

   Teens are in emotional turmoil. Of course, many adults are, too, we just label it as stress. It is impossible to suppress, hide and deny real feelings without self-medicating, creating chaos in our lives and relationships, or causing disease – 'dis-ease' – in the body.

   Keep in mind that teens are experiencing a whirlpool of emotions colored by hormones and an ever-shifting identity, all for the first time. They can feel afraid, unlovable, and terminally different, then flip flop to outrageously excited about life and, just as quickly, back to lonely and isolated.

   To tell teens (or anyone for that matter) that what they're feeling is wrong creates great conflict. Feelings are just feelings, and they happen without our initial ability to control them.

To criticize someone for having a feeling creates shame about who he or she is.

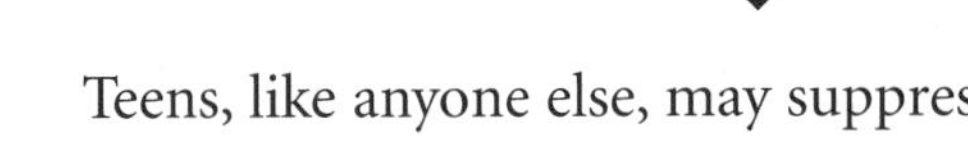

Teens, like anyone else, may suppress and deny to themselves what they are really feeling when they have been told their feelings are wrong. They will lose the ability to accurately identify what they really feel and become far more susceptible to others telling them what to do. When teens no longer trust their own feelings and awareness, peer pressure has considerably more power to influence them. Poor life choices are an expected outcome if teens do not find a safe and sane place to express their feelings without reprisal or shame.

Keep in mind that when teens passionately express outrageous opinions, they are seeking attention and searching for a unique identity. They may be testing how a parent will respond, enjoying the ability to have an impact or even control the situation. They may just be absorbed in adolescent idealism or rebellion. **They usually have no intention of acting on everything they say.**

Make an effort to understand what motivates their outburst. Have you given them enough positive attention? By resisting the Don'ts, you will be better able to grasp what your teens are actually expressing and be able to talk to them about their feelings, actually helping reduce confusion, anger and fears for both of you.

If you can't help but yell and argue, or you feel compelled to try to control their thinking with decrees or criticism, **consider having a more detached adult available to do the talking.** Ask an adult your teen likes or trusts to participate in the conversation – an aunt or uncle, the parent of a teen's friend, a counselor, a therapist, someone with the ability to listen without reacting who will share the common sense solutions you really want your teen to hear and heed.

Remember, the only cure for adolescence is time! You cannot force teens to think the way you want them to, you can only set an example, expectations and consequences. Trust the process. We got through it; they will too.

Now try these positive communication skills:
DO's of Teen Communication

1. **Do be aware of your body language.**

Remember, your body speaks long before your mouth does! Teens, like all human beings, react first to your body language and facial expressions. Body language that says you are listening with an attitude of compassion and patience encourages communication while an imposing physical stance or puckered face says you want to punish, control, change or fix.

Certain body language can project willingness to "understand." I consciously choose how I stand and put a neutral, relaxed expression on my face when talking with teens so they will find me non-threatening and feel safe opening up to me. I choose voice tone and physical gestures that are encouraging.

I make the choice to suspend judgment of them and, instead, remind myself that teens are inexperienced in life and doing the best they can with the circumstances they come from. As a result, adolescents have shared their most secret fears, thoughts and experiences with me over the years.

Teens as well as adults can actually change the way they react and think about one another by practicing open and encouraging body language. Our physicality has dramatic influence on our emotions.

Have you ever had someone help you turn a negative, angry frame of mind around by simply suggesting you put a smile on your face? You may have hated the thought and the intrusion on your mood, but if you actually did smile and kept smiling for a few minutes, your mood picked up. The body is wired to connect smile muscles with a release of endorphins that lift our mood and attitude.

The same principal is valuable when conversing with your teen. Their mind is wired to read your body language and react accordingly. If you have a scowl on your face, a wrinkled brow, and arms tightly crossed across your chest, do not expect your teen to open up to you. They are hard-wired to protect themselves from the angry energy you are clearly prepared to release on them.

Instead, whether you feel loving and open or not, choose to adopt a less threatening physical stance before you start a conversation with your teen.

- **Expression Empowerment:** Smile – yes, to yourself, to a mirror, to the cat or the dog. If necessary, open the refrigerator and look at your favorite food! Smiling brings the brain back into the present rather than out in the future with fearful imaginings. Hold the smile for at least 42 seconds, the length of time it takes for muscles to get the message and impact your mood.
- **Shoulder Savvy:** Lift your shoulders toward your ears and then let them drop into your back. Do this 3 to 5 times so the tension doesn't pool in your "attack zone" – the neck, shoulders and arms from which physical punches are thrown.
- **Standing Statements:** Practice standing evenly on both feet

rather than mostly on one foot. The "hip-out, one-foot" stance projects irritation and judgment.

- **Arm Adjustments:** Make an effort to drop your arms by your sides. Uncrossed, relaxed arms are far more inviting than crossed arms. One hand on a hip or aggressive waving of a hand in the air is clearly threatening and can imply violence.

To maintain relaxed, non-threatening body language requires a conscious choice and concentration.

◆

- **Eye Encouragement:** Lastly, look your teen in the eye as you make the effort to maintain a calm expression. You may find yourself more inclined to listen, and your teen more inclined to communicate honestly and calmly as well.

  If you practice these simple tips, youth *will* open up. They hunger for the experience, insights and suggestions of a caring, accepting adult. Situations regularly baffle and overwhelm teens and they deeply desire direction and validation.

2. **Share your own story.**

Teens will share in excruciating detail once they feel safe. To prime their "talking pump," share stories from your own life on the subject.

When I want a teen to share about current choices on alcohol, drugs, sex, depression, cutting or suicide, I share a story about kids in similar situations whom I have met. I also share freely from my own life experience.

When I do share from my own past, I share not just about the pains but also about the healing of my feelings. I share how I, too, had feelings of bitterness, self-pity, suicidal thoughts and anger. I continue with how I learned to turn the hurt, hate and rage into understanding and acceptance of the things I was powerless over — how I learned that alcoholism/addiction is a disease and that I was not the cause, could not control it, nor could I cure it in someone else.

Basically, I share my experience, strength and hope as

opposed to being stuck thinking of myself as a victim (concepts from Al-Anon Family Groups).

Using stories is basic to human communication dating back to the caveman. So, look for stories from your own childhood or come up with a composite story of several different people you know. Teens will get the point more powerfully and more eagerly from your stories that show the consequences of other's good and bad choices.

REMEMBER: As important as it is to share about consequences, share what the underlying feelings were that motivated your choices and those of the people in your stories.

Teens always relate to the feelings. They know that their own choices are often entirely motivated by feelings!

---

3. **Ask for their opinions.**

Conclude your stories by asking a teen for his/her opinion, "Do you know someone who went through something like that?" "What is your opinion of what happened?"

Teens are often more willing to talk about a touchy subject when asked to share about "a friend." Teens often broach communicating with an adult as though they have a friend with a problem. Once they feel they won't be attacked or rejected, teens will reveal they are really talking about themselves. Then, give them an opportunity to exercise their own thinking. You might ask, "What do you think is a better way to handle that situation?" And then, of course, let them know you aren't giving up on them: "How can I help?"

4. **Give them time to process and get the lesson.**

Typically, teens may not immediately trust your motives. It may take several attempts at compassionate communication before you see a teen respond in kind. Though you may maintain a positive body language and fervently resist the urge to push for immediate answers, your teen may still give you the "shrug" or an "I dunno" response. Now is *your* lesson – an opportunity to practice patience, and try again another day!

Rather than react critically, offer to talk more about the issue when and if they want to. Then casually bring it up again a few days to a week later.

Consider asking tough questions with an open mind!

"Have you thought any more about (binge drinking, driving drunk, drinking at parties, getting stoned, having sex, cutting on yourself, oral sex)? What's your opinion? Do you have any friends you are concerned about?"

In the case where you get another shoulder shrug, an "I dunno" or a blank stare, take the moment to share another brief story illustrating choice and consequences you or a friend of yours experienced. Give them situations to think about that illustrate why people choose what they choose and to evaluate the outcomes of those choices. Through examples, teens learn how to handle real life situations as they occur in their own lives.

5. **Give them safe passage to talk.**

Make it safe for your children and teens to express what they are feeling and what is on their minds. Allow them the right to an opinion without calling that opinion "stupid" or "wrong," even if it scares you! We do not have the power to control their thinking, but we can get them to think!

- Share meaningful stories.
- Role-play pressure situations and practice how to say "no" when peers pressure them.
- Acknowledge how tough these moments can be.
- Share your expectations and hopes for them.

By allowing children to express opinions and state feelings from a young age, they will be more receptive communicators when they reach the rebellious teen years.

Teach them how to recognize initial feelings by making it OK to express them.

Help them stop, think and talk over their choices before they act. It all begins with open and safe communication coupled with fair and consistent consequences.

6. **Play fair and praise often.**

   Straightforward, non-judgmental communication also reduces parental stress. Dominating, nagging, scolding and complaining does not control teens, nor improve a teen's self-esteem.

   - Try praising often.
   - Help them set attainable yet challenging goals through open discussion.
   - Release unrealistic expectations of them.
   - Create rules and discuss in advance the consequences of breaking them.
   - Don't impose harsh or unexpected new punishments.
   - Don't let the rule-breaker off the hook.

In return for the courage, time and energy you invest in teens, you will find uncommon success in common kindnesses.

"It is not subjects which are controversial, but the manner in which we communicate about them and the elements of personal blame we add to them in anger."

(*Dilemma of the Alcoholic Marriage* from Al-Anon Family Groups)

CHAPTER TWENTY-ONE
Stress is as Dangerous to Teens as it is to Adults

At some time or another, we have all reached out to less than the best of activities – alcohol, drugs, food, inappropriate companions or other compulsions – to deal with stress. Models of emotional overwhelm, escapist behaviors, and rebellion in the face of excess stress are prolific in our society. So, why are we surprised when our teens make similar choices?

Teens are seriously stressed. Stress is inherent to adolescence: emotional excesses; sexual overwhelm; fear of finding a future; both positive and negative expectations from parents, school, coaches and society; peer pressure to fit in plus rampant gossip, bullying, a daily barrage of scrutiny of high energy, competitive, critical peers. Lest we ever forget what being a teen was like – it's no walk in the park!

Over 13 years of speaking in schools, from inner city to blue-ribbon private, and at conferences for teen leaders, I've given stress management workshops to tens of thousands of teens. They unanimously respond with deep appreciation! Few have ever experienced a quiet mind, free of fear, worry or anger. Sharing a taste of yoga, guided meditation and positive self-talk, teens soak in the incredible sensation of serenity.

When asked to define stress, teens from at-risk to high-achievers identify a common barrage of uncomfortable emotions: disappointment, overwhelm, worry, fear, anger, disillusionment, hopelessness, loneliness, confusion, desperation, and more. They also define stress through their behaviors and the behaviors of the adults around them: rage - their own and that of their parents including physical violence, isolating, smoking pot and tobacco, alcohol and other drug use, emotional hurt and hurting of others, and, in recent years, an upsurge in self-harm. Clearly, stress has a major impact – not only on adults – but on our children as well.

As stress increases in the lives of us adults, it vents at home, on the job, in the streets, and even in our play. Alcohol and drug use – both prescription and illegal – increase as well. These two factors correlate as readily in teens' lives as they do in adults'.

The vast majority of teens say the greatest stressor in their lives is their parents!

Teens stress over what their parents think of them. They question whether their parents really love them. They stress heavily when regularly criticized by a parent and worry over a parent's unrealistically high or low expectations of them.

Dozens of teens have e-mailed me about severe stress, if not depression, due to the demanding expectations of their parents. A teen leader e-mailed, saying:

> *"My parents are always on my back to do good, graduate and be a perfect little girl. I plan on graduating, but they are always on my case if I don't do better than a C in only one of my classes. I am trying hard, but I just feel like there is a lot of pressure on me, and usually I cry myself to sleep at night."*

Teens, including high achievers, complain that their parents don't appreciate that they have put considerable effort into their grades or into resisting "bad" friends, only to be criticized and told that their efforts aren't good enough. Even top-achievers have painfully admitted feeling suicidal because they never seem to satisfy their demanding and critical parents.

Teens, in general, feel stressed when parents do not acknowledge their efforts. Regardless of whether or not they may come up short of parental expectations. Teens ask, "Why can't they at least see that I'm trying?!" Teens need parents to help them do better in school, rather than *expect* that the teen should know the way.

◆

Detrimental impact of a critical mother on one particular teen:

An at-risk Hispanic high school girl shared her story with me. She lived with her mother, stepdad and a younger, mentally challenged sister. Her stepdad teased and ridiculed her; her mother got angry that she wasn't doing better in school.

She had been a latch-key child for years, home from school for several hours before either parent returned from work. She was required to babysit her mentally-challenged little sister. Her mother fully expected her to become a lawyer, "because she was so good at arguing," Mom often said. Yet, her mother never helped her when she struggled with math, history or English. Her mother barely graduated from high school herself and hoped that by simply placing expectations on her daughter, she would figure out exactly what it took to become that lawyer.

I watched as this pressured girl slowly but surely gave up on school. She struggled with feeling she had already failed her mother by the age of 16. By that time, she found boys and was readily popular with her outgoing personality and well-developed womanly body. Why struggle to do better in school when her stepdad expected her to be pregnant by 17 and a high-school dropout like her mom?

Parents place spoken and unspoken expectations on their teens, and teens take them as gospel. Though they may argue back when a parent tells them they expect better grades, it is recorded as a definite measure of how capable they are. **Many enduring opinions of ourselves are forged in the inadvertent comments our parents make to us.**

Most teens recognize that a good deal of criticism and verbal abuse from home comes from their parents' own stress! Teens do recognize that their parents are coping with financial insecurity, inadequacy and overwhelm of their own. Certainly, plenty of parents have had their own self-esteem rattled by divorce, abandonment, loss of a job, new baby and more! **But it is not a teen's job to be responsible for a parent's self-esteem or well-being by compensating for parental problems.**

Teenage stressors, from grades, critical peers, adolescent sexuality, social pressures, jobs, extra-curricular activities and more, leave them feeling vulnerable and overwhelmed. When adult stress collides with equally stressed teens, communication between the two quickly disintegrates. Often neither one recognizes the underlying cause of their miscommunication: stress induced impatience, martyrdom, unrealistic expectations and exaggeration of problems.

FEAR is a mighty and sometimes dangerous motivator.

Stress is actually the biological response to *fear*. When teens or adults feel fear from real or perceived threat, it causes chemical reactions in the body and mind. A school confrontation with a peer; a parent on a teen's case for bad grades; tryouts for high school sports or cheerleading; an argument with a love interest; or an unfaithful boy/girl friend are all powerful teen stressors. And for adults, a job review; argument with a spouse; overdue bills; college tuition for kids; a new baby; a new home; health problems and many, many more concerns activate excess adult stress.

Subconsciously, many teens and adults convert fear into anger, self-pity, perfectionism, depression, bullying, blame, jealousy, rage or a variety of other alienating and discomforting emotions in an attempt to control fear. A simple outside stressor can become a complex play of emotions and attitudes. The outcome can be overreaction, resentments and destructive actions toward others.

FEAR can disguise itself as a battle of WILLS!

Emotions rooted in fear are not loving, compassionate, patient or kind. They do not promote courteous and thoughtful communication. Instead, fear provokes arguments and a battle of wills.

Everyone can recall arguments between a teen and a parent, perhaps even from your own adolescence. Did either parent or teen ever admit their fears, even to themselves, much less to one another? Probably not. Instead, a battle of wills ensued as fear instantly morphed into self-righteous anger, indignation, arrogance, self-pity, blaming, nagging, complaining, scolding and whatever else it took to hold one's ground or prove that they were right. When in fear, it is a natural human instinct to fight for control – even a false sense of control!

To avoid such common pitfalls, teens and adults can make a commitment to acknowledging their OWN stress levels. Both teens and adults can learn and apply simple tools to reduce the stress in their lives. The outcome will be improved communication, love and support between you and your teen.

Treat stress as the dangerously disabling threat it is to health, healthy choices and loving relationships in our lives.

Reduce the stress on your relationship with your teen by combating fear with the HALT Principle!

1. The HALT Principle:
When too Hungry, Angry, Lonely or Tired – *HALT!*

Hungry:

Hunger leaves us vulnerable to chemical changes that produce fearful irrational thoughts and depressive, angry feelings. Make it a priority to eat healthy. Keep snacks in backpacks, glove compartments, purses and sports bags to avert angry or poor-me reactions just because someone is too hungry!

Angry:

Become aware of when anger is brewing; and HALT. Take a time-out to allow the physical, biological fight or flight response to calm down. It will take a full 30 minutes for the body to reduce the chemical reactions, unless another fearful event occurs in the meantime. Then we can get stuck in the stress cycle. So, take the time to walk and talk out your anger. Uncover your underlying fears BEFORE reacting. Find someone who can help you identify your choices as well as the consequences.

You may uncover unrealistically high expectations of either you or your teen that create constant anxiety and a critical attitude about yourself and others. Being human, you may also have made unconscious assumptions about what others are thinking. Perhaps you assumed the worst and are now in a constant state of turmoil. You may be stuck in the obsessive pattern of self-righteous determination and find yourself at a loss of faith in a higher power or anyone else. All of these patterns are destructive to communication between you and your teen.

Look for choices, even if it is letting go of having to be right!

Lonely:

When lonely, meet with an understanding friend rather than isolating into deeper despair. The majority of teens do not know that other teens, and even parents, have had similar feelings or circumstances in their lives. Remember that teens do not have years of experience to refer to for perspective on problems. New situations in life will loom large and a teen is bound to overreact just out of lack of experience. As a result, they may blow rejection from another teen way out of proportion or not recognize the seriousness of smoking a joint or cutting on themselves to handle feelings of alienation.

Tired:

Research shows that a teenager actually needs nine hours of sleep to function well. They also are programmed with a body clock that encourages them to stay up into the wee hours of the morning! Combine that with school that starts at 7:30 AM, you have a consistently tired teen. The urge to sleep in late is actually a natural response in adolescence. So, give them a break and allow them that occasional Saturday snooze until noon without assuming and labeling them lazy. For that matter, give yourself a break, and make room for that power nap, especially when parenting wears thin on your nerves!

2. Make a List of De-Stressors

To tackle the ever-present intensity of life, make a list of ten healthy activities you find relaxing, which distract your mind and alter your attitude from the glass looking half-empty to half-full. Keep your list handy for moments when stress has engulfed you in a miserable mood and a dismal outlook on life. Then:

Take the right actions, even when you don't feel like doing them!

"Take the action, and the feelings will follow," says Al-Anon Family Groups in coping with overwhelm in life. A more optimistic outlook will materialize by changing the things you can in the moment. Regrets over the past or projecting fear at the future is unproductive, even destructive. Thoughts and energy focused on problems can turn to choices for today and a renewed hope.

Consider the following De-Stressors:

- Hobbies that fully absorb your attention. Tap into the right brain (intuitive, creative, abstract) by drawing, painting, singing, writing poetry, dancing or gardening.

- Get PHYSICAL! Take walks to clear your mind. Engage in sports or fitness activities, including strength and flexibility options. As you release stress from your muscles, you will relax the mind. Consider yoga, Pilates and Tai Chi.
- Allow yourself a quiet half-hour each day to recharge your spirit. Read something that encourages you and builds your relationship with the higher power of your choice. Spiritually uplifting material releases the hold that fear, disappointment and disillusionment have on your outlook or your teen's outlook.
- Meditate 15 to 30 minutes once or twice a day. Through brain imaging, researcher Richard Davidson of the University of Wisconsin at Madison has shown that regular meditation can re-orient the brain "from a stressful fight-or-flight mode to one of acceptance, a shift that increases contentment."
- Journaling is a great help to both teens and adults when life is overwhelming. Write down the fears, angers, resentments, grief, sorrow, shame, blame and projection that take your mind prisoner. Journaling can stop the mind from over-analyzing and obsessing. Then share your writing with a safe, non-judgemental person (minister, counselor, self-help group) to feel accepted and release the shame or blame.

There are a great many tools for relieving adult and teen stress. The key is to recognize that stress is serious business and takes a toll on your health, your children, your relationships and the very satisfaction in your lives.

For more details and stress reduction tools, visit **www.legacyofhope.com**. Check out our stress management products and *De-Stress for Success® Workshops*. In addition, websites abound on stress management. See our website for information on yoga and meditation.

CHAPTER TWENTY-TWO
Stop the "Rumor Mill" From Chewing Up Your Children

While most rumors and gossip blow over in time, the damage done to a teen's self-esteem can sear for a lifetime. Be there for your teen in these painful moments and, at the same time, teach your children to express their feelings and needs rather than gossip about others. Help them become a positive contributor to life, finding things to do that develop their own talents and self esteem instead of focusing on others.

Ask any middle school crowd how many of them have been the object of gossip and 85 percent will wave their hands wildly. Then ask those same teens how many have gossiped about someone else and every hand will sheepishly go up. Finally, ask how many believe gossip and rumors hurt them and their friends, and, again, you will get unanimous agreement. It is clear that gossip begins in earnest sometime during the 6th or 7th grade; and every one of our teens is affected, if not afflicted, by it today.

Today's brand of gossip is more ruthless than ever and dispensed without remorse. I think we adults have allowed our youth to be trained in – and numbed by – a rumor mill out of control. Children and teens are exposed to constant "professional" gossip under the guise of entertainment and news. Today, we are bombarded by a myriad of TV programs that delve ruthlessly into the lives of the famous; news broadcasts that mercilessly exploit everyday people's lives; reality shows that applaud self-centered ruthlessness and dissect every aspect of a person's flaws; and a plethora of magazines at grocery check-out stands that spread outrageous rumors without consequence.

A large number of teens and young adults today have a serious lack of empathy and compassion. This empathetic deficiency may be at the root of what we adults perceive as "a lack of respect" in teens. **But remember, empathy and compassion are learned character traits.**

These more evolved human qualities are developed in our character from the time we are toddlers. Empathy is taught when parents guide us to put ourselves in another person's shoes. For example, you may remember when you were 3 years of age and mom or dad showed you "how it feels" when we bit a sibling on the arm or pulled the dog's ears?

Empathy starts at home.

I observed a simple but important illustration in empathy education over dinner with a family including children ages 5, 10, and eleven.

The 10-year-old daughter blurted across the table at her five-year-old brother, "I hate you!"

Their mother immediately instructed her daughter to notice how it made her brother feel. His chin was trembling, his eyes teary. He had started the incident by flicking a napkin near his sister's eye. She reacted with fear, which quickly turned to anger. She then verbally lashed out. The boy was properly reprimanded for his dangerous antics. But when his older sister retaliated with an emotional dagger, her mother recognized the wounding of her daughter's words as well.

Mom was quick to step in before the damage to her younger son's self-esteem could take hold. She helped her daughter see that words can cut and damage another's self-esteem. She also made sure her son saw how his napkin antics created fear and reaction in others. Both learned a lesson in empathy for one another.

Much to the parents' credit, they did not tell their 10-year-old daughter she was wrong for feeling angry. Instead, they talked about ways to express anger and how damaging reactionary, unkind words can be. To their 10-year-old's credit, she gave a genuine apology to her brother, and he offered his in return.

Our hyper-speed lives, dual-working parents, and increased social trauma puts tremendous strain on families. The pace and pressures can contribute to teens being ridiculed and criticized by parents or siblings. An unfortunate number of teens have shared with me that their parents make brutal remarks to them like "I don't care about you," or "I never wanted you anyway." These statements leave life-long and festering emotional wounds.

In some households, children are taught from an early age to emotionally attack others rather than respond with

understanding, empathy and compassion.

Where Bullying is Born

In homes where one or both parents vent their anger by blaming, shaming, arguing, hitting, or degrading, children learn to do the same. When children see adults or older siblings take their frustrations and feelings out on others, particularly someone younger and weaker, they learn to vent their own anger as verbal or physical attacks on others. They learn to pass the blame to others and become bullies with anger management and self-esteem problems.

Fast forward now to middle school and high school, when preteens and teens live in a constant sea of peer judgment and criticism. Their emotional arsenal is armed and ready. Gossip, bullying and ugly rumors are common among teens. These acts are simply another form of venting low self-esteem, anger and rage on others. Preteens today are notorious for spreading horrendous and groundless rumors. A girl who is too cute, a boy who is very sensitive, a new student, an overweight peer, an intelligent studious peer ... any teen can become the target.

One teen, in particular, stands out in my e-mail exchanges, and illustrates how some teens desperately need compassion and empathy from others rather than rejection and gossip.
She emailed:

Dear Susie,

I am a 15-year-old female. I was at the FCCLA state meeting last weekend and I saw your performance on stage. The part that really caught my attention was the act about the gangster Julio. It reminded me of my life and how it is going at the moment.

I have been in a gang for 5 years now and I know it is bad. I first got involved because I felt like I fit in with these people. They are Hispanic just like me. I thought if I joined I would feel more comfortable with people because I am not a very athletic person and my parents don't have all that much money, so some other girls talked about me and said I don't belong there.

I thought I would fit in better in the gang. I got involved and we did some bad things and most of my friends got sent to juvenile hall. My parents are disappointed in me because they thought I would be a better person than they are. I want to change and be a better person and make my parents proud of me but it is very hard.

I joined FCCLA at my school for that purpose – to change. But I still feel left out of things. My advisor didn't tell me about the Star events but she told other people in my freshman class. She didn't tell me about competing for regional officer but she told others in my class. And other things that I join in I don't get told about events that may happen.

I feel like I am being racially discriminated. And those are the reasons why I feel like staying in this gang.

I feel neglected in school because of who I am. But I feel loved in this gang because they are more like me.

I don't know how I can possibly change now if I am being gossiped about and discriminated in school. Please help me and give me some advice. D.

I responded to her, saying:

Dear D.,

I want to complement you on your good thinking about joining FCCLA (Family, Career and Community Leaders of America). I think you joined for the right reasons and that it does have the potential to help you be the kind of person you and your parents can be proud of.

Yes, gang life has many pitfalls and negative consequences. I am glad you did not end up in juvenile hall like your friends. I bet you have heard and seen some things, however, you wish you never had. Gangs make tough demands on members, and often compromise our values and morals, even if they give us a place to belong.

So what do you do? First of all, I think it is important to understand that our cultural upbringing impacts the way we think and communicate and can sometimes create miscommunication with people from other cultures. For instance, in the Hispanic culture, many girls tend to be less assertive with authority figures than Caucasian girls. I believe it is a respectful attitude amongst Hispanic girls, but it can hinder them. What I would recommend is to go talk directly to your advisor and be honest. Tell her:

1. Why you joined FCCLA.
2. How you feel left out and were not told about opportunities to compete.
3. What you would like, what competitions you want to be a part of.

I don't necessarily think it is discrimination. I think it is probably a lack of understanding on your advisor's part about your cultural background. If your advisor does not see you assert yourself (show positive enthusiasm and request to be included), she may assume you don't want to try that hard, or that you are not interested. The key is to speak up without attacking or even defending. Just ask for what you need: to be invited to participate in all the events.

It takes courage to reach beyond your norm, beyond what feels familiar. Everyday I am on the road, I walk into a new school, a new state, a different set of cultures and attitudes. Sometimes when I go into a school, they are very unfriendly and act like they could care less about my being there. But I don't take it personally. Instead, I stay friendly, and go after what I need. I go directly to the gym, set up my sound equipment and props, start to stretch and do what I am *there* for – present a great assembly. Finally, I remind myself, **"What they think of me is none of my business. What *I* think of me is my business!"** Remind yourself, at the end of the day, the most important person to care about you is YOU!

Every time I go after an opportunity in life and give it my best, I find people who like me, show me kindness and friendship. So, don't give up. Have a MISSION. A GOAL. Don't give up on FCCLA fun and growth based on other people's attitudes. My GOAL is to have a life based on strong morals, values, self-respect, love and tolerance, and support of others in their positive choices.

YOU MIGHT CONSIDER THIS GOAL:

Help others at school feel less on the outside. Suggest your FCCLA club put on a CULTURAL DIVERSITY DAY. Schools where I live do this because we have many cultures in Southern California. Kids from each culture tend to separate during lunch time and at social events. Like you, they may feel they don't fit in and fear gossip and rejection.

A DIVERSITY Day or Multi-Cultural Club can help. Schools dedicate a day for students to share dances, foods, music and holiday rituals from their native countries. In one day, I saw Ballet Folklorico from Mexico, folk dance from Poland, ate French and Vietnamese food, learned about Christmas in Scandinavia, and gained insight into Latin America culture all in one school. Everyone got along much better afterward. Random gossip was replaced by new friends and interesting conversations.

Another idea for you to consider: Do an FCCLA project like "Helping Hispanic Kids Read." I know reading is a big area of interest in FCCLA. Why not get some club members to help you read to children who are just learning English? Or read to adults who came from Mexico and know very little English. What a gift that would be to them and it would help non-Hispanic FCCLA members feel closer to the Hispanic community as they get to know and give aid to individuals.

I think you have the potential to make a really big and important difference. Just don't give up! And don't give in to the poor-me's!!! That can bring us down. Fight a negative attitude by keeping encouragers around you. You can count ME in!

Your Encourager,
Susie Vanderlip

I was thrilled when D. let me know:

Mrs. Vanderlip,

I have talked with my advisor about the reading project

and she thinks it is a great idea.

You were right. All I needed to do was speak up.

She told me that she was wondering when I was gonna ask to do something. I told her well I figured you were going to give me something to do since that's what you told the others. She thought that maybe since I hadn't talked to her that I wouldn't want to do such a project.

But she is very pleased that I have gone to talk to her. I can't start the project this school year because it is almost over. But she told me to keep it in mind and next year she would help me out. She also told me that while I'm on summer break to start thinking about how I will do the project. I am sooo excited and sooo anxious to begin.

I guess I do want to be loved.

God loves you,

D.

So what do you tell a teen that's been chewed up in the rumor mill, feeling left out and like a misfit?

1. First and foremost, offer *compassion*. They may doubt that anyone cares when vicious rumors about them are swirling around school. A little reflective listening goes a long way. "I'll bet you feel really hurt by these rumors," can help.
2. Be direct and ask them how they feel. Many teens are so hopeless and alienated when bullied or the object of cruel gossip that they become convinced there is no way out. Suicide, drugs, alcohol, self-mutilation or sexual attentions appear to be the only way to reduce the emotional pain.
3. Getting the truth up and out is a huge relief to a hurting teen. Assure them they are neither crazy nor wrong for their feelings. Sometimes it is difficult for teens to identify, much less admit to themselves, the hurt they feel. To know that a parent or other supportive adult is there for them is a great reassurance.
4. Share your own tales of woe when you were gossiped about in your life. Describe how it stung and the way you got over it. Teens are hungry to understand and cope with life. Your stories or other people's experiences often reach them best. Through

your stories, they will grasp that they are not alone in their feelings and that they, too, can get through this tough moment.

5. Lay the groundwork of empathetic communication by simply offering, "I'm so sorry you are going through this. I think you are a terrific person and love you no matter what."
6. Help teens grasp that if they have done nothing to hurt someone else, then it is not their fault that someone is bullying them or gossiping about them. A cruel or thoughtless peer is probably motivated by his/her own low self-esteem, anger, and hurt from a home life of abuse or neglect. **Help your teen see gossip and rumors for what they are: one finger pointing at someone else, while three fingers of fear, anger, and low self-esteem point back at the gossiper or bully!**
7. Coach a teen to confront the gossiper. Suggest to your teen that he/she tell their abuser, "I am uncomfortable with you spreading rumors about me. They are not true; and it hurts my feelings. Why are you saying those things? Have I hurt you in some way? If so, tell me and I'll apologize. Otherwise, stop spreading rumors about me or I will report you to the office."

   Though a teen may or may not get a positive reaction, it can help to assert rather than suppress feelings. Knowing that he or she has done what he/she can to stop the gossiper reduces a teen's feelings of being victimized. It helps a teen detach from the gossip.
8. Encourage them to avoid the troublesome teen as much as possible; let the gossip blow over. Should the gossip or bullying continue, assist your teen in reporting the situation to a school administrator. Request the school talk to the bully and his/her parents. Ask the school to set appropriate consequences for past behaviors and future incidents.

It is our job as adults to find balance between what we handle for teens and what we require them to handle on their own. The best we can do is teach teens the communication and life skills to deal with irksome people and situations. With lessons in asserting themselves, it will be easier to deal with life as an adult.

In striking that balance, however, do not overestimate the emotional maturity of even the most capable teen. Identifying what we feel, and finding healthy ways of handling those feelings can take a lifetime of practice.

I encourage you not to underestimate a teen's need for emotional protection and support.

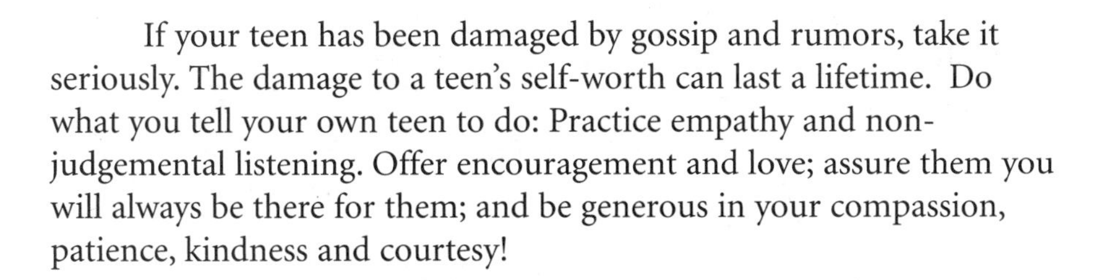

If your teen has been damaged by gossip and rumors, take it seriously. The damage to a teen's self-worth can last a lifetime. Do what you tell your own teen to do: Practice empathy and non-judgemental listening. Offer encouragement and love; assure them you will always be there for them; and be generous in your compassion, patience, kindness and courtesy!

CHAPTER TWENTY-THREE
No Teen is an Island — Isolation is a Dangerous Coping Mechanism

We can all expect a few gloomy days in our lives and that of our children. But when gloomy silence builds a wall between you and your teen, take action. Isolation can be a dangerous coping mechanism.

I received an e-mail this week from a teen who saw my school assembly:

> *"I am going to resort to the option I know best ... isolation. I will keep my mouth closed, and keep all the crazy things locked up. Then one day I will have a massive breakdown, because I won't be able to handle everything locked up anymore. The outcome of that ... I'm not sure ... I assume I will just wait and find out when it happens."*

While it may seem to some that this teen is overreacting, it is not uncommon for teens to feel exactly this way about busy parents. Teens cannot perceive how absorbing the demands of a family and job can be. They do not know the emotions their parents keep hidden under a lack of expression. Instead, teens take their parents' words and actions quite personally. They easily feel rejected, to blame, confused, fearful and abjectly helpless when ignored, nagged, scolded or criticized. At some point, teens may become despondent, depressed or discouraged which drives them to withdraw and isolate.

If belittled, or degraded by either peer or parent, teens may run from the embarrassment and shame. If teens have difficulty trusting the adults in their home, they will hide out in their rooms. Their self-appointed isolation magnifies the belief that no one understands or cares how they feel. A common response is to feel 'terminally unique,' a particularly common perception of children of alcoholics.

Unfortunately, the habit of isolating to cope with feelings can be dangerous for a teen. Teens who escape find it an easy step to alcohol, drug abuse and other social ills to help tune the world out.

Isolation is a self-imposed sentence to wallow in self-pity.

When teens regularly escape to their room and refuse to communicate, it may be a sign of deeper troubles. The troubles may be rooted in drug and alcohol use by the teen or within the family, perhaps across several generations. It is a sign of distrust and communication problems between parents and teen that develops when both judge and resent one another.

If a teen has made a poor decision about alcohol, drugs, sexuality, gangs, cheating, etc., he or she may isolate out of fear of losing the love and respect of parents. Teens will often hide rather than risk honesty and possible rejection and criticism.

Teenage isolation is not cured through nagging, scolding, dominating, demanding or complaining. These tools only reinforce their reasons to isolate. **Instead, try these relationship building techniques:**

1. Turn off the cell phone when you are in the car with your teen.
2. Take time out of your busy life to make a dinner date with your teen, just you and your child.
3. Set dates on both your calendars for the weeks ahead to continue parent-teen "dates."
4. Show interest in their interests, even their music!
5. Ask questions to get to know them rather than interrogate them:
   - What's up with their sports or hobbies?
   - How are things going at school and with friends?
   - Are they pressuring you in any way?
   - Has anything happened that makes you uncomfortable?

Rather than press for details, let them share, and just listen – Listen – LISTEN! Practice keeping your mouth shut and your mind open! Accept mini-dialogues on their hobbies, classes and social lives. Don't expect too much too fast.

Carve out time together and add a pinch of patience.
These show a teen you really care.

Of course, teens can be skeptical. Numerous teens e-mail me astounded I actually respond to their messages as promised.

Apparently, teens have had many promises broken by adults. It may take awhile for them to let down their guard and trust. It is our job to model patience and unconditional love if we want our teens to get it. Go out for a hamburger or pizza, and open your heart and your mind to your teen!

Teen suicide can be the dangerous outcome of denying or ignoring teen troubles.

If a teen is consistently withdrawn, you are not being disloyal or a poor parent to question them about alcohol or drug use, depression or suicidal thoughts. Listen to your gut and take that uncomfortable possibility seriously. Suicide is the third leading cause of death for 15- to 24-year-olds, and the sixth leading cause of death for 5- to 14-year-olds. (For more data, go to the American Academy of Child and Adolescent Psychiatry website: **www.aacap.org/publications/factsfam/suicide.htm**)

Thousands of teens and preteens grades 6 thru 12 have shared with me serious thoughts of suicide and, in some cases, multiple failed attempts. Over the past 13 years, we have administered our *Survey of Hope* to some 25,000 teens in 20 states, asking teens if they would be helped by a support group to deal with depression and suicidal thoughts. The statistics speak for themselves:

In 2003, the *Survey of Hope* results from an upstate New York school district revealed:

- **Over 40 percent of teens in 10th grade and 38.5 percent in 11th grade wanted help for depression.**
- **16.8 percent of the 10th grade and 12.1 percent by 12th grade wanted help for suicidal feelings.**

These numbers may vary, but rarely do I find a school where teen concern over depression is less than 20 percent and suicidal concerns less than 15 percent.

Everyone has disappointments and hopeless moments, but teens that don't feel safe reaching out to others to talk about these feelings end up on a dangerous path. It is, certainly, more important to save a teen's life than to hide in denial for fear of failure, shame and blame.

Parents can begin the process by acting courageously.

Reach out and ask for help from a school counselor or a teen's favorite teacher, coach, pastor, aunt, uncle or other adult your teen gravitates to. Seek professional help for your teen and rehab when alcohol or drug abuse are involved. Relief, understanding, parenting help, and hope are your right, not your punishment!

Constant isolation is neither friend nor solution for teenage angst and problems. It is a prison from which a trusted parent or adult mentor can have the key!

Additional resources:

- **www.legacyofhope.com**, "Ask Susie" or "Resources of Help" from homepage for hotlines and other helpful websites
- **www.aacap.org/publications/factsfam/suicide** – Facts for families on teen suicide.
- **www.psych.org/public_info/teen.cfm** – *Let's Talk Facts About Teen Suicide*, from the American Psychiatric Association
- **www.kidshealth.org/parent/emotions/behavior/suicide.html** – Learn more about teen suicide, including warning signs and how to provide help to a teen who is at risk.

CHAPTER TWENTY-FOUR
How Emotions Can Trigger Teen Drug Use

Sometimes, self-reliant teens take on too much responsibility. Teens may try to be too brave or too adult too fast. Teens may try to protect their parent(s) by handling problems themselves. Their fear of being a nuisance or their desire to be a "good kid" can be a threat to their well-being. First born children are especially susceptible.

Not more than a year ago, I sat on the grass in front of a high school with a 15-year-old boy I will call Jeremy, munching on sandwiches, grapes and chocolate chip cookies, chatting about school, hobbies, friends, interests, and plans for the future. Jeremy was a pleasure to talk to. A bright freshman, he was exceptionally aware, analytical and maturely conscious of his feelings.

Jeremy was perplexed, though, about why he had recently used pot with friends for the first time. He got caught, too, and felt a good dose of embarrassment and shame. As an Advanced Placement (AP) student with excellent grades from a very attentive and supportive family; a volunteer in the community; a young man gifted with and appreciative of the best of everything; it was not readily apparent to him or to me what motivated his experimentation.

I made no judgments; rather, I just listened and prompted him to think back – back to the past year when he started to hang out with these new friends who were more rebellious and daring than any in his past. I asked him to remember how he felt about home, his sister and his parents around the incident. As he thought it over, an "ah-ha!" flickered across his face.

Over the past year and a half, trauma had struck the family. His sister was struck with a debilitating illness that defied diagnosis. His parents were in and out of hospitals, and to and from doctors with his sister. He had made every attempt to be helpful and thoughtful, fully aware of the strain on his parents and the fear they were going through.

But then came a day in the hospital when he was keeping an eye on his sister while his parents consulted a doctor. She had been anxious that day. Feeling poorly, she yelled at him for what seemed like no reason. Under normal conditions he would just have brushed it off, but this time it hurt to the core. He had tried so hard to be supportive, and in the process, he had hidden his own needs and loneliness even from himself.

As he recalled the incident, his eyes began to well with tears. "I didn't know I had so much feeling about this!" he murmured.

After all these many months of being "the good kid," intentionally staying out of the way, keeping his focus on school, maintaining good grades, spending nights at friends' homes when his parents were at the hospital, he felt unappreciated by his sister and forgotten by his parents.

Jeremy's face filled with emotion as the memories surfaced, and he winced under the flood of feelings. He finally acknowledged that he felt resentful about her being the center of attention for so long. He had told himself then and now that he "shouldn't" feel that way. He had watched her struggle with being sick. But his heart said, "I matter, too! Doesn't anybody notice ME any more?!"

When ignored by the family, teens find other solutions.

It was about that time that Jeremy recalled seeking out a new friend. This new friend was the most popular guy in his class, a guy known to "party." Jeremy had never drunk alcohol nor used drugs, but he began to talk to 'Mister Popular' about pot and drinking since that was what he seemed most interested in.

It was nice to be noticed by the most popular guy in the class. Jeremy liked the way so many other peers began to notice him, too, since hanging with this new friend. He also realized that he had begun to like the attitude this new crowd conveyed – if they got mad, they hit somebody; if they were sick of responsibilities, they smoked a joint.

"It sounds like you felt you weren't supposed to be angry over the attention your sister was getting," I shared. "Do you suppose these new friends acted out your anger?"

"Yeah, I do!" Jeremy enthusiastically responded. "It felt good not to be such a good kid all the time, especially when it didn't seem to get me what I needed."

"And what was it you needed?" I asked.

"To feel loved," he said with the clarity, honesty and directness that makes teenagers so precious and so profound.

Even high-achieving teens from caring and loving families have a tender, vulnerable underbelly; that ever present need to be loved, noticed and acknowledged.

As Jeremy began to see the situation for what it was, his anger and resentments from the past year and the fear beneath it began to surface.

"What if I don't really matter as much to my parents as my sister?" he implored.

How could he go to them with his fear of not fitting in while his parents were afraid his sister might not get well? And he feared the changes in the family that used to be so predictable. Worse yet, he, too, feared for his sister's life.

Fear and anger are very potent forces in the life of a teenage boy or girl. Fear and anger are frightening to admit, much less share with stressed and distracted parents.

Once he acknowledged and expressed his real feelings, the anger lost its power over him. We talked about the assumptions he made that contributed to the anger. "Yeah, I assumed my parents didn't *want* me to need them anymore, that they were too busy with my sister. And I assumed they wouldn't understand that I still need their love even if I am 15," he surmised.

Jeremy went home that afternoon ready to let his mom know he was sorry about his wrong choice, but not ashamed to need her attention and her love. She understood and responded with a kind heart, open arms, and firm restrictions until he was sure his judgment in friends was well restored!

And to my delight, his older sister, well once again, gave him good guidance:

> *"When your friends are offering you pot or alcohol, tell them you want to think about it. Take five minutes; decide if you are doing it to be liked, because you feel lonely, or because you are mad at us. If you are, tell them thanks but you aren't*

interested and come on home. We're here for you, Jeremy!" Ozzie and Harriet couldn't do better than that!

SECTION FIVE

Do You Know What Your Teens Are Up To?

Teenage alcohol and drug use, gang involvement, teen sexuality, debilitating stress of high-achievers, suicidal thoughts and attempts, self-harm/cutting and other heartbreaking troubles still abound in the world of teenager's today. It is easy to ignore these issues until it comes home to roost. Even then, a parent's denial, as well as teen denial, can be tough to break through. The best protection and prevention begins with being well-informed about the dangers. Know the options for responding to a teen in need, who to turn to, and the wealth of support for determined and caring adults.

Tanya, 19-year-old party girl from *Legacy of Hope®* presentation:

He says he loves me. I met him at a party and I went just to go dancing. He was surrounded by a bunch of cheap girls, only he wanted me, ME! And, no, I did not sleep with him ... that night! I finally have somebody to love. And I'm gonna make him so happy. I gave him some money to buy clothes for a job interview and he came back with some CDs. He said they were a gift for me, for when we move in together. Hey, he'll have a job by then and quit drinking, too. He promised.

CHAPTER TWENTY-FIVE
Reality Check

The National Survey on Drug Use & Health produces a profusion of data and conclusions about our kids every year. Specific substance use and abuse are measured across a wide set of variables. The Center for Substance Abuse Prevention utilizes these numbers to rally Congress around funding for Safe and Drug Free Schools, No Child Left Behind dollars and a plethora of community anti-drug coalitions across America. Teen pregnancy statistics are monitored on an annual basis by such organizations as the National Campaign to Prevent Teen Pregnancy, helping to funnel dollars into prevention programs nationwide.

Throughout 2001 thru 2003, teen violence statistics generated significant funding for projects such as the Stop the Violence campaign of the school service club FCCLA (Family, Career and Community Leaders of America, previously known as Future Homemakers of America). In this time frame, FCCLA rallied more than 100,000 secondary school members to be alert to anger management problems in peers, report potential violence, and achieve a reduction in teen violence.

While touring schools and youth conferences, I have watched teen issues come and go. **As the media covers a new destructive trend, the public becomes more aware and government funding gets directed to fix the current problem of choice.** Survey statistics generate direct funding dollars into the issue.

I have seen how public concern has rallied around AIDS, teen violence, drugs, pot, painkillers, sixth-graders engaged in oral sex and more, around the block and back on specific drugs en vogue: heroine, cocaine, ecstasy, methamphetamines in America's heartland, pot as "harmless" to pot as "gateway drug", and prescription painkillers now being stolen from the elderly on their way out of pharmacies in urban communities.

It was in 1996 that I ran across my first enclave of middle school girls who admitted performing oral sex on teen boys. However, this issue did not surface into public awareness until 2002. Throughout spring of 2003, middle school counselors begged me to address oral sex in assemblies to 6th, 7th and 8th grade girls; it had become so prevalent.

> *"Please," a middle school counselor begged me, "give our girls the hint that oral sex is more significant than kissing! Above and beyond their naive desire to be liked, there are serious potential physical and psychological consequences. Many of our girls will do anything to get attention from the boys. So many come from homes where they are neglected or just feel unimportant and unloved. And many boys receive no training at home on how to respect and treat a girl any more. Our society tells them, 'Why not let the girls do it if it feels good?' "*

Reality in the trenches of middle schools and high schools across our country is far more brutal, physical, sexual, rife with Internet gossip and violent bullying, alcohol and drug abuse, and emotional trauma than most parents would like to believe. Beyond school counselors and some conscious and involved teachers and administrators, I have found that most adults just choose not to believe.

So, the statistics increase and decrease with the rise and fall of media attention and public awareness. Generally, news stories on new teenage drugs-of-choice surface when they become sufficiently trendy or create a tragic incident. By then, such drugs are prolific and readily available to our youth.

About Drugs

It can all jumble together into an overwhelming fear for our kids. A great many adults just numb out to the issue or suppress their fears by naively assuming alcohol, bullying, pot, sexual experimentation and other drug use are just normal rights of passage for teens. More naively yet, some adults resort to denial: "*Our* kids know better. *Our* kids are too strong to be sucked into what the other kids are doing." National statistics on youth don't generally mean much to us personally unless the problem becomes our own.

Not My Child!

Everything changes, however, when your own child becomes a

statistic or, as in my case and in the lives of school counselors, you run across numerous teens succumbing to these problems in your everyday work life. When one or more of these issues affects your own family, the numbers give way to feelings and fears that overshadow everything else in your life.

Unfortunately, my years of experience as well as the statistics warn us that every child is at risk today, from those in the most abusive family system to the high achievers. It is because of the sheer amount of daily exposure every teen has to peers who are indulging, escaping, glorifying, inviting and endangering the well-being of your kids. After awhile, curiosity and a natural urge for teens to rebel – even just a little, the availability and the "I just want to have fun!" urge – impacts every teen.

Then, add the grand sell-out of American consumerism where success means profits, regardless of the moral and ethical impact on families and children. Our teens are inundated with images of sex, violence and quick-fix promotions.

Teen marketing is (1) sexualizing every item a pre-teen and teen might want, and (2) aggrandizing normal teen rebellion as the route to popularity and power. Capitalism has morphed into the promotion of selfishness, self-absorption and guiltless greed to our young. Every teen's adolescent fears, desires, and need to be loved are exploited by big business to sell products, including cigarettes and alcohol in innumerable sizes, shapes and flavors.

We cannot afford to shrink from the challenges of raising teens by thinking "It won't happen to my kids." Whether you want to see the numbers or not, be assured that life-threatening options are in your teen's face on a regular basis. Teen ills are not just happening in urban cities and suburbs either. Some of the grimmest teen issues are occurring in "America's homeland" where isolation and boredom breed far more than wholesome family values.

In the next two chapters, the reading may be uncomfortable, but I urge you to have the courage to pay attention and think about how you can be part of the solution.

As you read these stories, you may be inclined to think that your teen or the teens you know will never go this far. Unfortunately, many of the kids I write about here start out bright, assertive, self-confident and involved in their education.

Addiction isn't picky; it chooses youth from all ages, races, religions, genders, incomes and living conditions.

CHAPTER TWENTY-SIX
Get Your Facts Straight: Survey on Substance Abuse and Study on Teen Binge Drinking

Since I began speaking in 1991 on teen issues, I have seen the drugs of choice vary by geography from state to state, town to town, even school to school, depending upon local economics, parent education, religiosity within a community, cultures and diversity, age and gender. Certain influences have a constant affect such as the popularity of certain drugs and sexual activities due to movies, magazines and music. Drug use can also decrease when it is made less popular by the news media and public awareness campaigns that focus on the dangers and consequences of particular substances.

However, when it comes to substance abuse, ignorance is not bliss!

Here are some of the latest national statistics that wake us up and also offer surprising hope.

Many of my "frontline" observations have been substantiated by excellent federal surveys such as the *National Survey of American Attitudes on Substance Abuse,* an annual survey conducted by CASA (National Center on Addiction and Substance Abuse at Columbia University).

A Rising Concern

Twenty-nine percent of teens in the survey said drugs, including alcohol and tobacco, are their biggest concern, up from 26 percent in 2000. Teens in all 46 states I have toured tell me that it is impossible to attend a party where alcohol and marijuana are not present and a majority of teens at these parties are using and abusing. Many schools sponsor sober and drug free dances, lock-ins and teen clubs, but most weekends, teens have no choice but to stay home or spend the evening with a small circle of friends if they want to avoid the heavy drinking and drug scene.

Rising Issue: Siblings as 'pushers.'

Twelve percent of teens in the 2002 Survey also reported that an older sibling offered them illegal drugs or encouraged their use when they were between 10 and 12 years of age. Often, the older sibling insisted they try it. For some preteens, it made them feel grown up and accepted. According to CASA, this proved to make such teens twice as likely to have a substance abuse problem as the average teen without a "pusher" in the home.

When the survey termed the older sibling a "pusher," it shocked me for a moment. Doesn't the term "pusher" conjure up images of a dark alley, seedy looking character in the shadows, selling crack or heroine for exorbitant prices to wretched souls? Well, today's "pusher" may be a preppy teen on campus, student leader or quarterback – a popular teen with an outgoing personality or a loner looking for a means of gaining attention. There are no stereotypes any more.

Gangs push drugs even in "Hometown America."

I had an eye-opening experience in mid-America. The student body had a central plains persona: predominately white, blond, and more conservatively dressed in jeans and Ts as opposed to the exposed bellies of coastal urban city teens. The student audience was respectful and attentive, lacking the initial taunts and arrogance of more affluent urban schools. I felt comfortable in front of these kids. I felt respected and listened to. From every appearance, it was the idyllic high school, full of well-fed, sports-oriented, wholesome all-American teens.

After the assembly, however, I was in for a surprise. A senior boy approached and asked to talk. He proceeded to tell me he was a member of a gang, right there in the middle of a middle-class farming community. He wore slightly more sagged pants than the norm, but certainly no gang colors, beanie or machismo swagger. On the surface, he looked much like a typical all-American boy. He continued:

> *"I'm in this gang that supplies all the pot and meth around here. There are seven of us. Like you described, my Dad is a drug addict. He beat me and my Mom ever since I was a little kid. She left us about four years ago. She lives with some boyfriend across town. She's a drunk and didn't want us kids.*

All seven of us guys in the gang got families like that. So we made enough money off the drugs to buy a trailer; and now we all live there together.

"I'm good at math so I'm considered the smart one. I do the books. The group is saving up to send me to college so I can learn accounting and handle the money. Problem is I'm starting to think I want out of the gang. But I know this gang is in every city across the country. If I leave, I'm dead cuz I'm one of the leaders; and I know too much. Only chance I've got is to move to Europe or, when I turn 23, get grandfathered out by promising my kids to the gang."

He painted a very frightening and dismal picture. Whether his perceptions are accurate or not, he made me aware that gangs and drug abuse are everywhere and that young people who join gangs to replace dysfunctional families or for the allure of the money pay a horrible price.

It is critical that we all be conscious of the serious family problems many young people cope with today and understand that *their* problems impact *everyone's* kids. Recognizing the severe impact that parental substance abuse has on the children is as important as teen substance abuse, because it is often the underlying painful cause. Then, and only then, will we have the conviction and guts to get involved and create community coalitions that address all aspects of the substance abuse problem.

With knowledge and commitment, it is easier to talk to our kids as well as the kids of others about our expectations of them, their choices and the consequences. We gain the strength with involvement and the support of other involved adults around us to follow through on the boundaries we set for them – this includes getting our children help for the emotional turmoil that motivates the destruction of their lives and others around them.

Pot is or can be easily purchased with unexpected effects.

Another eye-opening fact revealed in the survey was that for the first time, a higher percentage of teens found marijuana easier to buy than cigarettes and alcohol. In August 2003, additional information on the availability of marijuana came out of the White House Office of National Drug Control Policy's National Youth Anti-Drug Media Campaign. Their research revealed that in 2003 and still today, marijuana has become the most widely used illicit drug among American youth.

Some parents may misconstrue this as a plus, thinking back to their college days when pot seemed fun and harmless. Parents make a big mistake to underestimate the potency, psychological addiction factors and serious underachievement caused by habitual marijuana use. "The research shows," says The Anti-Drug Campaign, "that youth marijuana use can lead to significant health, social, learning and behavioral problems at a crucial time in kids' lives, when their young bodies and minds are still developing."

I, too, have met a myriad of teens caught in pot's spell. These kids cannot understand how they ended up on probation, in alternative education, or why they struggle to hold down jobs and keep relationships. All they know is that they cannot get through the day without smoking a joint every few hours. This is serious psychological addiction.

Since 2003, the vast majority of teens, agree that pot is easy – if not easier – to get on a daily basis from their peers or older brothers and sisters than alcohol. So many teen girls moan about boyfriends who are smoking pot everyday:

> *"My boyfriend says it's no big deal and that it's just something he likes to do. But he's stopped being as loving to me. It's like he's always off with his buddies smoking dope after school. I just don't feel like he loves me as much anymore because he just doesn't think I'm as important as smoking pot. His grades aren't even as important to him. He says he wants to go to college, but his grades aren't so good now either. We used to talk about getting married in a couple years. I'm so worried about him."*

Over and over, teens who are concerned about their friends and even themselves, tell me:

> *"EVERYBODY'S doing pot. Even the Advanced Placement students and the student body leaders. It's at EVERY party.*

I've even seen kids smoking at lunchtime and lots of them after school."

From every high school where I speak, teen feedback confirms that marijuana is used across the student population from at-risk to high-achievers and leaders. It is perceived harmless, even safer than alcohol. And parents continue to discount the use as normal teen experimentation, "Come on, we tried it in our day," they say. Parents may prefer to avoid one of the tougher parts of parenting: facing a teen's drug use. They delude themselves when they compare their college experimentation with today's teen pot use.

And younger teens are at most risk. Teens between the ages of 12 and 16 are almost 500 percent more at risk of substance abuse, says the *National Survey of American Attitudes on Substance Abuse VII: Teens, Parents and Siblings.*

Most teens who use alcohol, cigarettes and marijuana begin use between age 12 and 16.

- 95 percent who smoke cigarettes start at or before age 15. Average age of first use is $12^1/_4$.
- 93 percent who drink alcohol start at or before age 15. Average age of first use for these teens is $12^1/_2$.
- 86 percent who smoke pot start at or before age 15. Average age of first use for these teens is $13^1/_2$.

"A child who reaches age 21 without smoking, abusing alcohol or using drugs is virtually certain never to do so."
Joseph A. Califano, Jr., CASA Chairman and President

For many children, parents are the single biggest determinant as to whether teens drink, do drugs or are sexually irresponsible!

◆

With that as a goal, CASA encourages parents:
"For many children, parents are the single biggest determinant in these decisions – stronger than that of friends, teachers and media."

More teens who don't use marijuana (42 percent) credit their parents over any other influence. Parents, YOU DO make a difference!

Every current prevention resource agrees:

Parents should get involved with

- **Homework;**
- **Parent-children projects;**
- **Extracurricular activities;**
- **Attending religious services together.**

Study links health problems to teen binge drinking.

Binge drinking is a dangerous and serious aspect to teen drinking. Binge drinking is defined as 5 or more drinks in a row for males and 4 for females. According to the U.S. Department of Health and Human Services, 10 million youth between the ages of 12 and 20 drink and 20% binge drink. The National Institute on Alcohol Abuse and Alcoholism says that binge drinking even a single time can cause irreparable damage to the adolescent brain since it is in a significant growth phase from 12 to 24 years of age.

The *Journal of Studies on Alcohol* released additional research in 2004 regarding binge drinking. Their research finds in addition to brain damage, the overall health of our young adult children is severely affected by this dangerous teenage drinking pattern. If an individual begins binge drinking at age 13 and continues throughout the teen years, he or she is nearly 4 times more likely to be overweight or obese and 3½ times more likely to have high blood pressure at 24-years-old than people who never or rarely drank heavily during adolescence.

"Young adults' history of binge drinking during the teenage years appears to have serious effects on their health by age 24," said Sabrina Oesterle, lead author of the study and research associate at University of Washington's Social Development Research Group.

Given that boys, on average, try alcohol for the first time at 11 years old and girls at 13, we are looking at serious life-long healthcare implications for our youth. Drinking is affecting a far greater number of our adolescents than most parents wish to think, starting at younger ages than most care to believe, drinking episodes of much greater quantities than parents choose to accept, and having more far-reaching consequences than our society as a whole is willing to believe.

Dinner table stops them cold.

It may sound incredibly simple, but *The 2002 National*

Survey also found some encouraging actions parents can take to discourage teen drinking and binging. One of the best things parents can do for the well-being of their children, according to The Study, is to regularly eat dinner together!

> *"Among teens who eat dinner with their parents six or seven times a week, 93 percent say they have not smoked a cigarette in the last month. The same can be said for drinking: more than half of students who eat dinner with their parents six or seven times a week have not been to drinking parties in the last six months."*

Clearly, some of the simplest activities with your teens can have the biggest impact.

Consistency and practical expressions of love make for powerful parenting.

The regular expectation of participating in a family meal, the accountability that occurs in daily conversation as a family, and the deep investment of parents' time all demonstrate love to a teen and build the resistance traits of self-esteem and self-respect. For more parenting tips, visit, **www.casacolumbia.org** and search on 'surveys' for additional details.

It's never too late, and never too early! Believe in "Parent Power," it works!

CHAPTER TWENTY-SEVEN
The Ostrich Approach Isn't Helping Our Teens

Denial in teens is one thing, but when adults deny alcohol and drug abuse in their schools and homes, the problem can easily mushroom into a devastating issue. It's time we took our heads out of the sand.

Every October schools celebrate Red Ribbon Week. From kindergarten through high school, students receive a mega dose of alcohol and drug abuse prevention education. As a result, I am very busy that month giving assemblies, speaking in classrooms, and talking one-on-one with troubled teens about their alcoholic families and their personal use.

While in schools that week, I have observed many superb activities and lots of teen enthusiasm. Designating at least one week each school year to educate and alert teens to the dangers of alcohol and drug use is excellent. However, the use messages from the tobacco and alcohol industries are *constant.* Illegal drugs saturate teen parties and are dealt on many school campuses. I firmly believe some sort of prevention message every month would not be over doing the counter-use effort, whether it be on violence, teen sexuality, gangs, suicide, depression, drugs or alcohol. (For more information on the Legacy of Hope® programs in schools, see our website at **www.legacyofhope.com**.)

When politics get in the way.

When it comes to alcohol prevention in high schools, I sometimes run into a frustrating issue I call a case of the "Chicken Politics."

Principals and parents, particularly in more affluent communities, tend to claim that their high school students do not have such problems with alcohol and drugs. As long as their teens are performing academically, being accepted into the best universities and their schools are meeting and exceeding national standards, alcohol and pot are non-issues. Partying is written off as "sowing oats" and "normal experimentation." WHY a youth uses or abuses alcohol or drugs becomes irrelevant; family issues remain secret and forbidden territory.

The Denial can be thick:
"We don't have those kinds of problems here,"
I have heard principals say. "Our Parent Teacher Organization doesn't believe we need to address alcohol and drug issues; our focus is on academics."

Yet, in each and every case, the school counselor, school nurse and students on these campuses claim otherwise.

I have met principals who will acknowledge the need to talk about alcoholism and addiction as a family disease. They admit that children of alcoholics have damaged self-esteem that can have grave negative impact on academic performance. They may even recognize the need to talk about teen drinking and drug use as an escape from stress and feelings. Yet, when it is time to schedule a prevention assembly, that very same principal isn't sure the kids will respond or can't find the money for a prevention event.

A parent of a high school teen shared that her daughter came home from a weekend party disturbed that a number of her friends in Advanced Placement (AP) classes were experimenting with Ecstasy. Her daughter thought it was "stupid" of them to risk their futures. She implored her mom to see if the school would have an assembly on drug use, stress, emotional intelligence, parent alcohol abuse, and related pressures from home. She felt if her peers understood their motives and the consequences of their behaviors, they might stop and think.

To help, I contacted the counselor and school nurse who were enthusiastic and excited about the assembly. The school district was pleased to earmark funding from Safe and Drug Free Schools monies to fund the assembly. Everyone loved the idea, but the principal had reservations. Both the school nurse and district representative were frustrated and confused. The grapevine finally revealed the issue: the principal feared upsetting parents, particularly those making significant donations to the school and did not want these issues addressed.

Denying substance abuse does not make it go away.

Yes, politics are a part of life. Alcohol and drug abuse in affluent families are often denied and kept a secret. It is unfortunate, that some young person will have to fall further and harder at a later date due to undetected or denied substance abuse when a high school might have been just the neutral source to provide intervention and prevention. Middle school and high school campuses are often the only opportunity for a teen to hear about alcoholism and addiction at an early age, offering a real opportunity for awareness that can blossom into recovery.

I encourage administrators, Parent Teacher Organization presidents, school counselors and school nurses to err on the side of excess prevention education. Protecting and placating parents in denial is not helping today's teens.

Alcoholism and drug addiction respect no man, woman or child regardless of income, talent, intelligence or success level in society.

◆

Opt instead for community programs, parent education and health fairs that can expand knowledge and awareness in parents and educators alike. Our kids are just too precious to hide our heads in the sand.

CHAPTER TWENTY-EIGHT
Gateway Drugs at Twelve Are Best Taken Seriously

Alcohol, pot and tobacco are the "gateway" drugs, starter kits for lifetime addictions. They are sinking their fangs into our children at increasingly younger ages. Here's how to recognize the downward spiral and get help.

A parent spoke to me after a Community and Parent Awareness program I brought to her town about teen alcohol and drug abuse. She shared about her living hell, a parent's nightmare that had come true in her own home. She is the mother of a teen who had been a bright, dependable, loving son at age 12. She shared in anguish, however, how he had become a holy terror by 15 and a deplorable addict by 16.

At 15, her son refused to go to school and slept in until noon after she left for work. He raged at her attempts to direct him. "I hate you!" he screamed at her on a daily basis. Soon he was stealing both money and credit cards from her purse. Then, by 16, came the nights when he left in a fit of rage and did not return for several days. Worse yet, he wound up in police custody on multiple occasions for being intoxicated, stealing from his friends' parents, breaking and entering, or in the possession of a stolen car with dope stashed in the glove box.

Just one more out-of-control alcohol and drug addicted family story? No, this was a well-respected community member sharing the saga of her only son and his addiction to drugs and alcohol. And then I had the chance to hear the son, now in recovery at age 20, tell his story. It, too, broke my heart.

He shared that, like so many who end up alcoholics and addicts in their adult years, he started drinking at age 12. He first snuck alcohol from the home liquor cabinet. He gave an insight into the disease of alcoholism as he shared what he felt at age 12 after the first time he was drunk. Now at 20, he looked back and knew without a shadow of a doubt that he had inherited this merciless disease. Alcohol became his immediate best friend.

Now a well-groomed, competent 20-year-old young man, he

shared how far down his alcoholism took him in his teens. Even he was surprised at how quickly alcohol came to dominate his thoughts and his life. Expanding his repertoire to pot and other drugs had been an easy step. **If he felt that good on alcohol alone, he was certain he would feel even better adding other drugs.**

Getting stoned on pot became a close second, while alcohol remained the god that ruled his body, mind and spirit. School became irrelevant. Long-held hopes to go to college and to make his parents proud were faint memories that elicited no interest any more.

I encourage you parents of addicted teens: Get support today!

This mother shared how she found support in Al-Anon, the 12-step self-help program begun 50 years ago by the spouses of the founders of Alcoholics Anonymous. It was at the free and confidential Al-Anon meetings that she found help.

Initially, she admitted to being very anxious and embarrassed, if not ashamed to go to such a place. She had assumed her son's addictions and demeaning behaviors were the result of her failure as a mother. To her surprise, the people in the Al-Anon meetings neither judged her nor gave her advice. They were all equals, communicating on a playing field leveled by incredible despair over someone else's drinking; and, clearly, her son's drinking had torn her life apart.

Using the tools of the Al-Anon program, she experienced unparalleled support where she was unconditionally loved, no strings or rules attached. She received insights and encouragement from the sharing of others ahead of her in the process of healing and handling life with an addicted child. She identified with other people's pain and similar situations. She knew she had found a place where she could be open and honest about her son's devastating drug and alcohol afflictions, manipulative and baffling behaviors, and her own anguish and insanity.

As parents who attend Al-Anon meetings come to understand, this mom grasped that she had not caused her son's addictions; she could not cure them, nor could she control them. Through compassionate conversations and the suggestions of an Al-Anon sponsor, she was able to make a choice she felt appropriate. She calmly confronted her son: he must go to rehabilitation or leave her home. He chose rehab; however, within two weeks of his return, he was back on the streets getting stoned, loaded and wasted.

"Soon," he said, "any high was better than real life."

Real life meant acknowledging the mess he'd made of his life. He'd been kicked out of school, had a criminal record at 18, had seriously hurt his parents, and had friends who could no longer stand to have him around. To cope with all that his drinking behavior had ruined, he got high before he got out of bed. Any household product in an aerosol can would do; any pill in the medicine cabinet was worth a try. Soon he was again trading household appliances, sneakers, and whatever he could get his hands on for alcohol and drugs.

His mom shared how she survived by living the Al-Anon slogan "One Day at a Time," turning her mind to the tasks in front of her on a daily basis in spite of the havoc in her son's life. She clung to the spiritual support from the slogan "Let go and Let God," turning her son over to the care of a loving Higher Power who could do for her son what she clearly could not do by herself: make him want recovery. She was ready when he turned 18 to insist he leave her home as long as he continued to drink or use drugs.

This young man's addictions rapidly took him deeper into the depths of degradation. He remembered manipulating his way into the house of friend after friend, finding a place to stay for a day, maybe a week. Then he'd be kicked out again for stealing from his closest friends. He hit the streets until he found himself in a heroine den sharing needles with a room full of other lost souls.

Your teen has to make the decision for help.

Not until the night he was on the streets at 2 a.m., 18-years-old with no place left to go and no friends or family left willing to lend a hand, that he called his mom and at last admitted he needed help.

He continued to speak about his past, but now the tone changed as he shared about the greatest accomplishment of his young life, two years sober and clean in Alcoholics Anonymous (AA). Still, he was very clear that he was always just one day away from a relapse should he ever get complacent.

This recovering young man now attends an AA meeting and does service work with his AA friends each and every day. He is nervous and careful with his fragile two-year sobriety. He readily admits that alcoholism is cunning, baffling and manipulative. It has the power to destroy him in the wink of an eye.

As I listened to this mother and son share their two sides of the story, my stomach churned from the obvious tragedy of teens caught in the nightmare of alcoholism and its partner, drug addiction. I was hopeful, though, that here is one of the lucky winners in recovery. Mom will continue to be able to face come-what-may as she has committed to remain actively involved in Al-Anon regardless of her son's sobriety or relapse.

Predisposition is nothing to scoff at.

Kids in families where a parent, grandparent, aunt or uncle have drinking or drug problems commonly carry the physical predisposition to be alcoholics. Some research claims that any teen with a family history of alcoholism has a 50 percent chance of becoming alcoholic should he or she start drinking. Girls with an alcoholic mom or any history of molestation are highly vulnerable to alcoholism. Some statistics suggest that a large percentage of women alcoholics were molested as girls.

Points worth remembering:

- **Damage to a girl's sexual identity creates severe long-term shame, guilt and depression that may lead teens as well as adult women to alcohol and/or drug abuse** in an effort to alleviate the gut-wrenching emotional trauma and low self-esteem.
- Research has also discovered that **teens most susceptible to a drinking problem are boys from families in which either parent has a drinking problem.**
- Young people who begin drinking before age 15 are four times more likely to develop alcoholism than those who begin drinking at age 21 according to the National Institute of Alcohol Abuse and Alcoholism.

- Alcohol is still the most widely used and abused drug among youth, often referred to as a "gateway drug" because its use so often precedes the use of other illicit substances.
- **Pot is now considered a drug with serious addiction potential in and of itself. It is no longer merely a gateway drug.** This may be related to both the increased accessibility and the increased hybrid potency of THC, the active ingredient in marijuana.

Youth drinking and pot use require our significant attention. Not only can they lead to other drug use, but alcohol and pot alone inflict extensive human tragedy on vulnerable youth and their heartbroken families.

CHAPTER TWENTY-NINE
Lessons in Teen Sex Learned on the Dance Floor

As the keynote speaker at numerous youth conferences, I have had a number of opportunities to attend teen dances. I am 5 feet tall, 103 pounds, with 25 years as a teacher and performer in jazz and modern dance. I can slip into a teen crowd at a dance fairly inconspicuously! In fact, teens have often warmly welcomed me into the "eye of the storm" at the center of their dance floor to trade a few moves.

As a lifelong dancer, it is a thrill to learn current dance steps from teens; and I am honored that teens generally enjoy having an adult (other than one of their parents, of course!) who can do their moves. As a result, I have gotten a unique birds-eye view of life today in the teenage dance scene.

Teen dances can be fun, and, by all means, hopefully for your teen!

Not long ago, I chaperoned a teen dance at a youth conference. I expected several chaperones, though I found myself the only adult present with 100 teens for a period of time. So, I joined in some of the dancing as a way to move about the floor and keep an eye on the event. I found myself privy to an inside view of the teen world as I found a handful of preteen boys huddled in a corner, reluctant to participate.

Dancing is, of course, a tortuous rite of passage for some teens. Feeling self-conscious and uncoordinated is a gruesome experience at any age! With all my years teaching dance, the least I could do was to alleviate some of their misery. So I asked if they'd like me to teach them how to dance. They appreciatively nodded in unison.

I helped them find the base beat and their own natural body rhythms.

"Put your weight on the balls of your feet like you would in basketball, baseball or in football. Shift your shoulders, add a bob, and exaggerate your attitude. Now you've got it! Get out there!"

Armed with a few moves and a gut full of courage, they were no longer condemned to the sidelines with envy and defeat.

At that point, my attention was drawn from the impromptu

dance class to a writhing mass on the center of the dance floor. Four 13-year-old boys were taking turns positioning themselves behind two 12-year-old girls, unselfconsciously 'grinding,' also known as 'freaking.' For those unfamiliar with this dance form, a boy places his crotch up against the girl's behind; and they gyrate together. Then, the girl turns around and they grind crotch to crotch It's not unusual to have 2 boys with one girl sandwiched in-between or 2 girls and one boy. Certainly not the "coke-bottle-apart" requirement of my teen years.

The young teens at this dance were imitating dance styles they had seen on MTV and modeled for them by older teens. Of course, teens have been tantalized and taught more and more outrageous moves on television since Band Stand and Elvis Presley. We all recognize that adolescence is characterized by raging hormones. The question becomes when should adults draw the line as to what is appropriate in public? Even if teens revert to sexually provocative dance moves when adults are not around, shouldn't adults at least set boundaries for them to consider when we are present?

I have seen teachers and parents chaperoning school dances act completely oblivious to sexually explicit couples on the dance floor. **Why chaperone if we adults are not there to guide our youth in appropriate social behaviors?** Why accept blatant teen sexuality as beyond a chaperone's control? Teachers tell me that 'freaking' has become the norm and must be acceptable to teen parents since none of them show up at dances and object.

That night, I decided to draw the line at the objectification of these two 12-year-old girls.

I danced to the center circle and calmly reached for a hand of each girl. I danced them off the floor and out into the hallway where they gazed at me, naively, wide-eyed and oblivious as to why I had drawn them away from the innocent delight of so much male attention.

"Those boys freaking with you probably don't really care about you two girls," I began. "At their age, they are not thinking about you so much as doing what feels good and going as far as you will let them go. Their parents have probably never told them how to treat a girl with respect, or what is appropriate at a dance in public. So, it becomes your job as girls to demand respect for your own bodies. You have a choice about how you are treated and what you allow others to do with you. If you let those boys use your body this way at 12, what will you let them do when you are 14, 15, or 16?

Being cared for and loved by a boy is a lot more than letting them use your body. I urge you not to let boys freak with you at this age. They aren't going to respect you if you don't expect them to. Treat yourself with respect, and the boys will, too."

They looked at me incredulously. Perhaps they were shocked that an adult would be so direct and bold with them. I only wish today's pre-teens and teens were better prepared by parents to anticipate the choices and to understand the ingredients of self-respect.

Pay attention to the messages peers and the media are feeding your teens!

I encourage parents to watch a few MTV music videos each year and listen to rap lyrics. Much of today's music reduces girls to blatant sex objects, no more than body parts and sexual techniques, while boys are indoctrinated with messages of insensitivity. Both sexes are inundated with role models of lust rather than respect and commitments in love. And your teens will not know the difference unless we adults teach them.

It is a parent's job to stay informed on the influences in a teen's everyday life, especially in a world eager to exploit natural adolescent urges in order to sell products. The music and movie businesses make no excuses. If it's what the buying public (and your teen) "wants" (shock value and excitement), regardless of the ethical or moral impact, they'll supply it.

During the last half hour of the dance, parents began to arrive from the adult banquet bash to pick up their kids.

"Isn't my girl terrific!" one father remarked, exuding great pride for his 16-year-old daughter.

"I never have to worry about her. She's such a good girl," he beamed.

Unbeknownst to him, she had been unashamedly 'grinding' the

night away with attentive boys in a corner. Throughout the evening, I had danced my way to her side several times to gently remind her and her 18 to 20-year-old male partners to distance themselves and act as appropriate role models to the preteens and teens at the dance.

Get involved.

Just as I shared with this father, I encourage parents to stay involved and informed by volunteering to chaperone at a dance. Be visible. Make it your job to be aware of current trends and peer pressures on your teen. You will be in a better position to open up conversation with your teens and ask for their opinions. Then share with them your own life experiences at school dances, your values on appropriate sexual expression and behavior on the dance floor, your expectations of them, and a good dose of what is healthy self-respect.

Open up communication by asking for your teen's opinion on acceptable dancing. And, as uncomfortable as it may seem, start that critical dialogue on self-respect and sexuality: how a girl sets the pace by setting boundaries with a boy and demanding that he treat her body and her mind with respect; how a boy should learn to treat a girl, on and off the dance floor.

Parents of teens are often unfamiliar with current trends in teen sexual expression. They may remember more innocent times when they were teenagers. Parents sometimes mistakenly assume that their kids have absorbed their values and need not worry about their teen's choices. But, like the parent above, teens are very susceptible to doing what it takes to fit in. The fear of not being accepted runs very high in adolescents.

How many parents are conscious of the pressure on their teens to participate in oral sex, particularly in middle school? Shocking question? Here's an even more shocking answer:

In Spring of 2003, I was at a middle school where a counselor shared a disturbing statistic. Given her interactions with the girls at the school, she believed that close to 50 percent of the girls in 7th and 8th grades were readily performing oral sex on the middle school boys.

"The girls say it is not sex. I've heard that middle school

girls perform oral sex in full view of other friends at parties. The girls look at oral sex like kissing."

"These preteen girls may be totally uncomfortable having a conversation with a boy, but feel performing oral sex on him is ok!" the counselor despaired. "They do not connect emotionally nor have any comprehension of sex as an act of intimacy, just a way to get boys to like them."

The teens in this middle school were white, middle-to-upper-middle class preteens in an upscale community. According to the counselor, the parents are in grave denial, never imagining for a second that their precious little girls would degrade themselves in such a fashion, or that their respectable preteen boys would consider allowing themselves to be serviced in such a way.

I later heard similar tales from counselors in multiple other states across the country. Of course, the news has reported similar stories. However, when I meet real life, precocious, naïve, adorable preteens and realize these very same children are exposing themselves to both physical danger (STDs and AIDS) and emotional harm (low self-esteem, learning that love is compromising themselves), it was nauseating to think our society has so abandoned the moral fiber of our kids.

Teens today gravely need parental input and guidance on boundaries.

Talk with them about self-respect, how to protect and treat their own bodies, and what is respect from those around them. As you treat them with respect by setting boundaries and expectations for their inexperienced lives, it is then that they will settle for nothing less in their relationships with the opposite sex.

CHAPTER THIRTY
Achievement Pressures Can Exact a Serious Toll on Teen and College Athletes

Sometimes, even the highest achievers including "star" athletes resort to drugs and alcohol as a defense against the pressures they feel. Here's how to help a special niche of teens: dedicated athletes.

After numerous talks for high school and college athletes on substance abuse and stress, it has become clear that they can be at highest risk for alcohol and drug abuse problems of all students on campus.

The pressures on athletes are extreme and include making grades; individual scrutiny on a regular basis; and exceptionally high expectations from coaches, parents, peer group and teammates. Teen and young adult athletes have the added stress of schedule conflicts, competition, risk of injury, ego-based professional role models, and significant targeting by the alcohol industry: "Hey, stud, when you're hot and sweaty, what do you do? Get yourself an ice cold beer. Better yet, make that a six-pack."

Schools are caught between what's good for teens and what's good for revenues.

Many high schools have a tough time adhering to substance abuse protocol with athletes. A significant amount of vital school revenue is generated by athletic team booster clubs. When teams win, booster club and family attendance soars. When teams lose, attendance and concession food and soda purchases drop off.

School administrators are historically caught between dealing with a star athlete caught smoking pot or drunk at a party and the need to maintain revenues to run the school, which, in turn, pay for programs that numerous students benefit from. So, do we sacrifice one athlete and an important moral lesson for the financial good of the whole?

Teen and young adult athletes with alcohol and other substance abuse problems do become everybody's problem in time. In those not-so-rare occurrences of fatal drunk driving or debilitating accidents, every teen, teacher and administrator in a school is emotionally stunned and grieves.

Solutions need to be found. A few schools I have encountered have discovered a win-win combination. The more proactive school programs go to the source of alcohol and drug abuse issues with athletes. They will:

- Regularly provide special prevention messages for athletes.
- Give athletes training in coping with stresses of performance and competition as well as the stresses of expectations from themselves and those of others including family, coaches, fans and the media.
- Help them anticipate and recognize social and personal influences that will invariably encourage chemical use.
- Define clear policies and consequences for alcohol or substance use that are regularly communicated to both athletes and their parents. Then adhere to those practices consistently.

Take a walk in an athlete's shoes.

When speaking to groups of athletes, I can always expect several to show up afterward to talk about personal concerns. Many share that they related to the portrayals of excessive stress and suicidal thinking. I was surprised then pained when a strapping star male athlete admitted to being plagued with thoughts of suicide.

I now know that numerous college athletes, both male and female, have bouts of depression and suicidal thoughts. They say they feel persistent and intense pressure to perform. They fear disappointing teammates and parents. They fear losing athletic scholarships. And their families, their peers, coaches and they, themselves, often have unrealistic expectations of them.

The key is to explore with these athletes, both male and female, where their difficulty with these pressures may come from, especially assumptions about their self-worth that were set in childhood, long before the athletic achievements. When we talk about their families, quite often the athletes uncover a parent with an anger issue, drinking problem or critical attitude. I would be happy to find that the contributing cause is strictly an athlete with an out-of-control Type-A personality, or a male with a triple X chromosome. However, that is not what experience has revealed.

Parental alcohol abuse leads to abusive critical self-talk, even in star athletes.

Teen and young adult athletes who come from homes where parents or grandparents have had drinking problems exhibit excessive critical self-talk. Many high achievers come from alcoholic and/or critical families. The alcoholic family inheritance can be a drive for perfectionism and the attention denied them by a drunken, unavailable parent.

The chaos in an alcoholic home – unpredictability, broken promises, neglect, excessive criticism – drives many a teen athlete to overachieve in an effort to make up for the shattered self worth at home. It can also drive an athlete to drink, use drugs and contemplate suicide when left in the dark shadows of denial and shame. They never feel good enough in spite of successes. These athletes have the troublesome family legacy of pervading low self-esteem and a foreboding sense of failure because they never found the answer to the family shame.

Such athletes can experience serious self-loathing when they fail to reach unrealistic and perfectionist goals. They are also much relieved when they learn that these painful bouts of self-hate are a common side-affect of parental alcoholism. Athletes can develop a more balanced perspective once they comprehend the underlying emotional programming they acquired from family influences. Athletic departments can help their athletes cope by incorporating messages about the impact of being the child of an alcoholic or addict into their annual alcohol and drug prevention education.

Encourage athletes to support each other against substance abuse.

In addition, athletic departments can foster an atmosphere of team support that recognizes how chemical use problems can affect team morale, unity and performance. For example, the Massachusetts Interscholastic Athletic Association (MIAA) Partners in Prevention curriculum encourages athletes to take personal responsibility to talk to each other about health and performance problems, including chemical use. MIAA reminds athletes that they have a responsibility to seek help, both for themselves and for their teammates who are experiencing chemical use problems.

It's up to the leaders to lead the way.

Athletic abilities are a wonderful gift. Natural talents coupled with great coaching produce wondrous results that inspire every one of us. However "stardom" issues in athletes can lead to "doing what the older athletes do" by celebrating victories or drowning defeats. Athletes and coaches can create an environment that encourages positive role modeling and reduces the pressure to "party" and play the role of super star.

Coaches, trainers, parents and administrators hold the ultimate responsibility to create an environment of cooperation, responsibility, and support to teen athletes.

The result is a true winning team – a win of human spirit and talents serving the individual while serving the greater good.

CHAPTER THIRTY-ONE
Different Twists on the Alcohol and Drug Issues

The best parent is an informed parent. Be armed with the best tools and up-to-date information. There are Internet resources to help you understand drug use in teens, as well as important facts, indicators and therapeutic resources.

Drug testing – friend or foe?

Drug Testing is an aspect of prevention and intervention that is actively enforced under the drug and alcohol policy at some schools in an effort to intervene and screen youth with substance abuse problems. Sometimes the response is strictly punitive, in other more evolved policies, identifying those in need of intervention and/or rehabilitation is the goal. Some parents are pleased that a school will randomly test their teens. Others are very much opposed and consider it an invasion of privacy

Many youth and parents are uninformed about the different types of drug tests, who may test them, whether being around users – particularly marijuana users – will cause them to test positive even if they haven't used the drug themselves. This issue may not seem of great importance until you consider how often your own teen is surrounded by peers who are abusing.

A high school junior shared with me that he felt it was his responsibility to go with his drinking and drug-using pals to parties to be the designated driver and bring them home. Not only did he become an enabling caretaker, making it easier for his friends to use and abuse, he also became seriously stressed by looking out for and trying to fix his friends. Was he also making himself vulnerable to testing positive to marijuana by breathing in secondhand marijuana smoke, though he did not use himself?

Naturally, the best way to avoid a positive drug test is not to use drugs or hang with those who do. For more information, check out **www.theantidrug.com**.

Is the designated driver enabling or helping his/her friends?

It is equally important to talk to your teens about the

ramifications of being the designated driver again and again. To occasionally act as the designated driver is a responsible gesture. However, when a teen continually attends parties to intentionally watch over friends who are drinking or using drugs, then the choice becomes enabling for the abusing friend and destructive to the caretaking teen. A teen who takes on the responsibility of a friend's well-being can become resentful, martyred, angry and disgusted. He or she may feel an urge to fix his/her friend. An overly caring teen may become sick with worry, and anger over friends with addictions, often to the point of neglecting his or her own needs. Friends who are caught up in drinking or drug use can quickly become manipulative and annoying, not the kind of friend a teen is really looking for.

Many teenage girls have shared how they take turns keeping an eye out for one another at parties. One girl will be the designated driver and watchdog to make sure that an inebriated girlfriend doesn't become prey to boys eager to have sex with an out-of-control girl. In today's teen scene where alcohol and drugs flow freely, teens tell me that boys consider a drunken girl fair game for sexual favors. In generations past, such sexual predatory behavior was more likely on the college party scene. Today, high school culture is rife with such occurrences.

Our *Survey of Hope*, administered to over 25,000 teens around the country, indicates that up to 43.6 percent of 11th grade teens would be helped by a support group to deal with concern over friends' drinking or drug use. In 6th grade, 14.6 percent of teens had a similar concern. By 9th grade, it had risen to 36.9 percent.

Teens often come to me begging for suggestions to help a friend. Often, the friend is a girl teens have tried to talk to, scolded, and tried to control because of her drinking, drug use and/or irresponsible sexual behaviors while under the influence. Teens easily get caught up in the fear, guilt, and obsessive worry that accompany a friend's abuse problems. Such teens are helped by information about alcoholism and addiction. Without grasping the low self-esteem of an abusing friend and their own powerlessness to stop their behaviors, the anxiety can take a caring teen right down with the user.

I encourage you to talk to your teen about being an "enabler;" that resentment, worry and anger are harmful. Help your teen see alternative choices, like letting a friend know:

"I am uncomfortable with your drinking/drug use/sexual behavior. Do you think you have a problem?"

Asking a friend what they think is better than pointing an accusing finger at them. If they say, "No way! Just leave me alone!" Then encourage your teen to set a boundary that keeps him or her from being sucked too deeply into his/her friend's problems so that your own teen's life, grades and future do not suffer.

A teen can caringly say:

"If you choose to continue drinking/using/sleeping around, I need to let you know I won't hang around you when you are doing that. I care about you, and if you ever decide you want to stop or get help, I'll help. But until then, this is what I have to do to take care of me. It hurts too much to watch you hurt yourself."

A school support group for teens and Peer Assistance are great places to get information, emotional clarity and relief. Alateen, affiliated with Al-Anon Family Groups, is a self-help program for teens. Meetings can be found by contacting Al-Anon Family Groups at 888-425-2666 or online at www.al-anon.alateen.org

---

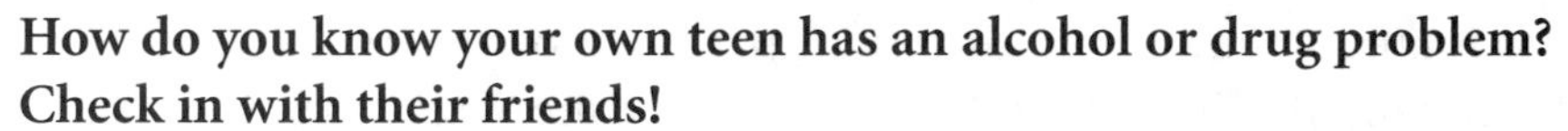

How do you know your own teen has an alcohol or drug problem? Check in with their friends!

If a teen expresses annoyance, worry, and high anxiety over a friend's drinking or drug use, this is very likely a clear message that the friend is a problem drinker, even an alcoholic or addict.

How a friend emotionally impacts others can be the barometer of whether he or she has a serious abuse problem.

If parents are concerned that their son or daughter has a drinking or drug problem, try talking to a significant girlfriend or boyfriend or other close friends about how *they* feel about your child. Are their friends worried? Are they angry that your child is acting irresponsibly? Do they feel your teen is breaking promises, not showing up or failing to keep commitments? Does your teen seem self-absorbed to friends? These are strong indicators that a drinking and/or drug abuse problem may already exist and that it *is* time to investigate rehabilitation options.

How a teen can tell a parent, "I have a problem."

Another article offers tips on how teens can tell their parents/caregivers about their substance or alcohol use. To a parent, having to advise a teen on how to tell them about their alcohol and drug use may seem silly.

"Of course they can come to me if they have a problem. They KNOW I would want them to and that I won't stop loving them," parents exclaim.

However, many teens get conflicting messages from parents.

Even at magnet schools and youth leadership conferences, high-achieving teens, athletic team captains and school officers have shared with me how they got started snorting cocaine or using methamphetamines "just for fun" at parties. However, now they can't stop craving it. They are addicted and know they are in trouble. Their grades may not yet be affected, but they don't know what to do and are in grave anxiety at the thought of telling their parents.

> *"My parents are so proud of me," a football captain and school president moaned to me. "How can I tell them I'm hooked on cocaine? I'm afraid of losing their respect and letting them down. I CAN'T tell them!"*

Of course, this teen's parents will be horribly upset and pained to find out, but they would be far more devastated to have their son's future destroyed by an addiction. This young man understood after we talked just how disastrous ignoring drug addiction can be, especially after I shared how my first husband died from addictions that included cocaine. This young man decided that keeping his problem a secret wasn't worth the potential consequences. Together we walked to the counselor's office where he shared his distressing reality. The counselor and the teen decided to call his parents into the counseling office so that together, they could share his addiction problem with his parents and offer options to help him.

This young man was one of the lucky ones. His secrets were revealed before they could destroy his life because he became willing to reach out and ask for help.

How can we help those teens who are still too afraid? Send teens to the helpful website: **www.everydaywarriors.com/teens/art_howtalkparentsdrugs.htm** and the article: *Coming Clean: How To Talk to Your Parents About Your Drug Use.* Teens will find ways to start the conversation, how to ask for help, and how to identify if they truly do have a serious problem. Also see link at **www.legacyofhope.com**

Rather than assume your child would never be afraid to talk with you, share the article with your teen so he/she and friends are well-equipped and encouraged to share with parents, should the need ever arise.

Parents tend to repeatedly underestimate use.

Most parents underestimate the use of drugs by their teens and are unaware of the signs. The drugs of choice can change so fast and show up in the most common of places that parents are hard-pressed to fully comprehend the reality of teen use and are undereducated on the signs of current popular drug use, including inhaling of common household products.

Sadly, heavy teen drinking is only recognized as the great deadly escape when a teen fatality involves alcohol. What if your teen isn't sure if his or her drinking or drug use has become a serious problem? A number of websites provide confidential assessment exercises for teens to identify if their own use or that of a friend is a serious problem. Get the power; face the truth.

Here are other misperceptions about teen drug use.

Adults may have the false perception that drugs like Ecstasy, Oxycontin, methamphetamines, cocaine, heroine and other club drugs are primarily the scourge of teens in cities. Traveling across the United States has shown me that many rural communities have pockets of serious use as well. Use can flourish because parents in rural, if not urban, communities like to believe "not my kids." They also underestimate parental use in rural America, where some parents even introduce their teens to drugs.

According to the Partnership for a Drug-Free America's annual report, while 92 percent of parents are aware of Ecstasy, nearly half would not be able to recognize its effects on their children. Signs of Ecstasy use include blurred vision, rapid eye movement, chills or sweating, dehydration, confusion, faintness, severe anxiety, grinding of teeth, and a trance-like state. Parents are naturally reluctant to think it can happen to their children.

The report found that only 1 percent of parents believe their child has ever tried Ecstasy, known as a "club drug" because of its popularity at rave dance parties.

"Millions of parents sincerely don't believe that their kids are the ones experimenting with drugs like Ecstasy," said Stephen J. Pasierb, President and Chief Executive Officer of the Partnership. "It's these assumptions that enable drug use to go undetected."

The Internet is chock full of information for any teen or parent eager to connect with accurate information and the experiences of others. Many websites offer up-to-the-minute research results from the Center for Substance Abuse Prevention (CSAP) such as **www.health.org**. I encourage you to take advantage of the resources your own tax dollars provide. I invite you to visit my website for additional valuable resources: **www.legacyofhope.com**.

Rural America poses special problems.

Many rural communities I've visited accept heavy alcohol consumption as a normal part of life for teens and adults. In towns where there is too little to do and nowhere to go, winters are long and wide open spaces abound, drinking fills the hours; and teens drink a lot.

Rural teen alcohol use is often seriously out-of-control as is pot and even methamphetamine use. Methamphetamines are easily manufactured in rural America where no one detects the smell, and pot is easily grown in fields including harvests in national forests.

These problems are magnified in rural America by parents in the community who bury their own boredom and/or hopelessness in alcohol and drugs. Indeed, there have been numerous teens across rural America who have told me that their parents started passing a joint across the kitchen table to them at age four or had them drink with them by age nine. Their parents claimed they wanted to be closer to their child by sharing getting high.

Teens have even shared how these same parents became infuriated when, as a teen, their child refused to participate any more. "What, you too good for me anymore?!" an angry inebriated and/or addicted parent has yelled at their teen. "You like to smoke dope with your friends more than ME? Bring them over here and we can all get high together. No? You don't wanna? Then, get OUT if you don't want to drink or smoke with me any more. See if your friends take care of you the way I have!"

No doubt, rural America has some special concerns that require total community involvement to solve. Community coalitions have been formed in communities, creating a united front of school personnel, law enforcement, religious community, mental health and parents to create awareness, prevention, intervention and rehab programs.

For examples of successful community coalitions, contact **Community Anti-Drug Coalitions of America** (CADCA) at **www.cadca.org.** CADCA is the expert in community coalition building and influencing Congress for funding of community programs since 1990. Their annual conference in Washington, D.C. brings together communities to network and share ideas that are working. Communities can also avail themselves of CADCA trainings throughout the year in coalition development, tracking outcomes, grant applications and successful strategies.

CHAPTER THIRTY-TWO
A 21st Century Epidemic: Teens Cutting on Themselves

Drug and alcohol prevention funding is at its highest, and the federal Anti-Drug Media Campaign in full swing. Now a new and foreboding teen enemy has surfaced. The 2003 thru 2005 school years brought a constant flow of teens up to the front of the stage to share with me after assemblies about their addictions with self-harm, otherwise known as 'cutting on themselves'.

Once you've had an adorable, blond, blue-eyed angelic 13-year-old girl shove her forearm in your face and have seen, first-hand, 50 fresh three-inch razor blade cuts carved into her arm, you'll never be the same. You can never go back to the naïve belief that teens are just being teens and don't really have severe emotional issues. You can't help but want to find whatever it takes to heal these wounded children.

Before the news caught wind of self-mutilation as a trend, I was seeing it on the bodies and in the daring eyes of teenage cutters who talked to me after assemblies. They said, "You're the first person who doesn't just say you should stop. You showed how I feel and why I like to do it. You're the first adult who understands. I cut because I feel better when I cut."

I was running into too many teenage girls, and especially young ones – 7th through 10th graders – who were cutting as a way to scream out to their parents and the world, "LOVE ME!"

But in the process of a desperate cry, telling parents they are overwhelmed by their fears and the pressures and their feelings, they got addicted to the rush of cutting. Their explosive, even suicidal, feelings abated when the razor cut into their arm. Their minds reinterpreted the physical pain as emotional relief, and now they cannot nor do not want to stop.

Middle school counselors tell me that it is epidemic with 7th and 8th grade girls. The word spreads that to cut shows you have intense feelings of inadequacy and are a victim. Nearly all preteens experience emotional fluctuations including moments of angst and identity crisis. Now, however, they have peers at school that model cutting as a means of relief from these emotional torments. So, more teens are trying it.

'Real' cutters are those who usually come from seriously neglectful, and/or abusive homes. They cut because their emotional turmoil includes dysfunction and legitimate victimization; they cut because their thoughts are constantly hopeless, black and suicidal; they cut to survive.

They cut to find an outlet for feelings they don't think they should have. Sometimes they cut, consciously and subconsciously motivated to get their parents' attention. They have no other way of letting them know that, though they look normal on the outside, they are crumbling on the inside. The cutting kills the pain; they can numb out, and don't need anyone, so they think.

The following are some approaches that have been found to help teens stop cutting:

Helping teens to stop cutting.

1. **Counseling** – Teens need a place to tell their story. They need an advocate to help them communicate with their parents the need for time and attention, unconditional love and affection regardless of performance in school, sports, or even at home. They and their families may need therapy for the underlying family issues and communication styles.
2. **Poetry** – Many teen cutters find that when they have the urge to cut, writing poetry releases their feelings and reduces the desire to a level they can resist. Sharing their poetry with counselors is excellent. The poetry is often dark and filled with reflections on a desire to be gone, to die, to leave a life that is so painful. But the poetry helps vent the feelings and creates a tool for exploring where their feelings come from. What is the loss so deeply etched into their

minds and hearts? Where is the criticism or neglect that leaves them feeling worthless?

3. **Support Partners** – I urge cutters to make a pact with another teen cutter and agree that when they feel like cutting, they will call each other and talk until the addictive urges pass. This mutual support is similar to sponsorship in 12-step programs like Alcoholics Anonymous, Narcotics Anonymous, Nar-Anon, Al-Anon and Alateen. And it works for many teens!
4. **Alternative Choice Lists** – I have encouraged teens to make a list of 10 things they can do when they feel like cutting. They have learned to turn to these lists and take contrary action rather than give in to the urge to cut. Their lists have included:
   - Listen to music
   - Play with a pet
   - Take a walk or jog
   - Go exercise
   - Draw or paint a picture
   - Play a musical instrument
   - Call a friend and talk about how they feel
   - Write poetry
   - E-mail
   - Talk to a parent or other adult a teen trusts
   - Sing or dance, and more
5. **Spiritual Practices** – Teens who cut generally tell me they used to pray to God to make things better in their lives, but nothing changed. They figured God didn't really care about them, forgot them, gave up on them, didn't really exist, or they gave up on God. When they are shown compassion by an adult and encouraged to see that that compassion as God in action, many become willing to revisit a spiritual relationship with a loving power greater than themselves. A number of teens found their obsession to cut gone when they finally found trust and faith in the God of their understanding.

No teen is too young to have emotional turmoil; therefore, no teen is too young to experiment with cutting.

Throughout the 2003-2004 school year, I asked 20,000 teens in assembly audiences if they knew someone who was cutting on themselves. 95 percent of hands went up regardless of locale across the United States. Clearly, teens are aware of peers and friends who mutilate themselves as a way to cope with feelings. This negative role modeling places all teens at risk and entreats every parent to recognize cutting as a very serious emotional problem. **Pay immediate attention to a teen who claims you never give them any attention or you don't seem to care. You can avoid a very dangerous and difficult obsession to break if you take the time to listen.**

CHAPTER THIRTY-THREE
Federal Funding and Grants Help You Provide Treatment to Community Teens

Incarceration of abusing teens can't help if they don't receive treatment, too. Here are several solutions that make it easy to support phenomenal, positive change in your own community.

What would you do if you found out your teen was using methamphetamines, ecstasy, pot and/or alcohol on a daily basis? What if your child had been arrested for drunk driving, stealing or breaking and entering while under the influence? Where would you turn? These are very real questions that thousands of American parents face annually.

One radical approach to stop addiction!

In striking contrast to our approach here in the United States, Kim Jong II, leader of North Korea, ordered on April 14, 2002 all drug users in his country be executed by shooting! "I will subject all those who sell or use illegal drugs to a firing squad, and have ordered that Chinese drug traders be beaten with sticks," said Kim.

Any parent whose child has become addicted to drugs, might consider such punishments within reason for the wicked drug traffickers that enmeshed their child. However, in the real world today, many of our teens acquire their drugs of choice from other teens at school and around town – teens that could also be one of your children. Does this mean we should lock our children up or, instead, look for more realistic approaches to teen addiction and drug-related crime?

Treatment is needed.

In my work with the Los Angeles County Sheriff's Department and the Orange County Juvenile Probation Department, I have met many teens incarcerated for drug-related crime. Many teen girls and boys have shared personal sagas with me filled with alcohol and drug abuse, which have led them to stealing and subsequent arrests for crimes while under the influence. It is heart-breaking to meet an 18-year-old facing a 3-strikes life-imprisonment sentence due to the impact of an addiction.

Without treatment, many return to the life they came from.

I have been encouraged by communities that create juvenile drug-courts, and sentence first-time offenders of non-violent crimes to addiction treatment instead of incarceration. The numbers indicate a great need for this approach. As an example, in 1999, the Arizona Department of Juvenile Corrections reported that 95.4 percent of the teens released from Arizona's detention facilities without treatment had a history of abusing substances.

In the early 1990s, I had a unique opportunity to talk with 100 teen boys incarcerated in a school of detention for 16- to 18-year-old male offenders and members of African American, Hispanic and White Supremacist gangs. In an hour of revealing conversation, every one of them admitted that they were under the influence of alcohol or alcohol and other drugs at the time of their crime. Perhaps more significantly, they also believed that if they had not been abusing alcohol and drugs, they probably would not have committed their crime.

It was with great dismay that I left that day, as 99 out of the 100 boys intended to return to their gangs upon release. **Back then, not one of them was in treatment for their addictions while incarcerated.** They would be released back to their hostile worlds with no ability to curb their alcohol and drug abuse and little awareness of how their abusive childhoods were motivating their choices. Sentenced to return to their home for a year of probation trapped these boys into the same gang environment.

A larger trap for these boys was that now they would be considered heroes by their gang. The "street" impression of serving time, was that they had endured cruel and tough treatment in detention, making them more of a man when they got out. Truth be told, most of these tough street gangbangers actually found detention a time of safety, structure, discipline, good food, and more constructive and positive feedback than anywhere else in their lives. If one of these boys chose to leave the gang on release from the detention facility, his "homeys" could not imagine anyone wanting out except for one and only one reason – to join a rival gang, which puts their lives in severe danger. Their "homeys" could not fathom someone wanting a different life. The trap was set for a life of violence and crime.

Communities can provide treatment with grant help.

Studies today are confirming that treatment for teens significantly reduces criminal activity. "*Treatment Reduces Drug Use, Crime*" an article on the Join Together website (**www.jointogether.org**), published September 11, 1998, confirmed that both substance use and criminal behavior is reduced for at least five years following inpatient, outpatient and residential drug abuse treatment.

I encourage communities to rally support for drug-courts and youth sentencing to treatment and rehab environments on first arrests for non-violent drug and alcohol related crimes.

Orange County Juvenile Probation Department in Orange County, California, offers a model program in their Youth and Family Resource Center (YFRC) where such teens attend high school under the supervision of Probation Officers with a ratio of one officer to every three teens. Studies include a full high school curriculum plus anger management classes, alcohol and drug support groups and therapy sessions, and social development activities including a Tolerance Class, as well as outings to the Museum of Tolerance in Los Angeles, California, and more.

Teens must qualify to attend YFRC by meeting certain criteria including referral from the courts after a first offense; have had gang exposure personally or through a family member; are known to use drugs and alcohol; and are behind in school credits. The goal is to ignite that spark of personal awareness in each teen that his or her life is valuable no matter the family or situation they come from.

Some juvenile courts also require parents/guardians to attend parenting classes and/or Al-Anon meetings to better understand the severe impact of an alcoholic parent, spouse or child on the family.

Millions of dollars in financial support are available through grants, particularly through Substance Abuse and Mental Health Services Administration (SAMHSA), to expand substance abuse treatment services provided by juvenile treatment drug courts. Information is available from SAMHSA's web site at **www.SAMHSA.gov** or by phone from **SAMHSA's National Clearinghouse for Alcohol and Drug Information** at 1-800-729-6686. *Reference Guidance for Applicants* (GFA No. TI 02-008).

Additional help is available through the federal agency CSAT, **Center for Substance Abuse Treatment**, which provides grant funding for community-based addiction treatment programs for youths. For example, Join Together reported that $5.84 million was awarded in 2002 by CSAT to programs that identified young people with addictions, referred them to treatment, and provided counseling and other services. Funds for treatment are continuing to increase as Congress is made more aware of treatments' ability to reduce crime.

SECTION SIX

Hope For the Future, Lies In Facing Tough Teen Troubles

In earlier sections, I shared insights from 20,000 conversations with teens regarding various common teen issues. You may have found a new approach to communicate with your teen and a preventative measure to help teens avoid the plethora of pitfalls in their world. It is in this section, however, that "the rubber meets the road."

Jenn, 14-year-old HIV positive from Legacy of Hope® presentation:

And like, I met this guy, Andy. He's 17 and has this awesome red car. And he took me to these bomb parties. You know, we'd smoke some bud; down some 40s; maybe do some E. And, like, there's always a room at these parties where couples go and take turns, you know. And Andy wanted to. I mean he is really hot ... I don't know, maybe I took sex too casual like my Mom says. Maybe way too casual. 'Cause now they say I've got HIV. No way! I thought Andy loved me. I thought all those guys loved me. I don't wanna die. But I don't know if anyone cares if I do, so why should I?

CHAPTER THIRTY-FOUR
A Nation in Denial

For quite some time I have wanted to bring the material in this section to the attention of mainstream America. I started writing this chapter in 1996 as a book unto itself, entitled "*A Nation in Denial*." The book was a primal scream from my gut to alert parents to the alarming number of teens I was meeting – tens of thousands who were buried under shame and deep grief vented as anger and rage.

From 1996 to the present, an excessively high volume of teens have revealed their secret feelings to me of inadequacy, perceptions of themselves as "losers," overwhelmed with chronic hopelessness, and consumed with self-blame for the ills that had befallen their families and their lives.

In middle schools and high schools all across the country, 15 to 50 teens would immediately reach out to talk with me after assemblies. Then, from 2000 to the present, the statistics from our post-assembly survey of teen audiences has revealed exceptionally high levels of emotional problems including depression; suicidal thoughts; rage/violent feelings; concern over their own alcohol and other substance use; and serious concern over friends' emotional states, substance abuse, and self harm.

Teens shared horrors about the family bedrock of rural Midwest. Six-foot, 180-pound white middle class athletes, Advanced Placement high achieving students, and macho Hispanic gangbangers were mutually admitting haunting thoughts of suicide. These teens shared how thoughts of suicide helped them cope with the pressure of parents who criticized them incessantly or whose expectations they could never meet. Teenagers felt like failures, regardless of achievements, because they had surmised that they could never be good enough to be loved by the most important influence in their lives, their parents.

Throngs of provocatively dressed 14-year-old middle school Hispanic girls have told me how their 18- to 24-year-old Latino boyfriends beat them or force them to have sex. Some of these older boyfriends had already abandoned these preteen girls with one, sometimes two, babies in tow. Even more disturbing were the Hispanic teen girls, usually the eldest daughters in the family, whose mothers nagged at them to forget their school studies and just care for their younger brothers and sisters.

> *"Why do you study?" a Latina mother railed on her daughter. "You're just going to get pregnant and have babies at 16. Now, go take care of your little brother and change your sister's diapers. Then come help me make dinner in the kitchen, you are such a lazy girl."*

After every assembly, regardless of what city or state I presented in, teen stories came at me fast and furiously. Their turmoil almost always had origins in family circumstances.

Many had parents who sounded like they, too, felt victimized or lost in obsessions, ambitions, addictions, self-absorption, overwhelm, and/or hopelessness of their own. The majority of these parents *did* care about their teens, but could not recognize, nor provide the emotional basics of security and esteem for their offspring.

My initial reaction was actually one of rage and distrust of parents. I was in my own state of grief and anger over the vast number of teens I met who were engrossed in dangerous escapism, already self-medicating emotional pain with record levels of drugs, alcohol, unprotected sex, self-mutilation and social violence.

As they told their life stories and family histories to me, it was clear that we had spawned a society where alcoholism, drug addiction, abuse and neglect were as much the norm as not. With divorce rates up to 70 percent in some areas, the highest teen pregnancy rates of any industrialized nation, and new extreme modes of acting out with each passing year, we had abandoned the basic laws of family decency and childhood stability. **We had become dazzled by "the having and the doing" of an affluent lifestyle and forgotten the value of consistently, compassionately and tenderly being there for one another.**

And our teens carry their emotional damage into every classroom in the country. From 1996 through 1999, I shouted from every platform:

> *"Wake up, parents of America! Wise up to the needs <u>inside</u> your kids. Face your own inner angst and the critical voices in your head. Figure out why you can't feel "it" – that critical key to a meaningful life ... self-love. Then take the baby steps to begin the process of your own healing so you can be a healthy parent, conscious and sensitive to the needs of your children."*

The message fell on many deaf ears.

The book that screamed to be written in 1997 and 1999 did not get written. I created outlines and book proposals, but got deterred by my own need to reach as many teens as I could with a message of emotional and spiritual healing that teens could begin for themselves. I feared I could not reach parents, so I sought to teach teens how to save themselves. The teens "got it." They understood the reality I portrayed; and they hungered and reached out for the hope and possibilities offered.

Throughout those years, I made attempts to recruit parents to the cause, but it became abundantly clear in the late '90s from conversations with middle-class peers that America was not ready to face these truths. The media would leak a story about a music star or athletic hero's drug addiction; AIDS hitting a high-profile figure or two; and certainly news-worthy violent acts were eagerly reported, such as the Littleton, Colorado school shootings. But the news media always addressed the symptoms – the shocking outcomes of youth desperation – rather than the cause.

For example, when school violence was reported, the media exclaimed, "*How* could this have happened?"

Broadcasters seemed to naively resist delving into the contributing parental factors of emotional neglect, self-absorption, alcoholism and substance abuse, verbal abuse and criticism of teens that I observed across our nation.

Nobody wanted to look more deeply inside our homes past the altar of materialism to the sacrifices the "god of stuff"demanded, stripping us of the values, time and energy required to raise resilient, secure children.

No one spoke of the decline in common courtesy in America's homes and the lack of respect for others. And what about the lack of time, energy and priority in parents' lives to set consistent, loving boundaries with clear consequences for children? We adults could hardly manage our own chaotic rat race. Our false gods devoured our values, compassion, patience, and kindness ... our spiritual centers. Middle-class America did not want to look at itself and remained in denial.

Middle-class America is in denial.

I recall a lunch I had in 1997 with some educated, comfortably well-off women who had children in 6th through 10th grades. The talk was naturally about the activities of their kids, redecorating of bedrooms, bathrooms and kitchens, and preparations for the holidays. Eventually, I was asked how I was doing. I shared from my recent speaking engagements across the US. I was honest about how I was emotionally aching for the thousands of teens who besieged me after assemblies.

I told these women how adolescents were readily and painfully identifying with my characters, sharing how desperate the teens were to find an adult who recognized they were emotionally wounded and stuck in layers of grief. I shared how overwhelmed I felt by the thousands of teens that year who had let out secrets to me about parents who were alcoholics, addicts, emotionally vicious, relentlessly critical and controlling, physically and even sexually abusive and how teens were trappped in these homes.

As I described how these teens coped through rampant drinking, drugging and sexual partnering, many at the age of 13 and 14, the women appeared stunned. Then they appeared irritated, if not appalled, that I might bring such atrocious tales to their seemingly secure and protected world. "Not MY kids," they thought. "I don't need to listen to some other negligent parent's problems." And then they changed the subject.

Denial of the power of peer pressure.

That was by no means the only time I experienced middle-class parents refusing to consider that *their* preteens and teens might be at-risk. They seemed oblivious to real life as it is for adolescents every school day, rubbing elbows with other troubled teens and the talk of escapades and opportunity for pot, alcohol and other drug use.

I have observed that if parents have discussed a topic such as alcohol and drug use or sex with their preteens and teens one or two times, many parents, especially white middle-class to wealthy, believe that their children know how they feel and will behave accordingly. But nearly all high school teens and many middle school teens are exposed on a weekly basis to peers using alcohol, pot and sex to give meaning to their lives. Such exposure can surely begin to make these choices look normal, if not fun.

In 1996, an 8th grade girl shared a chilling example of the power of peer pressure. At that time, the news was barely savvy to the fact that middle school teens were sexually active. It wasn't until 2003 that the media caught up with the trend of middle school girls performing oral sex on boys.

With this in mind, I was obviously taken aback in 1996 by the tale shared with me by this fourteen-year-old teenage girl:

> *"I was really afraid I was pregnant, but I feel better. I got my period a couple days ago. I'm only 14, so it's not all that regular. But two months ago I was out with my girlfriends; and we were hanging out and there were these guys – like 17, 18, you know. And my girlfriends say, 'Go scam with that guy. He is sooo fine!' So I did. And then my girlfriends said I should do it with him because one of them had, and said it makes you feel so good.*
>
> *"I didn't really want to, but they're my friends; and they thought I should. So, well I didn't really do it. I just jacked him off and his four friends, too. But one of them, like, did it close to me, and even though there's just a one in a million chance it got me pregnant, well, I was really worried."*

Disturbing, isn't it? A 14-year-old girl engaging in demeaning acts is a sad reflection of what our young teens find necessary as well as comfortable to do in order to feel accepted. Even more of a concern, however, is the influence peers-on-the-edge have on other naive teens. Not just peers, but friends, close friends, pushing a young girl to engage in sex with a stranger, and encouraging her to do so just because it felt good.

Or maybe her friends had a hidden agenda, pulling her into their world so that she would not appear better than them. Perhaps they wanted to have secrets to tell on her, creating a bond of trust that comes from shared and dangerous secrets. **This manipulation of friendship is intentional, sometimes to see just how far a good girl, a 'target,' can be pushed.** Clearly, teenagers are under regular pressure to engage in dangerous and demeaning activities from both friends and foes.

Family secrets put teens in peril, too.

Not only were middle-class parents in denial of the intensity and depth of peer pressures on their teens, they also were in denial of the family issues that put their teens at higher risk.

What about the secrets their own families harbor such as an

alcoholic parent, grandparent or child? Naturally, many parents – then and now – find it excruciating to admit such problems and fear how they reflect on them and the family. But without taking an honest and courageous inventory of their own inheritances, parents are raising their children blind, unable to provide the tools to be aware and provide warnings that might build resiliency into their young, rather than vulnerability.

Most adults who have shared stories of family alcoholism/ addiction with me acknowledge that they, like many teens today, are riddled with hidden shame and self-blame. **Most adults learned long ago to suppress and hide their own childhood traumas. Emotional wounds have long been considered weaknesses in society.** Many adults were made fun of as children and as teens for expressing hurt, sadness, or fear. As a result, some shut down, seeing themselves as victims; others as angry aggressors; still others just became obsessive and controlling to avoid looking at their own feelings.

Many adults had parents and siblings who used an admission of feelings against them. They learned that it was clearly not safe to let any emotion surface other than anger, love and lust. In so doing, **many adults have adopted survival skills of denial, suppression, and escape that create emotional handicaps and an inability to express unconditional love to their children.** Much of America's marketing and consumerism is driven by these deep-seated unresolved feelings that cause us to focus our lives and even our parenting on money, property and prestige rather than values, character and spirituality.

Emotions are complex, but they do make some sense. They are influenced, shaped and learned patterns, just as exercise shapes a muscle. Like muscles, a teen's patterns of victimization, low self-esteem, anger or violence, have the potential to be retrained, given early intervention and appropriate, compassionate care.

Wise and humble school counselors appeared like angels on my horizon!

From 1996 through 1999, I continued zealously to take the emotional awareness and prevention messages in Legacy of Hope® on the road. I prayed to find other adults aware and interested in these issues, as I sought support to stem the tide of troubled youth. Miraculously in 2000, I found an army of aware adults as eager as I to help save teen lives. They, too, worked to give today's teens and the next generation of children a chance at emotional well-being and hope. My journey led me to the American Counseling Association. There I found the collaboration I was desperately seeking. I teamed up with school counselors.

Counselors in middle schools and high schools across the country were seeing the same plague spreading like wildfire through their student populations.

Take time for an honest inventory.

Teens everywhere have been crying out for help even before I started in 1991; but the cry has become more desperate as escape options have increased. It is time we hear them. America IS ready. 9/11 taught us that we are not invulnerable. We know today that we are neither invincible nor guiltless. We have marvelous resources and assets as a nation and as parents; however, it is time we took a fearless moral inventory, as described in the twelve steps of Alcoholics Anonymous, Al-Anon, Alateen, Narcotics Anonymous, Marijuana Anonymous, Co-Dependents Anonymous, Gamblers Anonymous and Overeaters Anonymous.

Like a store that does not take a factual and honest inventory, our children will go morally, spiritually, and emotionally bankrupt if we do not take stock of the underlying emotional issues at home and in society that drive their choices.

With that, please strap on your seatbelts, open up your hearts and minds, and set aside guilt, shame and blame as we tour what has come to light in my trek across America.

CHAPTER THIRTY-FIVE
Stay Focused On Where You Can Make a Difference!

While the world focuses on global terrorism and international conflict, movie stars and reality shows, teens in our own country are fighting a daily battle against fears, isolation, peer pressure, parental abuse and more.

Though news media continues to broadcast stories on global terrorism, war, bombings, and international conflict, I recognize that my sphere of influence may not reach everyone around the world at the speed news broadcasts do. I, like most Americans, have much more impact on my family and friends. Despite media's focus, it is vital that we not forget to put our focus where it really counts – on our own families and children.

Pay attention to the children in your own home first.

Very real dangers still exist for youth in America. A 15-year-old girl from the South, whom I will call Sharla, reached out to me after an assembly. I noticed her out-stretched forearm, crisscrossed with a dozen half-inch shallow cuts, old and new. I remarked that I saw she had been cutting on her arm.

I was familiar with the look of self-mutilation from coaching other teens and was glad I was able to recognize Sharla using a destructive coping mechanism rather than judge her as a bad, or scary teen. I also knew from experience not to over-react. Instead, I talked calmly and openly with her about what I saw. Our conversation gave her a vital opportunity to express her honest feelings and vent about her family situation.

She spoke of a deep alienation from everyone in her home and at school. She was greatly relieved, even elated that someone finally grasped her heavy despair. Having established a level of trust with her, I suggested we go together to talk to the school counselor. She was initially reluctant, but gave in because being understood and listened to was such a great relief to her. We walked to the office and I introduced Sharla to the school counselor, where the two began to establish their own rapport.

A week later, I received an e-mail from Sharla. She sounded depressed and angry, even more insistent that her parents and sisters did not seem to notice how unhappy she was no matter what she did. She had tried to get attention by getting great grades, but felt her parents hardly acknowledged her. Sharla still feared trusting her school counselor, convinced that adults in her school didn't care any more about her than her parents appeared to.

Sharla was expressing what a great many other teens have also shared with me:

The biggest emotional trauma in their lives is the fear, if not the belief, that one or both of their parents do not really love them.

Sharla shared that she resorted to cutting on her arm again and then exposed her injured forearm at the breakfast table in an effort to get her parents' attention. She claimed that neither her mother, father or siblings even noticed. No one said a word to her about the self-inflicted wounds. She then became enraged and brought on a dramatic asthma attack. Her mother took her to the hospital, yet Sharla believed her mother did so out of obligation, since no loving words or hugs were exchanged between them.

A few days later, more e-mails arrived. Now Sharla wrote about ideas she was having about how to commit suicide. She was explicit and wrote about a gun in her parents' closet. She said she had even hidden the gun in her bedroom. Through our e-mail messages, it was clear that Sharla was obsessed with a desire to punish her family whom she felt had ignored and under-appreciated her. The atmosphere of denial, silence and withdrawal in her home had become intolerable.

I took swift action and contacted the school counselor to intervene.

The counselor immediately contacted Sharla's parents, met with them and Sharla, and helped find professional therapy for her before she could harm herself, her family, or, perhaps, even school mates. Clearly, this teen's sense of alienation and loneliness could have become everyone's problem. As it consumed her, the entire world became her enemy. The miracle of our meeting and the gift of e-mail may well have averted a teen suicide or, worse yet, a Columbine repeat.

During those days of interaction with Sharla, I continued to hear the media focus on national and international violence and terrorism. It was a sobering reminder that neglecting other people's pain, at home and around the world, can lead to being seen as a heartless enemy. A troubling parallel in an "all-American home."

A positive conclusion:

About a year later, Sharla e-mailed me again. Therapy had been "decent," in Sharla's opinion.

The therapy may well have kept her from taking drastic actions and given her new insights. Sharla also eagerly shared that her most dramatic change in attitude came from a spiritual experience that turned her thinking around.

Sharla wrote:

"*I went to a church camp two weeks ago and I accepted Christ into my life and I have never felt better. I have gotten rid of a lot of muck in my life and after 4 years I have finally found the strength to stop the cutting and it feels great. It is hard though to live a good Christian life with all the cruel pressures of high school but I am kinda looking forward to telling people what I stand for and what I believe in. It's very exhilarating. And I thank you so much because you really did help me out in the greatest way. You told me that I could do anything and that I shouldn't be afraid to try. As for things at home they are going better than I expected. I haven't been totally abused in any way. God has really protected me this summer and I know that he will continue to do so.*"

She fell as low as she could go without killing herself, and then she prayed.

There are many pathways to God; I will be forever grateful that one more hopeless teen found hers.

CHAPTER THIRTY-SIX
Help Teens When They Are In An Emotional Tailspin

When teens experience loss or rejection, they can easily become emotionally distraught and vulnerable. The simplest of emotional vulnerability that goes unrecognized or ignored by a parent can throw a seemingly stable teen into a downhill slide and into dangerous alternatives.

Of all the fears and feelings that terrorize teens, the fear of not fitting in with peers looms large.

Many teens are cruelly taunted or emotionally traumatized by gossip in middle school. Other teens have experienced family problems that lead to a lack of emotional support, grief, fear and anger. Teens in families where there has been abandonment by one or both parents, divorce, parental substance abuse, family violence, or even a move to a new school, town, or state, often feel different from other teens as well as unaccepted. Many teens are treated as misfits or unwelcome in new communities. Small towns in rural America with well-defined cliques are often the most difficult to gain acceptance in for a new teen in town.

Given the intrinsic human need to belong, teens find other ways to fit in by reaching out to other angry, hurting kids – joining gangs in the streets, involved in dangerous relationships over the Internet, or aligning themselves with other emotionally desperate teens, often leading to drugs, alcohol, fantasy, witchcraft or revenge to anesthetize their uncomfortable feelings. Loneliness and hopelessness pervade their lives.

Characteristic of adolescence is thinking that these intense feelings and the intolerable family/social situations are forever. A family that does not communicate about feelings leaves a teen depressed and angry, and substantiates a teen's sense of terminal gloom.

Ask any teen and you will find that they can identify plenty of kids at school who have these desperate feelings. I've asked crowds of 100 to 1,000 teens to acknowledge if they know someone who reminds them of one of my angry, lonely, grieving and desperate characters. Invariably, 80 to 90 percent of teens raise their hands in high schools across the country and 70 percent in middle schools.

Recent national survey statistics have confirmed my anecdotal observations. Information from the U.S. Department of Health and Human Services' *National Strategy for Suicide Prevention* and the Massachusetts Alliance of Samaritan Suicide Prevention Services has hence corroborated my experiences:

- Since 1970, teen/youth suicide rates have tripled.
- 60 percent of high school boys have thought about suicide; 9 percent have attempted suicide.
- For every successful teen suicide, there are 50 to 100 attempted suicides.
- Each year 5,000 young people, age 15-24, commit suicide.
- Suicide is the second leading cause of death among college students.

Unfortunately, as children progress into adolescence, they get the message from peers, society, and quite often from their own homes, that they are bad for having fear, loneliness, embarrassment, shame, and hopelessness – all the feelings that make us vulnerable and need the support of others. **The truth is that no one is bad for having feelings. What matters is what choices we make and what actions we take as a result of them.**

How teens (and adults) feel about themselves and our acceptability to others is very important to the quality and success of our lives. Feelings impact our attitudes and all of our choices, from who teens hang out with and who they date, to how well they do in school, whether they drink and do drugs, have sex, how they treat others, what music they listen to, what careers they choose, even what money they eventually make. Feelings significantly impact how your teens will someday parent your grandkids!

Feelings play an important role in what happens to teens. Hidden feelings intensify and create pressure from the inside out, pushing teens to escape into unhealthy choices.

◆

One teen's tale of hiding feelings that led her to the brink and back.

Emily was a teen who asked to talk to me after a Legacy of Hope® assembly at her school. She was a teen who could attend school for four years and graduate without ever being noticed. She was 50 pounds overweight. Her hair hung limp across her face. She had a timid doe-like look in her eyes. She spoke so softly, I hardly heard her as she shared about her life.

Like too many teens I meet, she shared that she drank and got drunk most weekends and used pot every day. Pot had become the easiest of all options to escape into. During the day, she merely slipped into the "right" bathroom to buy a joint, even take a hit or two between classes or behind the gym during lunch. She had tried ecstasy and speed and had already had her share of sexual encounters since becoming sexually active at 13 with older boys. She knew her life was out of balance but felt despondent and hopeless; being overwhelmed, she just went numb.

A willing listener became a lifeline.

From early childhood, Emily conveyed that she received little guidance, care or supervision. She had fed herself since four years of age as her single-parent mother lay daily in a drunken heap on the couch. Peanut butter and jelly sandwiches became her staple. Dinner might be potato chips. Breakfast was a glass of chocolate milk; it soothed her. With no parent to prepare food or teach her what to eat, she had no idea what was healthy either for her body, her mind or her spirit. She had thought the two dozen boys she had slept with would make her feel loved; instead she felt disgust for herself, worthless and deep despair.

Emily's thoughts were filled with failure and fantasies about suicide. Like Sharla, she desperately needed someone to listen to her tell her story – the whole story – without interruption, criticism, blame or shame.

She told me that her parents divorced when she was nine. Her father had been her hero. After the divorce, however, he disappeared out of her life. Her mother was too busy to give Emily attention and too bitter to show her affection. Worse yet, her mom criticized her mercilessly for being lazy when Emily was actually consumed by grief over the loss of her dad. She had no concept of why she had no energy, no interest in life, no happiness. She just felt sad and unmotivated as her unprocessed grief was treated with disgust and disinterest, or misinterpreted as belligerence by her mom.

> "*Just get over it,*" her mom would bellow when Emily asked about her dad. "*Your Dad is NEVER coming back, and if he does, you are not to see him. He's a loser; and I don't*

want you to have anything to do with him!"

To keep her mom from yelling, Emily held back the tears and stuffed her feelings with food. When she felt hurt or sad, she ate. When she liked a boy, it made her nervous and she ate more.

When she turned eleven, things got worse. It was a Friday night and her mother was on her case once again.

"STAY IN YOUR ROOM. I have a date coming over; and I don't want him to see you. You embarrass me; you're TOO FAT!" her mom yelled in a drunken rage.

Her mom and the date drank too much that night. As her mother dozed off on the couch, the date came knocking at Emily's bedroom door. He did the unspeakable – he raped this unprotected, preteen girl and stole whatever shred of self-esteem and hope she had left.

Emily was emotionally mangled. When she shared with me about her parents, it was the first time she recalled someone ever listening to her without criticizing, nagging, scolding or blaming. **She was starving for someone to appreciate her pain and her potential.** From our conversation, she felt an enormous sense of relief.

"I'm just a dumb kid at the school you did your show at today. I thought I should tell you that I lay awake at night, looking up at the ceiling, wondering "How should I kill myself?" Just having you listen to me at my school today makes me think maybe I don't have to do it," she e-mailed me that night.

It just takes baby steps.

In my return e-mail, I asked Emily how she'd like having someone at school to regularly talk with who would also treat her with respect and compassion.

"That would be great, but no one cares like that around here," she replied. *"I don't trust nobody, not even the counselor 'cause everybody always talks about me and I end up being made fun of."*

It is disturbing how often high school teens are afraid to speak to anyone at school about their problems. This may well be because troubled teens usually have had no experience of a trustworthy, compassionate adult in their lives, as in Emily's case. In most cases, the ratio of counselors to students in high schools is abominably and critically low.

With a little encouragement, however, Emily became willing to let me connect her with a very compassionate and willing school counselor. The counselor was a caring listener and offered options that gave Emily some sense of hope and control over her chaotic, imbalanced life.

The counselor put together a meeting with Emily, her mother, and the school psychologist. Emily's mother, though embroiled in her own emotional turmoil and chaos, recognized that Emily needed professional counseling and agreed to allow her to receive help from county services. The school counselor also scheduled Emily into a Family and Consumer Sciences class, enlisting more help from an insightful teacher.

The seeds of hope were planted. The Family and Consumer Sciences teacher taught Emily about balanced eating habits and how to cook and eat healthy meals. Her teacher coached Emily on make-up and dress. As she ate more proteins, fresh fruits and vegetables – a diet not based on sugars and carbohydrates – her energy improved and her depression lifted. She began to take small steps that included cutting the hair that hung in her face, enhancing her blue eyes with minimal make-up and lipstick. With small changes under the watchful eye of a devoted and encouraging teacher, Emily found the courage to step out of her isolation and join the school FCCLA Club (Family, Career, and Community Leaders of America).

Small steps can become major opportunities in a teen's life!

Participation in FCCLA brought out capabilities and talents in Emily she never knew she had. FCCLA, like 4H, KEY Club, FBLA and other national school clubs, promotes student projects, competitions, and abilities. FCCLA led Emily into regional Star events. She was even elected to a leadership position within her school club. Soon, she was traveling to state and regional conventions with other girls from school – girls she now trusted rather than feared, friends to laugh with and even share feelings with.

The beauty of teen involvement in service clubs like FCCLA is that, as they participate in helping others, they see their lives as meaningful and themselves as worthwhile. Emily's self-esteem grew under the healthy and well-balanced approach to living that FCCLA introduced her to. In her senior year, her peers voted her to be a peer helper, listening to others in isolation and pain, much like she had been just two years before.

How to help.

Help teens deal with feelings. If you have the skill, the compassion and the detachment to listen without judgment or attempting to control their choices, that's great. If not, encourage teens to reach out to other adults both you and they trust. It is not at all uncommon for a teen to prefer to talk to an aunt or an uncle, a coach or teacher, a parent's friends, or the parent of a friend.

You might enjoy the ideas in the book *For All Our Daughters – How Mentoring Helps Young Women and Girls Master the Art of Growing Up* by Pegine Echevarria, MSW. She also encourages parents to recognize that it is normal for a teen to be more open to advice from adults other than their parents, even when they are saying the very same things!

And by all means, access the resources available at school including school counselors, teen service clubs, athletic coaches, and involved teachers. Better yet, go to school functions, attend parent programs, and volunteer your services whenever possible. As you become involved and visible in your teen's world, your child will have more in common to share with you and more willingness to open up to you. You may even become that trustworthy, safe and supportive listener for someone else's teen in a time of need.

CHAPTER THIRTY-SEVEN
Let's Put a Stop to Rising Teen Pregnancy

There's more to teen pregnancy than today's relaxed, often negligent messages about sexuality. In most cases, teen girls are getting pregnant because they're looking for love. How can we, as adults and community members, support them in better choices for their lives and the lives of their unborn babies?

I was asked to a small rural central plains community to address a very pressing problem: unacceptably high teen pregnancy rates. No doubt, "nothing else to do" is a contributing factor, as some adults and teens claimed. The hotel clerk where I stayed, hit the nail on the head.

Now in her early 20s, this small town native had a baby in her teens. She shared with me:

> *"The teen girls here are just looking for somebody to love. They think the guys care, but they don't. The girls end up with a baby and think they have something that will love them forever...until they get into raising a kid. It's not all that easy!"*

Why worry about teen pregnancy in small town America? Won't grandparents help raise these grandkids? How big a deal is it? Obviously, it's a bigger deal than we'd like to think and this became quite apparent when talking with teens in the community.

A dozen or so teens wanted to talk about homes where they felt unloved and abused, sometimes verbally, often physically, and unfortunately, even sexually. Many of these teens were originally children of teen mothers. These teens had experienced homes where their struggling moms never married their "real" dads. Instead, their moms went through several traumatic relationships with unhealthy, irresponsible men, bearing an abundance of stepbrothers and stepsisters along the way.

Many teens today come from homes with multiple children from multiple fathers, none of whom are in their lives, while mothers juggle multiple jobs and multiple escape mechanisms from alcohol and drugs to a continuing string of men. Due to the expanded use of alcohol and drugs in the middle class over the last 30 years, this pattern is more prevalent across all boundaries.

I also had the opportunity to speak with teen mothers from similar circumstances on the West Coast. Several hundred girls attended. They were either expecting a child or had already given birth to one or more children. Three young Latinas, just 13, 14 and 15-years old, shared with me how they felt about already having had babies:

"I wanna be pregnant again," the boldest of the three spoke up, "'Cause I liked the feelings I had when I was pregnant. It felt like, you know, like my life meant something. My body mattered 'cause it had this baby growing in it. I just want to be pregnant, then I'll matter."

Her companions nodded in agreement. All three could clearly be expected to have more babies in their teens, irrelevant of any involved father, and without concern for the long-term consequences. Validation and meaning through pregnancy in the lives of these neglected, if not abused teens was, sadly, a need more potent than any dream (of which they had few) or love of self (of which they had none).

Angie told me an equally eye-opening story. She was a pretty, petite 15-year-old Caucasian girl in a middle-class high school. She wore an oversized baggy t-shirt and faded jeans, much like her peers, but her expression when she talked was obviously more mature, more telling. What she shared was disturbing:

"Well, I'm 15, but I really prefer older men, like 27 or 32." "That's because what I been through. Like, my Mom and real Dad are heroine addicts. Well, my Dad died from it when I was real little. Then I got taken away from my Mom 'cause of heroine and put in a foster home from 6 to 12. That was actually my best time. They were good to me in those different houses.

"Then my Mom gets outa jail and says she's clean, and she wants me back. So she gets my Aunt to get custody of me. She lied though, she wasn't off heroine and she was actually living in the streets. So I started living with my Mom on the streets and she got me into heroine, and then I started doing tricks to get money for my habit. Well, I met this 32 year-old guy who let me live in his trailer, and then he kept me locked in there and got me drugs and stuff.

"I finally escaped out and left, but you can see why I don't like guys my age 'cause like when I was loaded and on the

streets, I made it with lots of older guys and they made me do all sorts of sex tricks. So, like, boys my age are just too naive now for me.

"I just had an abortion. I got pregnant from that 32-year-old guy. I have to think of it not like it's a person or a kid, not like a baby, but like only a fetal thing. I'm not bad for killing this fetus 'thing.' I mean I don't feel good about killing it, but I don't want his baby. But I do want to get pregnant again someday. I was really happy when I was pregnant."

Angie's life was a sad extreme. Unfortunately, there are an alarming number of teens from East Coast to West Coast, Midwest and the South, that have lived extremes.

Many lessons can be gained from listening to a teenage girl whose life has been ravaged by drug addicted parents, street abuse, sexual abuse, or teen pregnancy. First and foremost, it is important to show your children how much you love them. Even girls from seemingly "good homes" can feel unloved. Parents can neglect their children for any number of "normal" reasons. Girls from every socio-economic bracket have been known to want to get pregnant just "to be loved," certainly not grasping the huge impact and demands of having a child.

Letting a teenage girl know how important she and her future are can help her want to defer children, even value the life of a future child to prevent an unwanted pregnancy now.

Protect our girls: Launch a dream in your child.

Find ways to light the fire of enthusiasm for life in the hearts and minds of teens. Help them find their dreams, the stuff that makes it worth holding off from sex until a more certain future, and, preferably, a stable marriage partner. Dreams come from exposure to possibilities, seeing others doing things in life that spark our interest and then grab at our hearts and souls. These are the prizes in the Cracker Jack box of our unique lives!

I learned the value of exposing youth to other ways of life as a deterrent to unwanted teen choices, not only for teen pregnancy, but even for violence and gangbanging. This lesson was driven home to me when I spoke at a school of detention for one hundred 16- to 18- year-old male offenders.

During my visit, I found that 45 of the boys were from the African-American gangs, 45 were from a wide-variety of Hispanic gangs, nine were from white supremacist groups and one was a non-gang-affiliated Hispanic boy.

Juan, the one Hispanic boy not affiliated with a specific gang, was the only boy who did not plan to join a gang when he got out, though he had hung on the fringe of joining for sometime. Juan told me with humility and confidence:

> *"My family takes me outside of my neighborhood to my uncle's house 300 miles away. I see that there are other ways to live and other places. We go to the beach and to the mountains, and I see my Uncle has a good life. I think I have another choice, so I won't join the gang when I get out."*

Unlike every one of the other 99 boys who had never been outside of the few blocks of their 'hood, Juan knew life offered more options. The other boys did not. The most shocking insight I got that day was how small and confined the lives of these gangbangers had been. Indoctrinated to believe that they would be shot if they wandered outside their small gang territory, none of these boys had experienced the beauty of the ocean nearby, the sunrise in the local mountains, or observed a successful family in process.

Over the years since that day at the detention facility, I have worked with many juvenile probation facilities and family resource centers and have seen a proactive attack on troubled youth's limited dreams and life goals. When a teen convicted of a crime is sentenced today, the facilities make every effort to rehab their drug and alcohol addictions *and* they take them on field trips from team-building camps in the mountains to an occasional sporting event. The results are heartwarming! As troubled teens see a future worth waiting and working for, they do make good choices.

Similarly, I met 13 boys on an Indian reservation in the Southwest, whose greatest desire were to be gangbangers! They lived two hours outside of a major city in the open high plains. Their town of 1,000 people had no hotel, so I stayed with a local family. And out in this remote community, these boys' greatest aspiration was to be in a gang – lives that had power and, therefore, meaning.

We, too, had a chance to talk and in so doing, I asked them,

"If you could blue sky it, dream BIG, and be ANYTHING you wanted to be, what would it really be?"

They thought for a brief moment or two and then almost unanimously replied, "Policemen!"

From gangbanger wanna-be's to police officers in the speed of thought!

It was not the rebellion of a gang that they most sought; it was the prestige and meaningfulness in their lives. But because they thought their true dream unattainable, they resorted to the next best thing on the wrong side of the law!

So we helped them dream! The group agreed that a ride-along with the nearby police department would be a dream come true for them and could certainly spark a new and more positive goal for their futures. The school and the boys came up with a plan to approach the police department for a ride-along. Multiple lives were changed that very day.

Communicate with your teens to help them avoid irresponsible sexuality.

Talk – talk – talk ... as differentiated from lecturing, nagging or scolding! Talk to teenage boys and girls about choices including sexual choices and their consequences.

The girls I met in this rural community were attentive and eager to communicate about family as well as sexual choice and relationships. They were hungry to hear honesty and truth from an adult about feelings and the impact of severe dysfunction in families that often goes unspoken in small towns.

Small town America is full of gossip. It makes kids and adults cautious about personal conversations. Having someone from out-of-town helped make it safer for the teens to be honest. I'd leave town and take their secrets with me. These teens shared their ever-present fear of the future, the chaos at home at night, and the lecherous stares of Mom's newest "roommate." What could they do outside of drugs, alcohol, and sexual relationships to stop those gnawing feelings: unlovable, insufficient, confused, overwhelmed, and unbearably hopeless? They felt their lives didn't matter.

We talked long into the afternoon about approaches to coping with life, especially because most of them had one or more alcoholic or drug-addicted parents and/or stepparents. We looked at what they had power over and what they did not – what choices they had. We bonded teens with other teens as well as with a counselor to start a support group to help these girls identify choices in their daily lives.

We talked about practicing new standards of decent behavior. This included:

- Not fueling the fire of poor communication at home by adding sarcasm or disgust to their interactions with the adults there.
- Practicing "Let go and Let God" when they couldn't change the way a parent might be acting out, drinking or using.
- Choosing to reach out and talk with other teens rather than isolate and feed their sense of victimization and self-pity.

I referred them to Internet resources including the National Campaign to Prevent Teen Pregnancy (NCPTP) at **www.teen pregnancy.org**. Recent research about parental influences on children's sexual behavior says that there really IS much parents and adults can do to reduce the risk of kids becoming pregnant before they've grown up.

> *"Many of these lessons will seem familiar because they articulate what parents already know from experience," says NCPTP, "like the importance of maintaining strong, close relationships with children and teens, setting clear expectations for them, and communicating honestly and often with them about important matters. Research supports these common-sense lessons: not only are they good ideas generally, but they can also help teens delay becoming sexually active, as well as encourage those who are having sex to use contraception carefully."*

Here's how to prevent teen pregnancy.

The National Campaign to Prevent Teen Pregnancy (NCPTP) has some clear and constructive advice. They suggest that parents and adults interacting with teens follow Ten Practical Tips available on their website. Here are some I thought extremely beneficial:

1. Be clear about your own sexual values and attitudes.

Communicating with your children about sex, love, and relationships is often more successful when you are certain in your own mind about these issues. To help clarify your attitudes and values, think about the following kinds of questions:

- What do you really think about school-aged teenagers being sexually active – perhaps even becoming parents?
- Who is responsible for setting sexual limits in a relationship and how is that done, realistically?
- Were you sexually active as a teenager and how do you feel about that now? Were you sexually active before you were married? What do such reflections lead you to say to your own children about these issues?
- What do you think about encouraging teenagers to abstain from sex?
- What do you think about teenagers using contraception?

2. Talk with your children early and often about sex, and be specific.

Kids have lots of questions about sex, and they often say that the source they'd most like to go to for answers is their parents. Start the conversation, and make sure that it is honest, open, and respectful. If you can't think of how to start the discussion, consider using situations shown on television or in movies as conversation starters.

Tell them candidly and confidently what you think and why you take these positions; if you're not sure about some issues, tell them that, too.

Be sure to have a two-way conversation, not a one-way lecture.

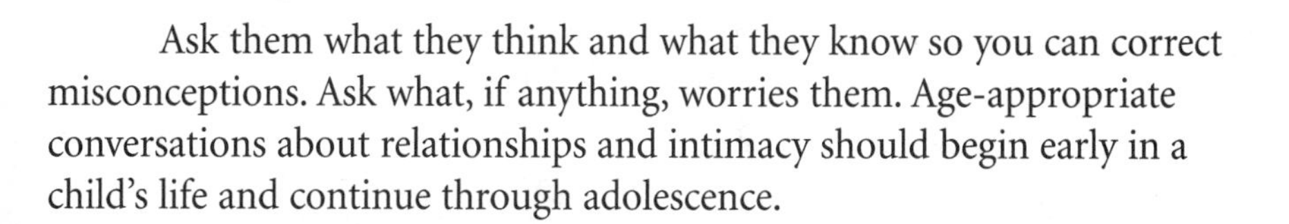

Ask them what they think and what they know so you can correct misconceptions. Ask what, if anything, worries them. Age-appropriate conversations about relationships and intimacy should begin early in a child's life and continue through adolescence.

Resist the idea that there should be just one conversation about all this – you know, "the talk."

The truth is that parents and kids should be talking about sex and love all along. This applies to both sons and daughters, and to mothers and fathers.

All kids need a lot of communication, guidance, and information about these issues, even if they sometimes don't appear to be interested in what you have to say. Many inexpensive books and videos are available to help with any detailed information you might need, but don't let your lack of technical information make you shy. Kids need as much help in understanding the meaning of sex as they do in understanding how all the body parts work.

Tell them about love and sex, and what the difference is. And remember to talk about the reasons that kids find sex interesting and enticing; discussing only the "downside" of unplanned pregnancy and disease misses many of the issues on teenagers' minds.

Here are the kinds of questions kids say they want to discuss:

1. How do I know if I'm in love? Will sex bring me closer to my girlfriend/boyfriend?
2. How will I know when I'm ready to have sex? Should I wait until marriage?
3. Will having sex make me popular? Will it make me more grown-up and open up more adult activities to me?
4. How do I tell my boyfriend that I don't want to have sex without losing him or hurting his feelings?
5. How do I manage pressure from my girlfriend to have sex? How do I tell her I don't want to have sex without her thinking I don't care about her or that I'm not "a man/macho?"
6. How does contraception work? Are some methods better than others? Are they safe?
7. How do I handle the disappointment when a boy drops me because I won't have sex with him?
8. Is abstinence worth it?
9. Can you get pregnant the first time?

3. In addition to being an "askable parent," be a parent with a point of view.

Tell your children what you think. Don't be reluctant to say, for example:

- I think kids in high school are too young to have sex, especially given today's risks. Whenever you do have sex, always use protection against pregnancy and sexually transmitted diseases until you are ready to have a child.
- It's okay to think about sex and to feel sexual desire. Everybody does! But it's not okay to get pregnant/get somebody pregnant as a teenager.
- Our family's religion says that sex should be an expression of love within marriage.
- Finding yourself in a sexually charged situation is not unusual; you need to think about how you'll handle it in advance. Have a plan. Will you say "no?" Will you use contraception? How will you negotiate all this?
- One of the many reasons I'm concerned about teens drinking and smoking pot is that it often leads to unprotected sex.

NCPTP concludes by stating:

> *"Research clearly shows that* ***talking with your children about sex does not encourage them to become sexually active.*** *And remember, too, that your own behavior should match your words. The "do as I say, not as I do" approach is bound to lose with children and teenagers, who are careful and constant observers of the adults in their lives."*

Not only do parents make a difference in the teen pregnancy rate of your town, but all adults can have an impact by relating better to the town's teens.

> *"For instance," says NCPTP, "parents – especially those who are single or working long hours – often turn to other adults for help in raising their children and teens. If all these caring adults are on the same "wavelength" about the issues covered here, young people are given more consistent messages, and that will make a difference."*

Of course we want to prevent teen pregnancy. Of equal importance is to guide a teen to proper resources if they do get pregnant. Practice one of my keys for hope and healthy choices in life: REACH OUT AND ASK FOR HELP from social services, medical care, and drug and alcohol rehab for a teen who is pregnant. Given that two lives are in the balance, helping a teen learn how to confront the situation can go a long way to better prepare her to treat her future child with unconditional love as well.

- Visit the NCPTP website at **www.teenpregnancy.org**
- Teens worried about being pregnant, can contact TEEN LINE, a hotline for teens 24/7 at Cedars Sinai Medical Hospital, Center for the Study of Youth – Call 310-855-HOPE, 310-855-4673 or 800-TLC-TEEN or visit **www.teenlineonline.org**

CHAPTER THIRTY-EIGHT
Warn Your Teens: AIDS Is Still Alive and Well; HIV Teens are Not

In today's amazing technological and bio-medically advanced world, we can get complacent and think that we have solved everything. Certainly, with all the turmoil and/or excitement in the world, we may also find ourselves guilty of "brushing AIDS under the rug" because if it is incurable and horrible, we don't want to believe it can happen to us. Meanwhile – and predominately because of this "brush it under the rug" attitude – AIDS is still spreading around the world; and here in the States, the fastest growth rate occurs in the 14- to 24-year-old age range. We may not be able to stop AIDS yet, but we can help stop its appetite for our children.

When I first started speaking to youth, the news media was awash in stories about AIDS. That was 1991, 10 years after it was primarily detected among homosexual men in the United States. Many were dying in 1991 from AIDS, and the disease was increasing through heterosexual encounters as well as by intravenous drug use. The top priority over the next few years was to educate teens about condom use.

Of course, there was a great controversy over whether educating teens about condoms also encouraged teen sex as well, "rubber"-stamping it as acceptable! As I traveled across America, the "abstinence only" message soon became the message that Parent Teacher Organizations (PTOs) and churches preferred in schools, particularly in middle-class white communities across the Midwest and the South. Large urban and inner-city schools continued to encourage safe-sex messages as a large percentage of their teen population was already sexually active. These schools felt, and many still do, that it is negligent if they refrain from educating teens on how to protect themselves from the deadly AIDS virus.

As time passed, I saw the media turn its focus and the public's attention to other pressing issues in American life. Teen violence in the schools became all consuming. AIDS soon lost its sense of immediacy.

Yet AIDS did not go away ...

World AIDS Day creates awareness.

Every year, December 1st is World AIDS Day. On this day, the media refocuses our collective national consciousness on AIDS and its serious danger to our teens. It is imperative we take notice for the safety of our kids and share with them. "Out of sight, out of mind" still holds true!

14- to 24-year-olds are most at risk.

In 1999, *Peer Educator Magazine* reported that AIDS was growing the fastest in the United States in 14- to 24-year-olds. The disease was said to be spreading the fastest in the heterosexual community, and most rapidly in the Hispanic and African American communities. Most disconcerting is the fact that **teens can be infected with HIV, yet not have symptoms for five to 10 years,** in the meantime infecting numerous other partners, who in turn infect partners.

Perhaps we can take some morbid comfort in that America's struggle with AIDS is nothing like that in Eastern Europe, Central Asia and Africa. AIDS authorities continue to expect that China and India are "AIDS time bombs." According to the Reuters article in 2002, "Already an estimated one million Chinese are infected with HIV and the United Nations said the number could reach 10 million people by the end of this decade."

In South Africa, the country hardest hit to date by AIDS, 30 million people (and increasing rapidly every day) are already infected with the disease, and millions of children have been orphaned. The disease impacts the daily life of every South African, whether infected with HIV/AIDS or not, as the economy falters with agricultural workers dying, cemetery space running out, and the fragile South African economy badly impacted by a huge flood of orphans, death of millions of workers, and unfathomable health costs.

AIDS easily crosses geographic borders, racial groups and economic lines.

It may be easier to ignore because we are not living in Africa, China, India or Eastern Europe, but we are a country with open borders, an adolescent population that embraces multi-culturalism, and a sexually permissive society. The disease will continue to grow in our country, and our youth remain at risk without proper precautions and guidance in abstinence.

Best weapon!

All the evidence says that our best weapon is a strong, loving relationship between parents and their teens. So, start communicating with your children while they are young. Make your expectations clear and consistent. Help them find value in themselves so the momentary pleasures are more easily deferred, and so that the hunger to be loved is not so desperate that it becomes a very real risk to their lives.

CHAPTER THIRTY-NINE
Teen Violence/Dating Abuse, the Legacy of a Violent Family

When teens abuse or take abuse in friendships or dating relationships, you don't have to look far to see from whence it comes. Don't let your children endure what you, yourself, hated in your own childhood. Here's how to break the chains of family violence:

I was at a high school freshman orientation with four hundred 9th graders and 100 upper classmen. Out of the crowd strolled a junior, I will call Michelle, who told me that two weeks previous, a girlfriend had set her up on a date with a 17 year-old boy she did not know.

From the beginning, he controlled the conversation, interrupting her and acting irritated if her attention left him. She took his behavior as a sign that he liked her, but soon she said she felt uncomfortable. As the night wore on, he forcefully kissed her and pushed further. She resisted, yet, he overpowered her.

"You know you want it," he snarled, and then he raped her.

As disturbing as the incident was, Michelle's fear of telling her mother about the rape was even more disturbing to me. She felt ashamed and to blame, but could not conceive of telling the police or her family.

Michelle's mother had been abandoned by Michelle's father when Michelle was just a baby. Her mother then married and divorced a physically abusive alcoholic. A string of physically abusive live-in boyfriends followed. Michelle's maternal grandfather had been an active alcoholic, beating both Michelle's mother and grandmother throughout her mother's childhood. Now, unbeknownst to her family, the third generation of abuse had begun.

Michelle's family was in denial about the impact that her grandfather's alcoholism and physical abuse had had on two successive generations of women. She was responding to the family pattern. She had already had an earlier boyfriend who had hit her. She joined ROTC at school to learn how to defend herself, become tougher and ultimately forewarn men to beware. Even in her ROTC class, however, the boys kicked her; she still had the bruises to show. No doubt, Michelle expected and accepted abuse from boys, a pattern several thousand other teenage girls from around the country have shared with me.

Teen dating violence has increased over the past two decades, as has alcohol and drug abuse. In fact, 80 percent of family violence is committed when the perpetrator is under the influence of alcohol or drugs.

But violence is also a learned response, a way to cope with feelings by blaming and dominating others. Boys learn by watching dads beat mothers, by being beaten themselves, or seeing it portrayed by other family members, on TV, or in movies. Once the pattern is established, it is a short distance to react similarly with a date. Teen girls have learned to expect physical abuse from dates and from boyfriends after many years of observing their mothers in repeated abusive relationships.

Michelle's family had assured her that she'd be the one to break the historic chain of abuse. This unrealistic expectation was just another example of family behaviors around the shame and blame of alcohol, drugs and family violence.

Sometimes families demand achievement upon achievement to fix the inadequacies and mistakes of the parents.

Like other teens carrying this heavy family burden, Michelle was prone to depression, which she continually generated by setting unrealistic goals and demanding unachievable perfection of herself. She admitted she felt a constant sense of failure. She focused on making her mother proud and lost awareness of her own needs and feelings. Without knowing what she felt, she found it difficult to know when to say no to abuse. By putting her mother's feelings before her own, she felt in constant conflict and found it impossible to put her own well being first.

Boyfriend-girlfriend relationships are more inclined to be violent today.

A 15-year-old girl came up to the stage after an assembly and reluctantly yet desperately asked for me to listen, her fear of breaking a boyfriend's confidence heavily hung over her head:

> *"I have this boyfriend and he, well, makes me do it when he wants to. He slaps me if I complain or grabs me by the neck and shoves me. Yeah, he's usually been drinking. And he says, 'Bitch, you do what I want!' But he's really sweet when he's*

sober. I feel upset about it, you know, but I love him. I don't know if it's OK or not."

With high school drinking at unprecedented levels such violent teen relationships are gut-wrenchingly common. It is alarming when the majority of teen girls in classroom conversations raise their hands to identify with similar treatment from inebriated boyfriends today. Many of these girls and many of the boyfriends involved acknowledge coming from families where their fathers drink heavily and inflict physical and verbal abuse. The pattern repeats, and the pattern escalates as the music, movies, TV, electronic and computer games all make violence more commonplace and familiar.

Teen girls are known to be violent against teen boys as well.

Though boys find it much harder to admit, they, too, are experiencing more violence from girlfriends. One 18-year-old boy shared with me,

> *"My girlfriend is possessive of me. She gets real jealous and she gets real hurt if I'm not interested in her, like when we're sitting on the couch watching TV and she want to kiss. Her little 2-year-old is sitting on the floor and asking her mom to pick her up. So I'll say, 'Hey, don't ignore her, and I'm not really in the mood.' She gets real hurt like I don't like her. She'll hit me and throw things at me. Do you think that's right? Like should she ignore her daughter? Should I have to put out every time she wants something? Like, I gotta fix her feelings every time?!"*

Clearly, the pattern of abuse repeats as readily in girls as it does in boys. Sadly, making her boyfriend responsible to "fix her feelings" was how this 17-year-old girlfriend acted out her feelings. She came from a home where her mother, who had been abandoned with a baby in her early teens as well, would hit her from early childhood. Her mother hit to relieve her own feelings of overwhelm, anger and despondency. Now, the girlfriend found it reasonable to demand from and punish her boyfriend while also neglecting her toddler.

Physical abuse between girls is on the rise and can include simple friendships.

A freshman in high school e-mailed me about a girlfriend who was "always poking, pinching, kicking, punching, slapping ... and never even said she was sorry." This teen was able to tell her friend she was uncomfortable with the way she physically treated her and, then, stopped spending time with the abusive friend who was unable to curb her physicality. This girl grasped that she had the right to refuse to be treated in a way she was not comfortable with and that she was not a "bad" friend to end the relationship. In fact, she had become a healthy friend to herself, a valuable life-long lesson.

Serious sibling violence should not be ignored either.

Serious sibling violence has been shared with me all across the country as well. A teen girl from a white middle-class family told me about her home life when I visited her school:

> *"My sister hits me with the phone and throws me down the stairs. She grabs me and pulls me back when I try to leave the house. And my Mom won't do anything about it!"* she cried.

Over and over, preteen boys as well as girls have reported sibling violence that parents seemingly ignore or deny. Preteens in these circumstances feel imprisoned in these situations and find themselves distracted at school if not acting out as their fear mounts about going home at the end of the day.

Speaking up about this behavior, as with any violence, is vital for teens. Without knowing they have the right and the responsibility to speak to school counselors or other authorities about such abuse, they are prisoners in torturous homes. Many preteens have great fear sharing about these violent family issues. They fear the consequences. Some fear an angry parent who may become equally abusive. Many fear hurting their parent by exposing the family violence and the possibility of being taken from the home.

Most preteens will not ask for help until the physical abuse becomes obvious and/or life threatening (as when a sibling chases them with a knife). The strongest motivator for a preteen to finally reach out and ask for help is when a sibling or parent threatens their younger brothers or sisters. They will bring the situation to the school counselor if they fear for the life of the younger ones they feel responsible to protect.

It's time to break the silence and denial.

The stories teens have shared about violence their parents have inflicted upon them are heart breaking, to say the least. They run the gamut and set up teens for a lifetime of struggle with self-esteem and a string of abusive relationships. **Teens get used to violent treatment, expect it, and assume it is the way life is and always will be.**

I encourage you not to discount violence in a family because it is something you think only happens to a particular ethnic group, in a specific geographic area, class of people or economic strata.

A teenage girl in the Midwest shared with me regarding her stepdad:

> *"It's not like a really big deal, he only rages like once every three to six months. Only he's starting up again. I'm kinda afraid. I know that he's working up to hitting me again. What should I do?"*

> A similarly all-American looking girlfriend jumped in to tell about her dad:
>
> *"It was worse when I told about my Dad hitting me and smacking me around. My friends saw the black and blue marks on my face. They weren't such a big deal, but I turned my head because, you know, one side of your face starts getting sore when he keeps smacking you so I went to turn my head and he got my nose. So my friends saw my nose because it got all swelled up and red. So they told the counselor and I got taken away from my Dad and put in a foster home. Only, they were even worse. They were abusive, too. A single woman who just left me in this apartment by myself for hours, all night, and then she swore at me and put me down."*

> *"Yeah, a lot of foster parents are just in it for the money,"* other girls chimed in.

Lastly, I was impacted by a conversation with a teen about her home in a growing suburban community:

> *"I don't trust nobody no more. I don't let no one get close to me. When they do, I walk away and won't talk to them any*

more. I don't like it, but I can't stop myself.

"My Dad, he hit me and beat me all the time I was growing up. He was alcoholic. A couple years ago he was hitting me so bad, I left and said, 'You are not my Father anymore!' He never drank again after that, but now, I feel nothing for him. I am the oldest, so still my parents say it is my responsibility to take care of all my younger brothers and sisters and my Mother. It is too much work. And they tell me I am being selfish because I do my school work instead of giving my little sisters a bath or feeding my brother. It is not fair; and I hate my home."

Here's how YOU can help:

- Become aware of physical abuse within your immediate family, grandparents and great grandparents. Learn about the patterns of family violence from the Internet (**www.health.org**) so you can examine your own attitudes and parenting behaviors.
- Learn the facts about alcoholism and drug abuse and how these problems contribute to foster family violence, generation after generation.
- Notice if physical and serious verbal abuse is used to control others or release anger in the home.
- Rather than hide in shame or react in blame, seek information from counseling.
- If you are the recipient of violence in any form, seek safety from crime prevention officers and shelters. If for nothing else, do this for your children.
- Then, please, educate your teens on what is acceptable treatment from others and what is NOT! Love your children enough to encourage them to say NO to unwanted advances and to leave abusive relationships or intimidating situations IMMEDIATELY.
- Support their healthy self-esteem by allowing them to be less than perfect in their grades, and to have their own dreams and goals so that they have the self-respect to walk away from demeaning and dangerous relationships.

Mindful parents can counteract the destructive forces that abound in a teen's world by providing extra encouragement, communication without criticism, listening without interruption, and role-playing as to how to protect themselves. With this "support net," your teen will feel safe to come to you in times of real need.

CHAPTER FORTY
A Day in the Life of Teen Reality

From conference to conference, school to school, and state to state, I've been listening to teens pour out their fears, and their worries. What follows is a just a sample of conversations to reveal to you a greater understanding of how teens feel, what some endure, and how tender, fragile and precious they remain.

Fortunately, I still see hope in teenagers' eyes every place I go, regardless of how tough their lives have been. They are amazingly resilient and admirably willing to ask for help and hope.

A tale from the upper Midwest.

In the midst of the 1,200 teens exiting the auditorium, a six-foot-two-inch, gangly high school boy caught my eye. He plowed upstream through the flood of teens to make it to the stage. He drew my attention by grabbing my hand and shoving a 20-page manuscript into my grasp. Then, just as swiftly, he turned on his heel and disappeared into the crowd.

I tried to stop him, "If you want to talk, I'll be in the counselor's off...", but he was gone and 12 other teens were already clamoring for an opportunity to be heard.

I sat them down in a compact row of chairs. They stared expectantly, looking for some answer to their own pain. Yet no one spoke. Teens are notoriously reluctant to open up in front of their peers. So, I began with what I know works with teens: acknowledging the obvious and telling the truth.

"So, you are all here because somebody else's drinking or drug use bothers you?"

All heads nod, some fast and furious, some slightly cocked to the side to avoid full eye contact. Either action speaks volumes of their emotions.

This dozen is just the tip of the iceberg of the volumes of teens that come out of the crowd ready to unload the weight of what's going on in their homes and in their lives.

I hear similar stories from teenage girls again and again: A separated mom's boyfriend lusts after the teen daughter, bosses her around after he's been drinking, taunting her with sarcasm and sexual innuendo – the fears that too often become reality as mom's boyfriend loses all semblance of respect for boundaries.

Stepbrothers and stepsisters share tales of two, three and more different fathers who continue to hang around or reappear after prison time, neglecting and abusing them. The feelings of worthlessness hang heavy in the crowd of teens around me.

They also have talk of fears, anger and resentments about their boyfriends, girlfriends and closest friends' drinking and drug use.

"How do I get them to quit?" They beg me, distraught and anxious, some resentful, bitter, mostly sad.

"You can't stop them. I am sorry," I say, "You are powerless over somebody else's drinking and drug use. And it may get worse before they see they have a problem and even worse before they are ready to quit. What you can do is learn how to help yourself so you don't drown in hurt and anger, worry and fear."

Then I ask about their parents.

Out flow the heart-breaking truths, the skeletons in the closet of so many American homes.

> Teen: *"Well, my Dad drinks a couple six packs once in awhile."*
>
> Me: "How often is that?"
>
> Teen: *"Oh, two or three times a week, but he never gets really drunk except maybe once or twice a month when my parents go out with friends."*
>
> Me: "Do your parents argue or yell very much?" I am looking for the clues, the symptoms of an alcohol problem in the family. The amount of alcohol is already suspicious.
>
> *Teen: "My parents are always on each other's case. My Dad moved out a couple times. And they're never around to talk to me or look after my little brother and sister, so I get stuck with it."*
>
> Me: "Do you try to talk to your mother about how you feel about what's going on?" "Ever ask her to go to lunch or maybe dinner, so the two of you can talk?"
>
> *Teen: "Yeah, I asked her a couple times and she says she just doesn't have time to spend with me. She's working two jobs to make up for my Dad who got fired."*

The pattern is all too typical in teen life stories. The kids don't identify the problem as alcoholism because American culture associates beer with a good time. Teens often think their dad or mom is simply going through a hard time. The truth is, the disease of alcoholism has invaded the home, seeping into every relationship in a teen's life.

Though I never heard from the boy again who gave me his 20 page life story, he clearly had grown up in a family riddled with alcoholism, abuse and neglect. His manuscript was a courageous attempt to document the pain, seek validation that he was not the 'crazy one,' and to reach out for help and healing.

Parents in chaos lose empathy for their children.

Absorbed and overwhelmed in her anger and misery, a mother can feel abandoned and rejected by her spouse; a husband of a problem drinker may feel ashamed that he cannot control or please his wife "as a husband should." As a result, moms or dads have no energy left after patrolling and controlling their out-of-control spouse. They receive no compassion or tenderness, then lose the ability to express either to the kids.

A home with an alcoholic parent is a home where compassion, patience, kindness and courtesy typically do not exist. And often, one or both parents have come from an alcoholic childhood themselves with its own history of neglect or abuse.

Parents in emotional turmoil over their own relationship often assume that teenagers can and should take care of themselves as well as take care of their younger siblings. Such parents often have no clue that their children feel emotionally abandoned, angry and lonely.

Look for the pattern repeating itself.

As I listen to teens, it is clear that this pattern repeats inter-generationally. Homes where a parent has a drinking problem is a home filled with resentment, anger, distrust and disappointments. Children grow up without a clue as to what is a healthy relationship. They become adults unfamiliar with respect, boundaries, consistency and compassion. They did not receive these courtesies as children and now haven't got it to give, even to their own children.

Armed with the knowledge of the pattern, I return to the adolescent girl whose boyfriend's drinking and drug use is gravely troubling her.

"Do you and your boyfriend argue much? Does he ever hit you?" I ask.

With her face down she slowly lifts her eyes to look into mine. She blinks several times, then answers nodding her head,

> *"Yes, we argue, but only over his drinking and using. He ignores me when he and his friends are all juiced up. It makes me mad and he has slapped me a couple times, but only because I made him really mad and really got in his face about how he was treating me."*

I shared with her,

"What you are describing to me is someone who has a drinking problem, both your boyfriend and your Dad. You see how the pattern repeats itself? Many girls learn as kids to expect a guy to drink to have a good time and relax because you saw your Dad do that. Without an understanding of alcoholism, most people don't recognize that the arguing and the hitting, are symptoms of the disease. We end up emotionally damaged by someone else's drinking problem ... and don't even know that's the cause."

You can't change someone else's chemistry.

Now the teenagers are listening with great care, identifying with the feelings and hungry for the facts.

"Drugs and alcohol change brain chemistry," I continue. "Somebody who drinks or does drugs or uses both just does not think the way a person does who doesn't use. Their brain is altered while using, and continues to be affected for days, months, years – sometimes permanently damaged depending upon what they use and for how long. The affects on their thinking can be there long after they are no longer using. Many drugs as well as long term drinking damage the brain permanently. They may never be able to reduce their anger or self-centeredness, or treat you with the kindness, tenderness, and thoughtfulness you want and deserve.

"We are powerless over their brain chemistry and whether they choose to drink or to use. Painful as it is, it is true. It's reasonable to hate their disease – their alcoholism and drug addiction. It is normal to be deeply sad. When we feel that grief, the loss of someone we love to alcohol or drugs, it is normal to hurt, to cry, to feel angry about it.

To admit having these feelings and share about it with others who understand, helps us accept reality, and then, to ask an important question: What do I need? Can I get the love I need in this relationship? If not, where can I get love that is not abusive, won't neglect or abandon me, won't dump me because I'm not perfect?

"You can look for another boyfriend who treats you better. But, truth is, boys are only human. What if you could find that love in a support group where that love is always present, regardless of the people who are there, regardless of the personalities? A place where no one judges, gossips, no one criticizes you, and no one tells you what to do?

"That probably sounds impossible, but it's not and it's been around for over 50 years! The spouses of the people who started Alcoholics Anonymous started their own groups to deal with their grief, hurt, loss, fear, sadness, anger – all those desperate and hopeless feelings that come from living with or loving an alcoholic or addict. These feelings can even drive you to drink or use drugs and go down the same awful path as your dad, mom, boyfriend or girlfriend.

"That group is called Al-Anon for adults and Alateen for teens and preteens. You can find it in the phone book or simply ask your school counselor. They will help you find a meeting near you.

"Go online and check it out at **www.al-non.alateen.org** where you can ask for an online meeting or for a pen pal. Ask them to send you some pamphlets to your home or a friend's house if you feel safer receiving information there. Your school or your church may also have a support group for children of alcoholics or for teens concerned about their friends' drinking or drug use.

"We are talking about the disease of alcoholism and addiction and its very real impact on your lives. It has affected you or you wouldn't be here to talk after the assembly. You are not bad for your feelings and you certainly are not alone. Just look around you. How many of your peers agree? And remember, whatever you've heard here and whomever you've seen here stays here. NO GOSSIP! No talk about someone you've seen here. Instead, talk about how you *feel* now, what you thought about *you* and *your* life from this meeting. **Keep the focus on what *you need* right now."**

Then I ask, "How many of you feel better?" All hands go up. Every face looks hopeful.

"What you are experiencing here is a support group meeting. How many of you would like to continue having meetings like this?" I ask. Again, all hands go up.

It's your choice to make.

"You have the choice. Do you want it?" I ask the group. They nod vigorously now.

"Then put your name on this piece of paper; and I'll talk to your counselors and principal to see if they will start a group here on campus. Will you go if they do?"

One last time, they are in agreement and on their way to the possibility of change. Unconditional love and accurate information combine to give teens hope where they had none, and choices where there was only paralyzing fear.

AN URGENT PLEA TO SCHOOLS, ADMINISTRATORS, SUPERINTENDENTS, LEGISLATORS, AND PARENTS:

Insist on funding for support groups in every middle school and high school. Make time for school counselors to do what many came into the field to do, counsel kids – even on the tough stuff of family and friends of alcoholics and addicts. School is very likely the *only* place a teen will have to confront these emotional issues. Without such help, academic achievement for *many* is a pipe dream, as teens under such pressures come to school with serious distraction and priorities focused on survival, not test scores.

CHAPTER FORTY-ONE
No Child Is Beyond Help

I have been blessed to meet and encourage a great many teens. Some of them remain etched in my mind and heart, like scenes from a battle zone, unforgettable memories of human tragedy. I get to see teens grasp the hope that can turn their lives around: I've met heroes in our schools and communities and watched them pick up the baton and fight for programs for troubled kids. I have seen hope come alive.

Here is one more compelling life story of a teenage girl who stepped forward after a school assembly. I met her on a typical high school campus.

A quiet, shy girl, Amelia as I shall call her, waited patiently while I talked with a dozen teens after the assembly. She looked more like a deer frozen in the headlights of a car than any human being I had ever seen. Her eyes wide, her body still as stone, she listened in silence, with huge rolling tears flowing like a river down her face. Amelia did not make the slightest attempt to staunch her tears. It was a disturbing and heart-breaking sight.

I took her hand halfway through the conversation with the other teens, hoping to reassure her. She responded by squeezing my hand as tightly as she could. Her eyes never met mine. But the pressure of her squeeze did not subside for over 30 minutes. Neither did her tears or doe-eyed, startled stare.

At the end of my time with the group, I spoke to Amelia alone, ever so softly, asking, "Are you hurting?"

She nodded a controlled yet vigorous, "Yes." It was obvious; Amelia had deep, dark wounds. Her wounds could be nothing less than some kind of serious physical or sexual abuse.

I delicately probed, "Did someone do something bad to you when you were a little girl?"

And now her nod was strong and certain. "Do you want to talk about it or tell me what happened?"

Now she shook her head, "No."

"If you're not ready," I spoke softly, "that's fine. I know that if something very hurtful happens to us when we are little, it can stick with us and make us want to hide. We may feel ashamed. Sometimes even think it is our fault and that we are bad. Do you feel that way?"

And now the flood of tears began again. She nodded another "Yes" but did not utter a sound or change the expression upon her angelic, still face. This petrified child had learned not to draw attention to herself.

Amelia's ability to still herself in the face of fright and pain was much like a wild animal hyper-alert to danger, listening and waiting. It was truly a frightening disfiguration of a precious child.

"Most importantly, Amelia, I want you to know that whatever happened to you was not your fault," I shared soothingly. "Do you want a hug?"

She released my hand and opened her arms wide. With no licensing laws to restrict me from showing this hurting child that I cared, I was extremely glad to be able to offer Amelia a hug. I am certain this distraught teenage girl had never experienced comfort from an unconditionally loving adult before.

After 10 minutes, she loosened her hug but continued to hold on tightly to my hand. I gently let her know it was important for her to talk further about what she had remembered today. I encouraged her to let me take her to the school counselor so she would have someone at school to talk to about these painful memories. Amelia's face finally softened; and her fight-or-flight animalistic reaction relaxed. Her fear visibly drained from her body as trust and hope trickled in; and her reasoning skills returned.

Amelia and I talked on about what might happen now that she had finally opened up to someone else and let help in. I told her:

"When we remember and share about the bad things in our past, we feel good to let it out, but a little later we can suddenly feel scared. Sometimes we can even feel like hurting ourselves because we are so scared and feel we made a big mistake, even though it's a very good thing to have shared. So, let's go talk to the counselor now so you have someone safe you know you can go to if you should feel afraid again. Tonight, tomorrow or anytime in the future. OK?"

She nodded "Yes", her eyes bright and face now full of expression. We walked down the hall and this once paralyzed little doe was handed over to a caring counseling professional with whom she could explore real feelings and hopeful healing.

I was grateful for the sensitivity and awareness of her school counselor. I knew Amelia was in the hands of a humble hero: a dedicated, compassionate, and knowledgeable school counselor who would dedicate herself to supporting and counseling this delicate teen child.

Throughout the many conversations I've had with troubled teens, the vast majority have been willing to connect with school counselors once they have experienced what it is to have a safe, open and non-critical conversation with an adult. They will risk their secrets once they have tasted acceptance and the renewed hope that comes from being treated with respect, listened to, and understood.

So, how many teens step forward to talk?

Sometimes a mere handful of teens come up after a school assembly, sometimes 50 to 100 over the course of a day. I know that even more have the need to talk but fear gossip and/or parental abuse for divulging family secrets. Our *Survey of Hope* is designed to give voice to the remaining volume of teens holding onto painful secrets.

Those that step forward are the teens courageous enough to forego peer pressure, in too much emotional pain to suppress their feelings any longer, and/or finally believe somebody out there just might understand how they really feel. Many have lived in hopeless isolation with a deep sense of interminable uniqueness. They believe no one could possibly understand or hurt the way they do.

As a result, **I am firmly committed to the establishment of support groups on school campuses for this epidemic of traumatized adolescents.** In a support group setting, teens find that they are not alone and discover new and positive options for handling life problems by listening to peers share their experience and hope.

Peer support gives them relief from the isolation they have used to protect themselves. Support groups give teens help in identifying appropriate choices in day-to-day situations and help in handling a barrage of emotions. Having a safe and sane anchor in their lives renews their hope and the resiliency necessary to not only survive the roller-coaster ride of their families, but succeed in life.

Support groups help. Therapeutic counseling groups at school are critical to keeping some teens in schools and others alive.

Counselors are essential in the battle to save teen lives and can be a major source of solutions. Counselors are the people on campus with the training and the mandate to counsel teens on emotional and family issues. Support groups and counseling in schools are critical stepping stones to greater academic achievement for many emotionally overwhelmed and underachieving teens.

I strongly urge legislators, boards of education, directors and principals to adequately fund counseling, school psychologists, peer programs, and student assistance support groups in every secondary school across America.

Thousands of the schools I have visited are seriously under-staffed with counselors. A ratio of 1,500 students to four counselors is not uncommon. As we adequately staff counseling departments in schools, they will become a sanctuary for more teens in need. Teen lives will be saved; academic achievement bolstered for many; and countless seeds planted for a more compassionate, non-violent and cooperative world.

Visit our website www.legacyofhope.com for resources, contact hotlines, order free pamphlets or visit similar websites and associations that are eager and available to provide further assistance to parents and teens

---

SECTION SEVEN

Hope And Help Are On the Way – What's Working And Who Are The Real Heroes

No matter what attitude or personality your teen may possess, and no matter what teen issue has challenged you, rest assured there are other parents, guardians, grandparents, coaches, teachers, mentors and concerned adults who have been there, too. Many of those who have been through troubles with teens are willing and able to offer you support and strength.

There are resources waiting to help you guide your teen through the overwhelming trials and pitfalls of adolescence into productive adulthood. This section includes some of the enlightened resources I have been privileged to know and work with along my journey. Each is effective, noteworthy and of high integrity.

The way back from the depths of despair for both teens and adults begins with the simple act of being willing:

- Willing to ask for help.
- Willing to listen and learn from others.
- Willing to change the things we can in this moment.

Hope and healing are not a solitary journey. They come from knowing there are no normal people in the world, only those who haven't shared their life story with us yet! Every life and every family will have challenges, if not now, then down the line. I welcome you into a world of support, acceptance, and unconditional love where no one need be held hostage by shame, blame, self-pity, depression, suicidal thoughts, resentment or rage, regardless of teen trials and tribulations!

Julio, the gangbanger from *Legacy of Hope*® presentation:

If someone's drinkin' or drug use, you know, is, like, bothering you, making you mad or sad or worry and stuff, I heard you could go to these support groups ... And when I got there I heard stuff I didn't expect to hear, man. You know, like, it's not my fault my old man, he drinks, or my cousin, she does drugs, or like my uncle. It's not my fault. Like, even when my old man, he says, "I'm drinkin' cause you're so stupid, you're such a screw up." I learned here just because an alcoholic says it, man, doesn't make it so. Now, that's a relief! And then I heard, like, I can't stop nobody from drinking or doing drugs. Better I go hang out with my sober and drug-free friends, get myself some hobbies like basketball or soccer or, like, my street dance, man. I like dat stuff, dat's good stuff!

CHAPTER FORTY-TWO
VIDA Boot Camp for Troubled Kids Offers Lessons and Changes Lives

There are many answers available for youth who are heading down the path of substance abuse. The more resources we can offer them at this fork in the road, the better the chance at getting them back on the right track.

How do we turn teens involved in drugs, alcohol, gangs, crime and violence back to a positive, productive life style? In my travels I have run into a myriad of programs that give teens new skills, new choices and new hope. A program that has been a stand out is VIDA, a boot camp for troubled teens developed and run by a small but dedicated team of Los Angeles County Deputy Sheriffs.

For several years, these committed deputy sheriffs have pulled together 20 to 40 teens at a time, referred by schools and parents, for a 16-consecutive-Saturday boot camp. They run the teens around the blacktop, bring in a wide variety of speakers like me, and bark commands while insisting upon respect for self and others. The deputy sheriffs devote themselves to adjusting teen attitudes and have been successful at convincing isolated, angry adolescents that expecting them to keep the rules is a genuine sign of caring. And the truth is – these deputies really *do* care.

I have spent a day at several boot camps speaking to the VIDA teens. It has been obvious that most of these teens really want to find a sense of self-worth. I have always been touched by their hungry expressions: hungry to be acknowledged, hungry for praise, hungry for self-respect.

By the time I was brought in to speak, a VIDA class was nine or more weeks into the program. By then, the teens had begun to experience consequences for small infractions of decorum and discipline. They had faced authority figures that demanded a task be repeated until done right. It was boot camp, but one run with compassion and concern clearly expressed by every deputy sheriff and volunteer involved.

On this occasion, the teens responded without "attitude" to the orders barked at them to sit up rather than slouch in their chairs. They showed me respect by paying avid attention and not chatting with their neighbors. It was refreshing and encouraging to see how readily they responded without argument, enthusiastically involved in our conversations. Attendance at the camp is strictly optional, so these edgy teens have shown significant commitment to improving their lives.

Voluntarily showing up every Saturday for 16 weeks and accepting the strong disciplinary approach of the VIDA deputy sheriffs and staff speaks volumes for the heart in each of these teens. For many, it was the first healthy discipline in their lives. The VIDA program showed them discipline that is motivated by caring and healthy boundaries rather than by anger, rage and alcohol common in many of their homes. For many, this was the first experience with adults who consistently care.

It was equally touching to hear the VIDA instructors, men from highly disciplined professions of law enforcement and military service, share stories of their victories and defeats with these teens. They become deeply vested in turning these teens around. They are equally disturbed when they fail to reach even one youth.

Several of the deputy sheriffs and volunteers said that they saw themselves in these teenagers. They wished someone had tried to reach them as teens when they felt isolated and alone in a raging, abusive world. Some of the men shared how they, too, had grown up in abusive alcoholic homes with belligerent and mean-spirited parents. Some of their own personal healings rested in the hope of saving these teens from the trouble they had gotten themselves into in their younger years. If the hearts and minds of the VIDA youth could be turned and if those teens could grasp the true value of their lives, these genuinely sensitive instructors saw a world of positive choices and potential awaiting these teens.

Observation about troubled teen girls.

The lead Deputy Sheriff made an interesting observation on my most recent day as a presenter for VIDA. After conducting several years of teen boot camps, the deputy saw a pattern among the adolescent girls in the program. Always the minority, but nonetheless on their way to serious trouble, the girls always seemed to start the sixteen week program lethargic and rebellious. As the weeks progressed, they began to trust the deputies and actually liked responding to their orders. They became eager to attend, and thrived on being recognized by adult male authority figures for being responsible and competent.

"They are missing a caring father-figure," he concluded. "One that tells them they deserve to be valued for other than just their sexuality ... an authority figure that treats them with respect, with no motive other than to see them accomplish their best.

"It is teaching me how to raise my own 5-year-old daughter," the Deputy Sheriff remarked with a flutter in his voice and a tear in his eye. "Little girls need to learn from their fathers that they are loved and valuable and not just for their bodies. That's how girls learn to expect proper treatment and respect from men when they grow up. I see it in the girls in the program. I see it in their eyes. Their fathers never showed them they are special or that they deserve to be respected and cherished. It's a sad thing."

A psychotherapist's insight into self-esteem of boys vs. girls.

His comments were reinforced by the statement I heard some 20 years ago by Dr. Pat Allen, a respected and knowledgeable clinical psychologist in Southern California, and bears repeating one more time.

**"For boys to grow up healthy,
they need to be respected by their mothers.
For girls to grow up healthy,
they need to be adored by their dads."**

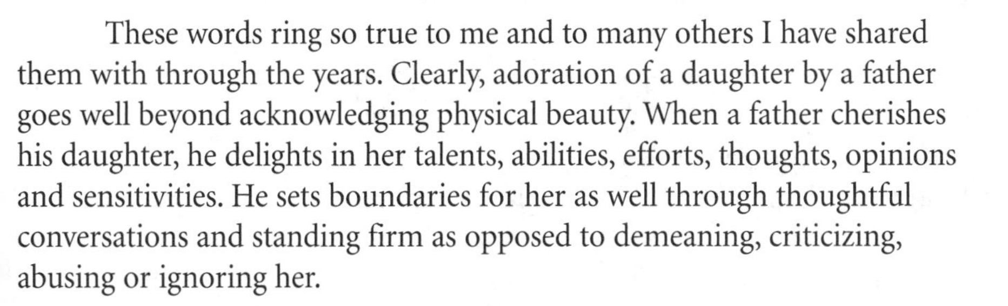

These words ring so true to me and to many others I have shared them with through the years. Clearly, adoration of a daughter by a father goes well beyond acknowledging physical beauty. When a father cherishes his daughter, he delights in her talents, abilities, efforts, thoughts, opinions and sensitivities. He sets boundaries for her as well through thoughtful conversations and standing firm as opposed to demeaning, criticizing, abusing or ignoring her.

A father who applauds his daughter's efforts and delights in her progress builds that healthy self-image.

In this way, she grows up expecting boys and then men to value her likewise and treat her accordingly. If they do not, her solid self-esteem will guide her to leave an unhealthy, abusive relationship and move on, expecting better. Parents can be more hopeful about the boys she eventually brings home!

It is equally important that boys be acknowledged by their mothers for their accomplishments and efforts. When mom treats her son respectfully, she lets a son face appropriate consequences for his actions rather than finding a way out, spoiling or coddling.

A mother builds respect in a son by similar respectful conversations, encouraging his dreams and interests. Sons develop healthy awareness of a man's role when mothers demonstrate respect for the boy's father.

If a son becomes his mother's emotional surrogate for an inattentive father, he may struggle with how to relate interdependently rather than co-dependently to women as an adult. A boy's relationship to mom impacts his confidence and the self-worth it takes to walk away from negative influences.

Recognizing how boys develop self-respect by capably meeting expectations, a deputy sheriff shared with me about a boy I'll call Manuel, who continually fidgeted and struggled to pay attention. Manuel constantly pushed against the expectations the deputies had of him. He felt picked on for the smallest of things and complained loudly.

Manuel came from a large low-income family in which his parents were overwhelmed and preoccupied with survival. His father worked long days at physically exhausting jobs, then home for a six-pack of beer and out with his compadres to walk the street after dinner. His mother was beaten down and worn out from bearing and raising eight children while living in meager and modest conditions.

Manuel was basically raising himself, all but forgotten in the struggle. He received little to no recognition or encouragement, no help with school, and had a great dearth of self-worth. "Mammacita" loved him, but had no energy left with eight children in tow to notice his talents or encourage his dreams.

"Why do you sweat the small stuff?" Manuel exclaimed to the deputy that Saturday.

The deputy sheriff's response was powerful.

"It IS the small things that matter. It is in following the small rules that you learn to respect yourself. By not breaking the small rules, you learn you CAN keep commitments and that you can trust yourself. In keeping the small rules, you gain the self-respect and the know-how to make good judgment in the big decisions of life."

"When you look at yourself in the mirror," he continued, *"you KNOW if you do or don't really respect yourself. It's not for me to decide. It doesn't feel good to look yourself in the eye and not feel proud of what you did that day. It starts with the small things."*

The deputy stated that he spent a good hour working one-on-one with Manuel that Saturday. He was rewarded by a glimmer of hope in the boy's eyes. He also saw when the curtain would fall; Manuel would lose focus and emotional control. The deputy knew the boy struggled and fought inwardly to hold onto an ounce of self-esteem. Manuel appeared to run the deputy's words through his mind as he regained some self-control. Manuel may well be a child with Attention Deficit Disorder; he certainly was a child who needed to feel loved and competent. In VIDA, he got a taste of both.

"It has taught me to care about myself. No one else ever did that."

VIDA – At-Risk Youth

CHAPTER FORTY-THREE
Juvenile Drug Courts Turning Kids Away from Life of Crime

When teens are truly headed down the wayward path – can they still be saved?

There are those within the judicial, probation and mental health systems that are betting they can.

Juvenile Drug Courts currently offer a select percentage of juveniles a second chance. The demands upon these teens are many and strict, the consequences of failing to meet expectations often greater than the average sentence to motivate teen effort. But the outcomes are convincing.

In Orange County, California, the Juvenile Drug Court is under the direction of the Honorable Judge Robert B. Hutson, Presiding Judge of Juvenile Court for the County of Orange, where 89 percent of teens that have gone through the program were still clean, sober and crime-free after one year. These are outstanding recidivism rates and results you may wish to use to help promote the implementation of a juvenile drug court in your home town!

How juvenile drug court works.

The Orange County Juvenile Drug Court is a docket within the juvenile court to which selected delinquency cases are referred for handling by a designated judge. The youth referred to juvenile drug courts are identified as having problems with alcohol and/or other drugs. The juvenile drug court judge maintains close oversight of each case through frequent (often weekly) status hearings with the parties involved. The judge both leads and works as a member of a team comprised of representatives from the Health Care Agency, the court, school and vocational training programs, the probation department, the prosecution, and the defense. Together, the team determines how best to address the substance abuse and related problems of the youth.

To enroll in the juvenile drug court program, a referral can be made by a probation officer, a public defender/private attorney or by the minor's own request. Any juvenile between the ages of 13 and 17 years who has been charged with a crime, other than a violent crime, drug sale or sexual offense, is eligible to be accepted into the Juvenile Drug Court Program.

Juveniles are screened for eligibility based upon their need for treatment, their commitment to the program and their past delinquency history.

Candidates who are accepted into the program participate on a voluntary basis. Should a juvenile fail to complete the program, he or she must then complete the original sentence for their crime. If the minor successfully completes the program, the charge or charges are dismissed, probation is terminated and previous jail sentence is vacated.

The juvenile drug court operates in four phases plus an initial 30-day orientation phase which will determine whether minors will be able to abide by the rules and guidelines of the program. During the first two phases, the participant receives intensive education and therapy, along with close supervision by the court. Probation monitors the juvenile's use through drug testing three times per week during the orientation and Phase One. Drug testing continues and eventually is administered on a random basis. The juveniles must also abide by specific curfews throughout the program.

The juvenile drug court program is a comprehensive program that also provides support to the entire family. Parents are encouraged to participate in parent support groups as well. There is currently a Spanish-language parent support group, Padres Unidos. An English-language parent support group is also available. Probation makes random home calls to monitor probationers, on occasion with the participation from the Health Care Agency to provide support and deal with possible mental health issues the minor's family may be experiencing.

The third and fourth phases focus on the participant taking responsibility for his or her actions, which includes being employed or enrolled in a training-to-work program. The youth must also be enrolled in school throughout all four phases.

How juvenile drug court makes a difference.

"We'll take chances on a kid in this business," says a veteran officer of Juvenile Probation.

Typically, teens in front of Judge Hutson for Drug Court sentencing are from lower income homes with many children; perhaps a single mother or two exhausted, overwhelmed hard-laboring parents; no guidance or life direction; a seriously truant youth using drugs and alcohol daily; running with a desperado crowd; angry, belligerent and prideful to a fault. Yet, these teens are also willing to adhere to a program that requires them to:

- Attend school regularly,
- Participate in counseling,
- Attend multiple Alcoholics Anonymous or Narcotics Anonymous meetings weekly,
- Work closely with their juvenile probation officer,
- Stay clean and sober,
- Adhere to curfews,
- Work toward employment or job training,
- Drug test, both scheduled and random,
- Report frequently back to Judge Hutson's courtroom for evaluation,
- Accept a more stringent custody sentence (perhaps up to 18 months) should they wash out of the program.

To see each teen through the Four-Phase Orange County program, a juvenile is assigned a probation officer with a caseload far less than the typical rate of 60 plus. At a reduced caseload of 20 or less juveniles, probation officers can make family visits and become a legitimate surrogate parent figure/support system to troubled and disenfranchised youth.

Mental health provides counseling and on-going evaluation. Parents are encouraged to participate in counseling groups, though parental involvement is usually quite low and a common contribution to a youth's delinquency in the first place. Juvenile probation visits the homes, works with parents with alcohol, drug and/or abuse issues, and helps find resources to stabilize the family when possible. The results are encouraging.

Involvement of teens in the Juvenile Drug Court program has not only shown to lower recidivism rates, but is increasing family stability. As probation officers visit the homes, they

- Talk to parents about parenting skills;
- Offer contacts and choices to help reduce family dependence on welfare;
- Recognize and alert the Health Care Agency to respond on issues from child abuse to parental alcohol or drug abuse, to needs of siblings, thereby deterring additional teens from crime and addiction.

And yet, Juvenile Drug Courts have their opponents who consider this approach "touchy-feely," and prefer a more punitive approach for those who have transgressed, especially since the Juvenile Drug Court approach requires considerably more resources per juvenile. Proponents argue in defense of drug courts, pointing to the thousands and thousands of dollars saved by rehabilitating a youth before he or she becomes a lifetime criminal, impacting victims, and costing society more when incarcerated throughout their adult lives.

The Juvenile Drug Court system in cities across the country is also successfully reducing the amount of services needed for each juvenile in the program, as well as for his or her entire family. As the drug-court probation officer visits the home and addresses parenting problems, including a parent's drinking and domestic abuse, violence in the home decreases and the number of calls to the police decrease as well.

"The public needs to see the individual care that goes into every case," says Judge Hutson, an enthusiastic advocate of the system. Juvenile Drug Courts fill in where parenting fell-off and abandoned a teen long ago.

Forty-eight teens who completed the Orange County program over one year ago – 89 percent of such teens – are still alcohol, drug and crime-free. Early intervention on drug and alcohol addictions *does* diminish crime and *does* create viable members of society! For what appears to be a lost-cause teen, it means a new life and a second chance. To society, it means a productive, tax-paying citizen rather than a convict that drains our public coffers for years.

Judge Robert B. Hutson is quite certain, "Drug courts are here to stay." Because they work!

Consider the positive impact a juvenile drug court can make in your community. Advocate for drug courts. **An investment of resources in Juvenile Drug Court systems now will save our tax dollars in the long run and save a youth's life in the present.**

CHAPTER FORTY-FOUR
Giving Credit Where Credit is Due: A Tribute to Teachers

At the beginning of every new school year, I gear up to go back to school as a motivational speaker educating our teens in emotional awareness and the downside of denial: alcohol and drug abuse, teen pregnancy, gangs, AIDS, violence, depression, suicide, self-harm and more. I am blessed to see miracles happen in our youth and in schools everyday I am on campus.

Certainly, the best of all miracles from this experience is to see hope glimmer in the eyes of a previously depressed, detached teen. Hope sprouts and nurtures the seeds of change.

Equally uplifting in my work and travels to schools is my exposure to the amazing, ingenious, ever-evolving programs that counselors, teachers and administrators in these schools have created and kept aloft each year all across our country. Few parents have any concept of the demands, time, energy and creativity these programs have required to create, administer, fund and pass through unwieldy bureaucracies. I have met inspired educational professionals who devote their lives to guide and heal our troubled youth. I have often been in awe of their devotion, humility and tenacious spirit, both of which go well beyond their modest salaries and job descriptions to help teens where parents and society have been lacking.

Imagine what it is like for a teacher today in a classroom filled with students who speak any number of different languages, many of whom are from broken homes or are "latch key kids," and acting out from abuse or neglect in the home. At younger and younger grade levels, pre-teens and teens are experimenting in ever-increasing excess with alcohol, drugs, sex, self-harm and violence. They bring these problems to school daily, making a teacher's job tougher and tougher, not to mention federal standards that leave little time in the classroom to deal with personal teen problems.

A Tribute to Teachers

I would very much like to pay tribute to those under-appreciated, often much maligned teachers by way of sharing an anonymous e-mail I received. From my travels across the educational landscape of America, I know it speaks the truth. Consider sharing it with your son or daughter's favorite teachers:

The 21st Century Teacher Applicant

"Let me see if I've got this right. You want me to go into that room with all those kids and fill their every moment with a love for learning. Not only that, I'm supposed to instill a sense of pride in their ethnicity, behaviorally modify disruptive behavior, and observe them for signs of abuse and T-shirt messages.

I am to fight the war on drugs and sexually transmitted diseases, check their backpacks for guns and raise their self-esteem. I'm to teach them patriotism, good citizenship, sportsmanship and fair play, how and where to register to vote, how to balance a checkbook and how to apply for a job.

I am to check their heads occasionally for lice, maintain a safe environment, recognize signs of potential antisocial behavior, offer advice, write letters of recommendation for student employment and scholarships, encourage respect for the cultural diversity of others, and, oh yeah, always make sure that I give the girls in my class 50 percent of my attention.

I'm asked by my contract to be working on my own time and expense in summer and evenings toward advance certification and a master's degree; and after school, I am to attend committee and faculty meetings and participate in staff development training to maintain my employment status.

I am to be a paragon of virtue larger than life, such that my very presence will awe my students into being obedient and respectful of authority. I am to pledge allegiance to supporting family values, a return to the basics, and to my current administration. I am to incorporate technology into the learning, and monitor all websites while providing a personal relationship with each student. I am to decide who might be potentially dangerous and/or liable to commit crimes in school or who is possibly being abused, and I can be sent to jail for not mentioning these suspicions.

I am to make sure all students pass the state and federally mandated testing and all classes, whether or not they attend school on a regular basis or complete any of the work assigned. Plus, I am expected to make sure that all of the students with handicaps are guaranteed a free and equal education, regardless of their mental or physical handicap.

I am to communicate frequently with each student's parent by letter, phone, newsletter and grade card.

I'm to do all of this with a piece of chalk, a computer, a few books, a bulletin board, a 45-minute planning period and a big smile, all on a starting salary that qualifies my family for food stamps in many states. And you want me to do all of this and expect me NOT TO PRAY?"
— Anonymous Internet Author

It is often said that there is no job tougher than being a parent. Second to that may be being a teacher or school counselor!

I especially honor all those teachers and counselors who take on the role of advisor to extra-curricular programs such as peer helpers, support groups, SADD, FCCLA, FBLA, KEY Club, FHA, VICA, and more. These responsibilities add long hours to their workday with little or no extra pay. These roles almost always demand an enormous personal and emotional investment into other people's kids; and I see so many teachers and counselors doing just that without expectation of recognition or appreciation, just the joy of watching your kids grow!

So, as you send your teen off to school each day, take note of those educators in middle school and high school who are taking on these extra roles. These are the educators you can count on. Why not thank a teacher or a counselor today? Better yet, take the time to stop by and talk.

Even in high school, teachers are willing to listen and discuss your son or daughter's progress, and appreciate a heads-up about changes taking place in the family that may affect your teenager's attitude or academic performance. Perhaps even offer to be of some small service in the classroom or to the school. I know much can be accomplished if your expectations of teachers are realistic and if parents communicate with them rather than make assumptions like everything's the teacher's fault.

Keep in mind that teachers are nothing less than parents' eyes and ears throughout the day. If you are willing to help out on campus or support an extra-curricular club, just think, you too, could be present to witness and enjoy the miracles as they happen!

CHAPTER FORTY-FIVE
Underrated School Resource: School Counselors Provide Unparalleled Support to Teens

School budget cuts occur every year in one state or another, most recently, all across the country. School resources considered less critical to meeting academic standards become the first target of cuts. Unfortunately, school counselors are commonly placed in this category. Whenever school funding tightens, counselors are shuttled from counseling activities into administrative tasks or back into the classroom to teach.

I have clearly observed from talking in-depth to over 20,000 plus teens, that school counselors are critical to the survival and academic success of many teens today in both middle and high school. **It is abundantly clear that our nation must recognize the emotional vulnerability and serious wounding of today's youth. We must speak up for more counseling services in secondary schools where we still have a chance to reclaim young lives.**

I have worked with school counselors at hundreds, if not thousands of schools to put on awareness assemblies, assessments and meet with troubled teens. I have also had the privilege of keynoting numerous state and local counseling association conferences. I've met and conversed at length with leaders and membership at statewide conferences in Arkansas, Florida, Kansas, Kentucky, Maine, Mississippi, Nebraska, New York, South Carolina, Virginia, Washington and West Virginia. At such events, the majority of participants are school counselors from middle and high schools voicing very similar concerns and very similar passions all across the country. These conferences have given me a clear perspective and great insight into school counseling issues. Significant today is the severe lack of funding from federal to local levels for enough counselors in the vast majority of middle schools and high schools all across America. In addition, soon many of the most experienced and senior school counselors will be retiring, leaving a critical need to recruit more caring people into the profession.

Having now met and worked with nearly 8,000 school counselors at conferences and schools, I can say without a doubt that school counselors are a deeply compassionate, sensitive, dedicated, and humble group of people. People in this profession are devoted to the emotional, social, and academic well-being of our kids, the operative word being "emotional."

School counselors are much more than academic schedulers, college application coordinators, and job placement advisors for our teens.

Every adult employed on middle and high school campuses is chartered with a different set of job responsibilities and priorities. The Principal functions as the Chief Executive Officer, imparting overall direction, final authority, and top-level leadership. The Vice Principal often has the arduous task of discipline and maintaining safety on campus so schools can be safe environments necessary for learning. The Teacher's role is to educate our youth in the subjects that create productive and contributing members of society. Athletic coaches are committed to developing the physical potential of our youth, imparting social skills of teamwork and sportsmanship. Everyone on a school campus, from custodial help to Principal has a designated role.

The School Counselor is the ONLY person with a depth of training in and responsibility for the emotional well-being of our children.

School counselors make a significant contribution to the academic success of our children, especially the many from problematic homes. Many parents and adults outside education seem to think secondary school counselors exist to do academic testing, coordinate student schedules, write recommendations for teens applying to colleges, and occasionally mediate with parents when a teen has messed up. But school counselor duties go well beyond these activities, both as a personal mission and by professional training. They fill in where parents and society have left off – if not left out – the emotional, social, and self-esteem building skills teens need to navigate adolescence and successfully acquire a high school diploma.

School counselors handle all the tough stuff.

The large majority of school counselors I work with at schools and conferences make an effort to stay informed about current social and mental health issues. They implement programs that deal with the emotional needs of youth including: coping skills; peer mediation; anger management; counseling for grief and parental divorce; current trends in alcohol and drug abuse; domestic violence and abuse; teen pregnancy; gangs; adolescent sexuality; suicide and depression; counseling the gifted; guiding the disabled; and stress management. They are aware of every hot teen topic long before it surfaces in the media. From bullying to self-mutilation, eating disorders, rampant oral sex, and violence between girls, counselors live with these issues at school each and every day!

If a trend is brewing in teens today, school counselors have probably seen it coming or heard of it first!

Secondary school counselors are trained and dedicated to deal with the tough stuff that an ever-increasing number of teens bring to school daily. When a school allots time and funding for a counselor to do their job, counselors will seek out, design and implement solutions to many of the problems plaguing adolescents. Peer-helping programs, anger management groups, grief groups, divorce groups and other sundry support groups are some of the most successful and my favorites.

I have also been greatly impressed with the inventive and successful programs counselors have created such as the faculty-freshman mentoring program started by the counseling staff at a high school in an East Coast school. Volunteer faculty were teamed up as mentors with incoming freshmen. This program gave substantial positive support to the students in adjusting to high school and starting off on a positive footing, and gave teachers a new sense of participation and involvement.

Then there's the class I observed at a high school in the Northwest where the counselor conducted a support group each and every day for teens from foster and group homes. This class was conducted as a Peer Assistance Program and offered an open and caring surrogate "family" clearly responsible for keeping several dozen teens in school.

Counselors have coordinated nearly all of the community

and parent awareness programs I have presented on campuses. They enthusiastically go well beyond the call of duty to coordinate evening programs for parents and community. In the hope of raising awareness about the serious and sensitive teen issues they see in their cramped offices on any given day, counselors go outside their job descriptions to garner support from local newspapers, community leaders, faith community, mental health facilities, police departments and parents. They have provided refreshments, solicited for door prizes, and stayed long into the evening after programs to counsel a parent and/or child in emotional need.

I have sat in many a counselor's office chatting when a series of teenagers have popped their heads in the door just to say, "Hi, I'm here," "Hangin' in there" or share a simple thumb's up. This brief interaction is often the one connection that keeps a troubled teen in school rather than out in the streets.

School counselors are often the one person in the life of a struggling teen that makes coming to school matter.

Counselors saving teens, one teen at a time.

I remember when a teen girl popped her head in to say, "Hey, Ms. Brady" to the high school counselor, then scurried off to class. Ms. Brady shared that the girl's father was in prison for grand larceny and drug trafficking, her mother was addicted to cocaine and rarely came home, and if she did, it was always with a different man in tow. This vulnerable teenage girl had no parental supervision and had lived on the streets for a period of time. She had run away on two occasions, dropped out of school for a while, but was intelligent and did well in class when she was there.

Ms. Brady had reached out and brought the teen into her office to ask what was going on in her life. Then, she asked the girl to be part of a peer education class that was learning about teen concerns and educating peers. This abandoned teenager started showing up at school again. A couple days a week, Ms. Brady just happens to have an extra sandwich which is readily devoured by the girl.

And every day, this salvaged child casually drops by Ms. Brady's office to let her know she's made it to school, or maybe just to get "the look" from her counselor that says, "Glad to see you're here." Ms. Brady was the first adult in this girl's life who truly seemed to care she was alive. This all-but-lost teen was going to graduate; and Ms. Brady was actively looking for scholarships to help her go on to college.

Ms. Brady is cut from the same cloth as innumerable other caring, dedicated and proactive school counselors I have been privileged to work with. School counselors, though humble in the lack of credit they take for impacting teen achievement and saving teen lives, also fight ferociously for mental health programs, awareness assemblies, assessments, support groups, peer programs and funding to help our kids. Many approach their jobs with the fearlessness and devotion of a protective parent but get little appreciation from actual parents of students. The list of remarkable school counselors I have been blessed to meet and work with throughout the years could go on and on.

Definition of a great school counselor:
The heart of a lion, the gentleness of a lamb and the wisdom of a Yoda!

School counselors are confidence-builders, confidence keepers.

In general, teens have no idea that a school counselor is well-trained and willing to help sort out their life problems. Teens from troubled homes and mangled lives have even less awareness than their peers that a school counselor might be a trusted confidante and mentor. Their general lack of trust of all adults keeps them wary and isolated to gangs or cliques with other disenfranchised youth. Many teens believe that their counselor doesn't really care since no adults have cared about them in the past. They assume it is just a job and that a counselor wants to be left alone to schedule classes and work with the "good" kids.

Counselors are mandated to report to social services any mention of physical or sexual abuse. But many go much further to seek solutions by communicating with teachers, administrators and coaches. I have observed that school counselors often have more professional training and depth of understanding on teen issues than anyone else on the school campus. **They regularly go beyond the call of duty to help solve personal and emotional problems for students in their schools.**

Of course, school counselors have legal limitations on what they can and cannot talk about to students. There's no imposing of personal values and no mention of religion or God in public schools. They must be cautious about physicality, even to the exclusion of helpful hugs in many settings. **Yet they do everything in their power to keep students in school: help them overcome behavioral and emotional problems; find ways to manage chaotic lives; create peer helping programs and support groups; and go beyond school borders to coordinate resources from community services to help wherever possible.**

From my observation, school counselors rarely have the time or inclination to blow their own horns. They tend to be empathetic, socially-concerned individuals, rather than Type A, assertive executive types. Unfortunately, that humility and gentleness of spirit seems to make counselors appear dispensable and the first to go under a budget crunch.

We must educate our kids in the academics that allow them to make a living and be productive adults, but we must also educate them in "emotional intelligence." It is the internal assets that make the entire journey of life worthwhile. And it is school counselors who are primed to address this aspect of our children's education.

If school counselors can salvage the self-esteem of an anguished, abused child, isn't this effort at least as valuable as passing English, History, or Math? In reality, such youth are NOT going to pass classes without relief from their emotional trauma, grief, depression and despair anyway. Every school counselor I know bemoans having too little time to deal with the magnitude of teens at his/her school in serious emotional turmoil.

Our *Survey of Hope* in 2003 and 2004 results revealed that up to 40 percent of tenth graders in normal middle class high schools requested support for feeling depressed. Should we leave all these teens to fend off their demons alone? It is unrecognized depression and other emotional traumas that motivate rampant use of alcohol, pot and other drugs in secondary schools and colleges, and makes our youth engage in self-harm, suicide, and, ultimately, poor academic performance.

Instead, let's face the two serious needs in school counseling nationwide, and take action to help!

1. Raise the awareness of state and national legislators, county and district superintendents, parents and voters to the importance of funding more school counseling positions, rather than less. Raise your own voice! Help make it clear that educating a child from today's complex and challenged families is more than just meeting academic standards. **We must provide sufficient psychological counseling services in school to children whose minds are overwhelmed by the dysfunctions of their families.**

2. Recruit more people into the school counseling profession by making the position more appealing and more respected. Many of the best and most experienced counselors will be reaching retirement over the next few years. To draw dedicated and caring individuals into counseling, schools and school districts must commit sufficient funds to hire enough administrative help so school counselors can do what they became counselors to do: counsel kids.

We must open our eyes and accept the fact that many adolescents are emotionally troubled, lack healthy coping mechanisms and proper adult support. Without help to handle their emotions, many will fail to academically achieve. More will fall prey to accessible social problems and, worse yet, become our social problems. We will ALL pay the price of increased cost to healthcare, crime and incarceration, teen deaths, and increasing number of dangerous influences on your children.

The GOOD NEWS!

School counselors and the life-changing programs they create on school campuses continue to make a difference, opening up futures, and saving teen lives.

So, get behind your school counselors.
Acknowledge them! Advocate for them!

CHAPTER FORTY-SIX
Teens Helping Teens - Powerful Peer Support and Personal Empowerment for Participants

As I travel, I search the country for programs that legitimately help teens resist the landmines of substance abuse, irresponsible sexuality, suicide and violence. One of the nation's most successful programs for guiding, coaching and influencing teens in healthy life choices is Peer Helping/Peer Education.

Teens who participate in peer mediation and peer education do even more than help their peers. Research shows they help themselves, too! Peer helpers increase their own self-esteem; their success rates in school rise substantially. Here's how Peer Helping programs, often designed and implemented by, guess who – school counselors – can be instrumental in your teen's school.

National Association of Peer Programs (NAPP) describes the program at **www.peerhelping.org:**

> *"Peer helping is simply people helping other people. When teens experience frustrations, worries, concerns, and other life events, they typically turn to their friends – not professionals or even parents – for help, advice, practical assistance and support."*
>
> *"Peer helpers provide teens with opportunities for learning, guidance, emotional support, and growth which translates to reduced drug and alcohol involvement, higher academic skills, reduced HIV/AIDS, and unwanted pregnancy, reduced conflict, and increased understanding of differences and service to others. By helping others, peer helpers increase their own self-esteem and personal functioning."*

The positive impact of peer programs firsthand.

A heartwarming example exists at a continuation high school that houses at-risk teens I have worked at over the span of several years. This alternative high school is for teens that have fallen behind academically in their traditional high schools due to poor choices, challenging lifestyles, home difficulties, and truancy. The school offers students the opportunity to change inappropriate behavior, unhealthful lifestyles, and/or to improve their attendance and catch up on their credits to return to their home schools or graduate from the continuation high school.

One very gutsy and insightful teacher decided to establish a peer assistance program including peer helping and peer education at this school. Many mainstream high schools across America are finding such peer assistance programs to have an extremely positive impact on teen participants. This teacher thought," Why not at an alternative high school?" Her dream was to immerse trained teens, though streetwise and from troubled backgrounds, into compassionate community service that might help them better cope with their own problems and lifestyles.

As expected in an alternative school setting, many of the students struggle to stay in school, some lack enthusiasm or hope for a positive future. Some have resorted to alcohol and drugs, self-harm and/or gangs in an effort to cope with life. As is part of peer helping programs, this committed teacher/peer-assistance-advisor taught the teens active listening and communication skills as well as ways to get along with all types of personalities. With the intention of assisting these teens with personal problems, she taught them about the dangers and consequences of dysfunctional families including domestic violence and abuse, alcoholism, drug abuse, troubled relationships, sexual and emotional abuse and self-mutilation. **Teen issues were discussed openly and peer assistance teens began sharing about their own challenges, difficulties, and heartaches as they felt understood and their life struggles appreciated, for the first time in many of their lives.**

Students practiced the listening skills they had been taught: to listen without interruption, criticism or breach of confidentiality. A "healthy family" atmosphere blossomed within the group. These teens became the role models of their school, looked up to by others and reaching out to fellow students on campus who needed a listening ear. I was invited in to present Legacy of Hope®" to help educate the peer assistance teens on a wide variety of youth issues, emotional awareness and healing. In this unique safe environment, the peer assistance teens found the opportunity to express long-withheld feelings and secrets. As a result, this peer assistance program created a spirit of camaraderie, team spirit, loyalty and love among the group — an outstanding byproduct of peer helping programs I have seen all across the country.

The next step was for the advising teacher to generate service opportunities for the peer assistance teens in the way of mentoring children in low-socioeconomic elementary schools and special-needs schools nearby. Because continuation school students are often misunderstood and labeled 'trouble,' the elementary school administrations took some convincing, but the teens took this opportunity quite seriously; and their advising teacher set stringent standards. To participate, the teen peer assistants had to refrain from drugs in order to work with students. Their attendance had to be 90% or above and they had to be succeeding academically in all of their classes. The teacher/advisor was successful in getting principals and teachers at the elementary schools and special-needs schools to give the peer assistants the opportunity to prove themselves, and they did!

Each Friday, providing they had been in school Monday thru Thursday, the peer assistants read to the elementary school children, assisted with academic assignments, projects, recess and P.E. The teens provided holiday gifts and activities for the children; and donned Santa and bunny suits to make holidays special for the children, giving presents to these needy children that they would otherwise not receive.

Seeing others less unfortunate than themselves helped the teen peer assistants to shift their focus and acquire the gift of gratitude! Through compassion for others, peer helping helped the participating teens turn their own lives around. Valuing the opportunity to be role models, peer assistant teens responded to the expectation that they act maturely and wisely. And they didn't want to let the little children down! **They came to see themselves as important, productive, and capable of tackling the challenges life puts before them. They rearranged priorities and established loftier goals.**

Six months later, I returned to the continuation school to share in the peer assistance program year-end luncheon. I was astounded at the changes in perspective and maturity the program had made on the students. Prior to being in peer assistants, the mindset of many teens was to get back with their homeys, to hang out and continue their negative and unhealthful lifestyles. Instead, I now saw teens prepared and excited to educate themselves to be teachers, counselors, psychologists, doctors and more. **Their self-respect and life goals had expanded dramatically as they found meaning and purpose through caring for others.**

All of the peer assistance program teens radiated love and enthusiasm for their school, the program and enormous gratitude and love for their dedicated teacher/advisor. The peer assistance program had been the primary key to keep many of these teens coming back to school, motivated and on track academically.

One teen summed it up for the entire group who all nodded in agreement,

"You get a really good feeling helping someone else who really needs it. I used to miss a lot of school, but since I became a peer assistant, I'm there every day. 'Cause to go help the little kids and see them smile, I don't want to miss that good feeling!"

Begin this powerful program in *your* schools!

This magic occurs everywhere I see peer programs in schools, and most dramatically in schools where peer helping becomes a class within the curriculum as a recognized and valuable part of teen education. These programs require a school counselor or teacher to be the advisor. To create and implement a strong peer education curriculum, these programs need funding and the support of parents, administration and community.

The investment is well worth it. Adults and parents in a community can help by encouraging school principals, superintendents, school boards, and counselors to implement peer programs on middle school and high school campuses. Consider attending the annual NAPP (National Association of Peer Programs) conference where valuable ideas are shared, and to get involved in the process, check out **www.peerhelping.org,** or call toll-free: 877-314-7337.

If peer programs already exist in your children's schools, offer to help by promoting the programs. Make them visible so more teens choose to participate.

CHAPTER FORTY-SEVEN
Journaling Clears Minds and Vents Teen Feelings

Self knowledge is true power: it gives us the ability to alter our attitudes and see the choices in our lives.

Teens, too, can discover their innermost feelings and find that important inner voice that guides them, that voice that many know as God, Allah or Higher Power. Encouraging youth to journal can encourage them to grasp and experience a vital spiritual connection.

I know the power of journaling from firsthand experience. So often I have felt compelled to journal after leaving a school or conference just to unload the painful stories teens and adults have shared that have laid heavy on my heart.

It is as though, by writing down the verbatim descriptions of the atrocities in their lives, I have shown proper respect for the pain in people's lives. By taking the time to write their stories, I acknowledged the enormous courage it has taken these teens and adults to remain alive in our troubling, unjust world. The journaling has also given me the material for this book that is intended to honor the youth and the families still struggling to find meaning, love and solace in life.

Most importantly, the journaling has helped me vent the sadness I have felt for the hurting souls I have met and my own personal feelings that resonate to their sadness. I have learned, you cannot touch others' deep and dark inner places without uncovering your own. And you cannot share in another's joys and self-discoveries without bringing greater meaning to your own life. I have seen journaling serve similar purposes in the lives of youth from ages 12 to 20 as well.

The teen years are swamped with emotional volatility. No better time to begin a journal or write poetry to clear the goblins from their minds!

Teens tell me that writing clears their minds and lowers the intensity of their feelings. For some, it reduces their sense of isolation, and gives them hope, especially when they share their painful journaling with a caring adult. And some have shared that journaling with me.

Usually, their writing is stark, desperate, full of rage and pain, and clearly feeling alone and painfully unique. Yet, as one young adult woman shared with me about her teen years:

"I had to write about it to understand."

She would sort out her thoughts and feelings in a journal.

"I'm not crazy. Things are not all my fault. And maybe I do need to tell someone how I feel."

Today she is a playwright and a professional speaker on college campuses.

Through journaling, poetry and prose, teens can identify the real cause of their problems and, when willing to look deeply, their own underlying motives and their contribution to their problems.

Encourage teens: Journal and share their thoughts with a caring adult in order to resolve their problems. Parents, supportive adults, counselors and coaches can be of great help.

As a parent, counselor, coach, grandparent, or other adult willing to aid a teen on the journey of self-discovery and healing:

- Offer to listen to a teen share portions of their journaling and to help them brainstorm solutions.
- Encourage them to write more about what they need to feel safe, lovable, hopeful and creative.
- Talk about options they might consider to temporarily, if not permanently, resolve their problems in a healthy way.

In the toughest of times, poetry is a teen's reliable friend.

"When there is no one else to talk to about what's going on, I write a poem," says a high school girl living in a group home after a series of abusive foster homes due to incarcerated parents. Writing never abandoned her. She could count on that part of herself to speak the truth on paper. The process reduced her sense of aloneness and abandonment. She said it helped her see that she had the courage to go on and, at times, gave her peace of mind.

Whether teen or adult, putting our inner thoughts to paper without censorship validates our feelings and our right to exist – whether we are in a good, bad or apathetic frame of mind. It gives us an option to connect with others. By sharing our uncensored, free-flow writing with a noncritical person, we can find an amazing sense of self-acceptance, safety, and uncommon relief. Teens are especially sensitive and hungry for this connection, as adolescence magnifies their separateness and the existence of a potentially cold, harsh, and lonely world.

Gift a journal to your favorite teen!

To encourage the journaling process, give your teen a journal and leave your expectations behind! Let it be up to him/her to journal when and if he/she chooses.

You may well surprise your teen. A journal says that you think his or her thoughts and feelings matter. That is the same as saying, "I think you are special." In turn, you will have given them a healthy tool for unleashing dreams, exploring passions, and confronting fears.

One caveat: Under NO circumstances invade their privacy and read their journal uninvited! The only exception: Should you have strong suspicions that a son or daughter is into drugs, criminal activity, or thinking of suicide, browsing their journal may be a lifesaver. By no means should you share anything you've read with anyone else. Many a teen has lost trust in adults as well as had self-esteem severely trampled by ridicule or gossip about a teen's very private feelings.

If a teen chooses to share writings and drawings with you, consider yourself honored and highly respected. Accept this teen's writing as an expression of thoughts that are not to be mistaken as actions. Your acceptance and recognition of his or her thoughts can have an enormous positive impact on self-esteem. Of course, show respect by neither criticizing nor correcting flaws in their ideas or syntax.

I encourage you to ask before offering suggestions, "Would you like my feedback or suggestions?"

Sometimes teens sharing is just because they want you to know who they are and how deeply they think about things. **It may be a declaration of how "grown-up" they have become or a desire for validation** as they ponder life from a more mature perspective.

They may also share because they want to startle you into seeing that they are struggling, hurting and need your help.

By no means dismiss writing about ways to commit suicide or fantasies of violence.

These messages are legitimate cries for help and attempts for your teen to get your attention.

Put your teen first and ask, "What do you need from me right now?"

- Is it merely a hug – something so simple, yet often very difficult for a teen to identify or ask for?
- Is it figuring out what to do about a specific problem that is overwhelming them?
- Is it grief over the loss of a relationship, friend, family, or a dream?
- Is it just to listen and be patient with them?
- Is it a desire for help to quiet unrelenting depression, despair, worry, rage, or a desire to be dead?

Teens have shared these needs with me after I have made them feel safe to reveal about themselves.

A common need among teens is to talk with an adult who is outside the immediate family, such as an aunt, uncle, family friend, parent of a friend, etc. You, as a parent, may have the closest of relationships with your teen. However, because their deepest, most basic of desires is to be loved by *you*, they may prefer revealing uncomfortable parts of themselves to someone more detached.

Should you be lucky enough to be invited into any teen's personal journaling, read beneath the words to the motives, the hidden feelings, their deepest dreams, and their hunger for love, understanding and help. Listen and learn about the remarkable mind and creativity of a child/soon-to-be-adult. Applaud their courage to share their truths, and you, too, may be inspired to journal and connect more deeply with yourself!

For specific instructions on journaling for you or your teen, visit the Legacy website **www.legacyofhope.com** and follow the 'Ask Susie' or 'Resources' link.

CHAPTER FORTY-EIGHT
The Internet Can Help Solve Teen Problems

While we all are mindful of the nasty stuff the Internet can expose our kids to, it also provides important benefits. In many cases, Internet help sites and counseling hotlines are supporting parent, church and school efforts in listening to our teens.

On a Wednesday morning a few years ago, I presented an assembly to 400 teens in a remote rural high school, similar to those I have visited all across America. I concluded my talk with an invitation to students, "If anyone wants to come talk with me personally, I will be in the back of the cafeteria for a couple of hours." That 'couple of hours' turned into a full day.

By 10:30 a.m., I was seated on an out-of-the-way bench in the corner of the cafeteria. Four girls arrived to talk. Soon two more arrived, then another and another and another, sharing stories of despair about unraveling families and lives of abuse, use, shame, blame, depression, obsession, and loss. I did not get up from that bench until 4:30 that afternoon as the flood of teenage "victims" poured through the cafeteria door.

The situations they shared were heartbreaking, but more disturbing to me was the painful lack of counseling and social services in this particular school and community. My only recourse that day was to leave many of these teens with a handful of Internet websites to log onto when they desperately needed to connect with someone who was caring, non-judgmental, and could help them decide what to do with their lives.

Since that day, I have teamed up with the American Counseling Association and school counselors across the country to advocate for on-campus therapy, support groups, and peer helping programs. But still, through proper Internet sites, no teen needs to handle life totally alone any more.

Teens have an alternative when there seems to be no adult around to trust. Though I have more school counselors helping with my cause, I also continue to rely on easy access to the Internet and steer teens to a select set of reliable, trustworthy websites. The net contains accurate information on every nightmare that binds them, and offers 24-7 access to competent hotlines for moments of fear, panic and an aching need. Many teens I meet today are on the Internet all hours of the night. I have e-mails from teens that have been logged on at 3:00 a.m., when they just couldn't sleep.

Teens and adults are welcome to check out up-to-date safe and supportive websites, hotlines, and self-help resources at my website **www.legacyofhope.com**, selecting the 'Ask Susie' or 'Resources' links.

Be wary of the Internet's down side.

> *Of course, it is equally important to educate teens on the dangers of the Internet. "The Internet is changing the way everybody does business, including the bad guys," U.S. Customs Services spokesman Dean Boyd says.*

Some teens will turn to suggestive chat rooms to fill the need for a caring conversation. Sexual predators are on the prowl in chat rooms. If a teen is looking for someone to care, an open chat room is not a likely source to find a professional therapeutic listener. You may want to share with your teen that **anyone truly dedicated to helping a teen evaluate a life problem and find healthy solutions will maintain a professional distance.** An adult who really wants to help rather than exploit a teen will keep a boundary by advising a teen to go directly to a parent, local school counselor or mental health facility for immediate help rather than offer to meet them themselves.

And, though the Internet is certainly capable of providing professional support and information to you and your teens, keep a watchful eye on "Favorite" sites. Ask your teen to show you some of his or her preferred websites; check out the bookmarks.

> *"It's all up for grabs (on the Internet). You can get almost anything you want if you are willing to look for it," says Robert Stephenson of the Substance Abuse and Mental Health Services Administration (SAMHSA).*

As Becky Mollenkamp states in her "Better Homes and Gardens" February, 2002 article *Drugs, the Internet, and Your Kids,*

> *"The days of needing to 'know someone' to score drugs are over. Children need only know how to use a computer."*

She suggests parents be watchful if a teen opens a post office box to receive packages and keep tabs on a teen with a credit card, check billing statements for unusual charges, and check out unmarked deliveries to the house.

Show your support for your teen's healthy use of the Internet by researching sites together and "book marking" those that can be of the most help. This assures that your teen is getting information that you approve.

CHAPTER FORTY-NINE
Fight Boredom and Denial – Create A Community Coalition and Gather Support!

Teen substance abuse problems exist in every community in every state. Teens that drink and/or binge on weekends may vary a few percentage points from place to place, and the amount of pot vs. other drugs will vary by geographic location and economics of the community. But there is no utopian community in America where our kids are safe from the ills of society.

Though I share a particular community's trials in this chapter, I would like to suggest you watch for the similarities to your environment rather than the differences. I hope you resist the urge to think, "Not MY community, not MY child!" As you accept that *all* youth are at risk today, then you may find yourself motivated to get involved in efforts to heal and protect *every* child in your neighborhood. Because – then and *only* – will your hometown be as safe as possible for your own teens.

I was speaking in a small farm community in the middle of thousands of acres of corn and soybeans. While in town to do school assemblies, I found the teens to be like teens in other rural mid-American towns from California to Maine, Alaska to Florida. They generally are more friendly, more courteous, a great majority involved in school activities, and more modestly dressed than their urban counterparts. They did, however, have a huge beef about living in rural America – THEY'RE BORED! The vast majority of rural teens envy life on the West Coast and its exciting lifestyle as proclaimed in movies and music videos. Except for the hunters, hikers and outdoorsmen of the bunch, many teens growing up in the most gorgeous remote natural settings on earth find country life boring and confining.

With no organized activity to occupy a teen's time, what *do* they do?

When asked, teens say they want shopping, theaters, dance clubs, and a teen center open on weekends until midnight. Small Town America can seriously lack these alternatives. So, they drink and/or smoke dope in the fields and the forests. Rural teens report that 80 percent of their high school seniors drink regularly on weekends and only a slightly lesser percent for undergrads. It is just something to do and has been a rite of passage in rural America for generations.

In addition to teen boredom, teens describe adult boredom as well. Many of their parents love their small-town atmospheres, nevertheless, resort to heavy drinking to fill empty hours after work or on weekends. Local drug and alcohol rehab facilities in rural America share with me how many parents in their towns grew up with drinking as their major entertainment, continue the habit as adults, and see little wrong with teens following in their footsteps. They do show concern over teens driving drunk, but do little to change how they model active drinking behavior, even after teen deaths in drunk-driving accidents.

Some parents may be accepting, but school and community adults are frustrated.

Local high school counselors and principals, on the other hand, respond with great concern because they see the emotional distress of the entire student body when a peer dies in a drunk-driving incident. Teens get depressed, grieve, and express deep anger at friends for taking grave chances every weekend. There are always teens who are disgusted and frustrated at how difficult it is to find sober and drug-free friends to hang out with on a Saturday night.

> *"I spend every weekend at home with my Mom and Dad," one girl shared. "I can't go to any party where there won't be kids falling down drunk or passing joints around. It just bugs me; and I don't like to go. I'll just invite a friend or two over. We'll rent a movie and order a pizza. Otherwise, there's pretty much nothing else to do around here on a Friday or Saturday night. Most kids are out in the field past the library just getting stoned and drunk." And she shrugged her shoulders as if to say, that's the way life is!*

I admire those teens making the choice to be alcohol and drug free. It is definitely not an easy choice. It can be a lonely and isolating choice.

School administrators and teachers from every sector of American life tell me they hear the Monday-morning bragging about teen drinking escapades on the weekend. They see the lethargic and bloated faces of weekend over-indulgence in their classrooms. A great many educators are disturbed by the trends and the obvious loss of focus and lost potential that alcohol and substance abuse inflict.

Principals, counselors and teachers in rural communities express a serious frustration over far too many parents who still look at teen drinking and drug experimentation as merely 'sowing wild oats.'

> *"I drank and smoked as a teen," parents commonly argue. "I'm not going to tell them not to. Every teen is going to experiment."*

The rebuttal from all prevention and rehab resources today is that today it is not the same. Today, a greater number of teens start experimenting with drugs and alcohol at younger ages, which also puts them at much greater risk of addiction and mental and physical damage. Preteens and teens have much easier access to marijuana today and use much stronger pot than their parents used.

Binge drinking in college, high school, and even middle school is far more the rage than ever before for both females and males. Add to this a greater assortment of readily available, more potent and brain-damaging drugs, and our youth are at much greater risk. **Today's youth have less supervision and less parental direction in values and ethics, so that the argument begins to look more and more like an excuse for parents to avoid the tough job of setting boundaries and staying actively involved in monitoring, communicating, and responsibly parenting their teens. Adults often do not want to look at their own use and abuse habits.**

In rural areas, drinking isn't the only issue of concern.

In rural America, social services are also more limited. As a result, teens share stories of being stuck in homes where parental substance and child abuse can be extreme. Rural teens have shared tales of going to authorities on their own to demand and beg to have themselves and their younger siblings removed from a neglectful/abusive parent(s)' home.

I have had several emotionally gut-wrenching conversations with teens in rural America. It still stuns me to hear 13- to 15-year-old girls and boys talk nonchalantly about childhood molestation at the hands of fathers, stepfathers, stepbrothers, cousins, and family friends who were, more often than not, inebriated at the time.

When I look at the results of the *Survey of Hope* from middle and high school teens in rural locations, these teens need as much help in support groups as teens anywhere else around the nation. Reduced funding for counselors in middle schools and high schools is extreme in small-town schools. A reduction in school counselors may mean no counselor or just one for hundreds of both middle and high school teens. Emotional trauma and unprocessed pain from familial abuse, loss and grief often goes ignored, and definitely under acknowledged. I hear from the teens in e-mails, cries for help, suicidal pleas.

Smaller communities can also mean bigger secrets.

Perhaps what seemed of special significance in one rural high school was the reluctance of teens to give their names on surveys when it came to participation in support groups that would deal with the large amount of depression, anger, and alcohol/substance abuse. Only 6 percent of the high school teens and 7 percent at the middle school gave their names to participate. The norm is 19 to 25 percent.

Some teens remarked on their surveys that they would like to give their name but were afraid to. Teens told me that they feared being gossiped about at school and in the community. Some feared reactions at home should their parents find out they were revealing a family problem. From verbal to physical abuse, teens were afraid to simply ask for help from other teens or professional adults.

Small town rural America can be a very hard place to be a teen.

Teen drinking, drug use and victimization from abuse in the home make teens hopeless and desperate. So they drink and use, act out sexually all the more. They keep it all a secret; and teens get sicker. These teens need at least one adult to encourage them to keep their hope alive so they can see a reason to break the pattern.

As adults, we have all had dreams that were dismissed or dashed. We have all had disappointments that changed the very course of our lives.

The greatest contribution we can make is NOT to pass fear and disillusionment on to the next generation. Instead, become an Encourager. Offer teens a wider vision of life with unlimited dreams!

Action steps adults can take:

- Ask your city council to create a teen advisory board. Give them a chance to add their creative ideas to finding solutions.
- Create a community anti-drug and alcohol coalition with youth and adults from all aspects of the community: school, business, law enforcement, mental health, PTO, etc. Join CADCA.
- Brainstorm about a Teen Center and the activities teens would participate in. (One small town in South Dakota created a skateboard park out in the middle of nowhere and attracted an enthusiastic group of preteens every day!) Put the word out that you are looking for someone to donate a facility for the Teen Center, fund activities or act as Director.

Be committed to creating options for your community's teens!

I encourage you to pick up the baton, take the action and contact Community Anti-Drug Coalitions of America (CADCA at **www.cadca.org**), the National Boys and Girls Clubs of America (**www.bgca.org**), and network with other communities that have been successful in these efforts.

A community anti-drug and alcohol coalition will bring issues to the forefront, create awareness and pull community resources together. Seek commitment from schools, law enforcement, local judicial systems, mental health services, liquor retailers, faith leaders, city councils, school district administrators, and parents. Then, involve local youth in the design and implementation so that teen drinking, drug use, related "secrets" and destructive choices will be reduced and precious futures reclaimed.

CHAPTER FIFTY
Children of Alcoholics Week Gives Community Opportunity to Get Involved

Because children of alcoholic or substance-abusing parents are at very great risk to repeat the pattern, it's important we step in with help and support. The National Children of Alcoholics (COA) Week in February gives adults an opportunity to explore Child of Alcoholic issues from their own childhood and the impact on their own children. In addition, there are suggestions for activities and involvement for adults to truly make a positive difference and experience the fulfillment from being of service.

When children grow up in a household with a substance-abusing parent they can develop problems that last a lifetime. These children are the highest risk population for developing substance-abuse problems of their own, as well as a host of related emotional and behavioral problems.

Each year, the second week of February is National Children of Alcoholics (COA) Week. It's a week entirely focused on raising community awareness of children or teens in need of support.

COA Week provides an opportunity to increase awareness in your own home of any impact a relative's addiction may have on your family, or to reach out to another family – especially the vulnerable children – from an alcoholic home situation.

To use this week as a character-building tool with your teens, CADCA (Community Anti-Drug Coalitions of America) offers free materials to build awareness of the impact of alcohol and drug abuse. As CADCA states:

> *"These resources may be used to impress on teachers, faith leaders, coaches, youth workers, counselors and others the influence they have in the lives of children affected by family addiction. They also can help give children clear messages that they are not to blame for their parents' abusive alcohol or drug use, that they are not alone, that there are many children just like them, and that help is available."*

Additionally, a **free brochure** entitled *"It's Not Your Fault!"* speaks to children of substance abusers, providing useful facts and suggestions on how kids can cope and get help. Obtain this brochure by calling (800) 788-2800 and at **www.health.org**. **Another brochure** developed by the Center for Substance Abuse Treatment is available for adult caregivers working with young people exposed to substance-dependent parents or guardians. Call (800) 788-2800 for a copy of "*You Can Help.*"

Consider asking a computer-savvy teen to explore **www.freevibe.com** for insights into family alcohol and drug addiction, then share with the family what interested them most. Web information for adults is located at **www.TheAntiDrug.com** and **www.nacoa.org**, so parents can have an informed exchange with their teenagers.

The Al-Anon/Alateen website has specific literature focused on children of alcoholics as well as adult children of alcoholics. Meetings around the world are listed on their website and may be attended at no cost and with the assurance of anonymity and no gossip, primary principals of the program (**www.al-anon.alateen.org**).

COA Week opens our eyes to kids in need around us.

According to CADCA, "*COA Week is a chance to speak openly about the pain and confusion, as well as the resilience and hope experienced by families impacted by parental substance abuse.*"

Know a teen that is regularly depressed or over-anxious?

Many teens feel awkward in social situations, but teens with a drug-dependent parent are often socially inept and viewed as outcasts or members of cliques considered misfits.

> "*Children of substance abusers may also feel isolated, embarrassed or afraid to bring friends home. Experts say these kids need caring adults to help them, maybe just to talk, to let them know they're not being disloyal to their family by talking.*
>
> *Trusted adults (such as relatives, friends, teachers, coaches or school nurses) can help children of substance abusers feel less alone and unloved or confused by their parent's actions.*"

Each of us must be willing to acknowledge the troubled kids in our community, noticing signs such as withdrawal, tardiness at school, plummeting academic or other performance, and/or physical ailments such as headaches or stomachaches with no apparent cause. Sometimes just talking about the problem at home or school is enough for a child.

Other times, kids need help through a support group such as Alateen.

One 12-year-old girl in a support program for children of substance abusers said,

> *"Group is like a family to me. I'm safe there and it's filled with young people who understand. Each time they remind me that it's not my fault and give me hope."*

Every parent who makes the effort to help a child also models to their teen the character traits of compassion and responsibility. We can all learn to care about our world by considering that the very child being affected by a substance-abusing parent could be your neighbor's child.

Adults who help the child of a substance abuser offer a lifeline that will last a lifetime.

CHAPTER FIFTY-ONE
FCCLA for Great Family Values, Uncovering Teen Talents and a Healthy Place to Belong

With strong family values at a premium today, what will our teens be like as adults? What kind of parents will they be? What kind of homes will they create when many have not experienced stability or an intact family themselves? Fortunately, FCCLA, a nationwide, service club at high schools across the country, is introducing teens to what it takes to build and maintain strong families, instilling healthy habits and values, and developing teens' talents and self-esteem. Is FCCLA in *your* school?

Catch some prime time news, TV sitcoms, MTV music videos, standard air play on a teen station, or browse a teen magazine and you may wonder if teens have half a chance of developing values that will steer them clear of society's ills. Can teens make it to 21 without an alcohol or drug-related car accident or abuse problem, an STD, unwanted pregnancy, suicide attempt, or AIDS? Will they be able to establish healthy marriages? Will they grow up to be self-absorbed takers and manipulators rather than contributors?

I have some encouraging news; and it may well be in your own backyard! FCCLA – Family, Career and Community Leaders of America – is a school club with local, state, regional and national structures that gives teens, in its own vernacular, "warm courage" and "high hope."

> **The FCCLA Creed guides teens to seek "precious values," and makes them "The builders of homes for America's future ... Homes where living will be an expression of everything that is good and fair ... Homes where truth and love and security and faith will be realities, not dreams."**

Now that's an encouraging vision; and a significant support to any parent's hopes and dreams for their children and future grand-children!

FCCLA is positively impacting more than 100,000 teens each year.

I have been privileged to keynote FCCLA conferences at national, regional, state and school events since 1997. I have always been revitalized and greatly encouraged by the consistent, disciplined, sound principles that are presented at the events and modeled by advisors and students alike. I've personally witnessed extraordinary transformations in teens from very troubled home lives. FCCLA has helped them channel and structure their lives; helped them fill their emotional need to belong and be safe; and made them productive and confident through achievement.

While many youth organization events and conferences make invaluable contributions to teen lives, FCCLA goes one step further by focusing on the very core of teen social problems: negative and neglectful families. FCCLA focuses on "personal growth" and putting *Families First*, a vital program of the organization to help teens understand what it truly takes to create strong families.

FCCLA, formerly known as Future Homemakers of America (FHA), was built from the committed dedication of Family and Consumer Sciences teachers (Home Economics teachers in my day). These dedicated teachers are the backbone of FCCLA. They talk to teens daily about what it takes to build and maintain relationships, nurture children, be resourceful earners, and continue to put our families first.

FCCLA offers healthy family modeling. *Families First* is my favorite program, though I've been impressed with many others including the national *Stop the Violence* campaign to programs that teach about finances and healthy physical self-care.

FCCLA's *Families First* teaches teens: "When families are strong and healthy, society as a whole is improved."

Obviously, in my work, I have observed that the lack of intact families across America is a major contributor to the ills that have befallen our teens and society. *Families First* gives teens a healthy family model when they have known none. They learn what it is to nurture and be nurtured socially, emotionally, mentally and physically.

Teens participate in projects that provide acknowledgement for small and large accomplishments, also missing in many homes. As teens attend regional and national conferences, their perception of what is possible grows. They compete in "Star Events" that develop skills and talents, and receive much needed recognition for effort and growth.

A case study of an FCCLA teen.

I have heard the stories from teens who found new hope and self-esteem through FCCLA. Much like Emily in Chapter Thirty Six, Sarah was a misfit from a very troubled family. She was petrified of rejection. The child of a cruel and critical mother and an emotionally withdrawn father, Sarah was riddled with self-loathing by the 9th grade. A pretty girl, she saw herself as abjectly ugly! She started smoking cigarettes as a freshman and toyed with marijuana. She had a boyfriend pressing her for sex; and her grades were miserable, though she spoke intelligently and seemed quite bright. When her counselor scheduled her for a Family and Consumer Sciences class, she reacted with disgust and threatened to ditch the class.

On the first day of class, her teacher, who was also the FCCLA Advisor, immediately figured Sarah out.

The teacher began by asking Sarah for help with small tasks in class, thus giving Sarah a sense of value and belonging.

Next, this caring and alert teacher invited Sarah to an FCCLA meeting after school. Sarah got involved in peer education training on families, and the denial and secrecy in her life began to melt away. Sarah channeled her pain into a passion for reaching younger teens teetering on the wrong path. Sarah is a marvelous success story, having graduated from high school with honors; in college studying to be a Family and Consumer Sciences teacher herself, alcohol and drug free; and engaged to marry her college sweetheart.

Kudos to FCCLA! If your high school has an FCCLA Club, get behind it and give it the support and financial backing it deserves. When your teen participates in a strong FCCLA Chapter, it will provide your child with enduring life skills and ethics, positive reinforcement through accomplishments, and help ensure his or her well-being by surrounding teens with equally well-directed, influential peers.

CHAPTER FIFTY-TWO
Spirituality Reduces Substance Abuse and Self-Destructive Teen Choices

Many of the world's best known and prestigious treatment programs for alcoholics and addicts and their families agree – **healing, hope and sustained recovery are most successful when we find and rely upon a Higher Power**. While I have no intention of sermonizing here, I have seen time and time again that belief in a caring, compassionate God breathes new life into families devastated by addictions, and creates on-going hopeful change.

At a time when even our Pledge of Allegiance is under attack for the mention of God, there is insurmountable evidence that spirituality is essential to overcoming life's most traumatic adversities.

Certainly, the Twelve Step programs of Alcoholics Anonymous, Narcotics Anonymous, Al-Anon/Alateen, Nar-Anon and others have been convinced for over 50 years that a spiritual healing is essential for recovery from alcoholism, drug addiction and the emotional damage of loving the afflicted. Faith in, and reliance on, a Higher Power greater than oneself is commonly the result of actively working the Twelve Steps, the backbone tool of these self-help programs. The National Center on Addiction and Substance Abuse (CASA) at Columbia University now has research to support the promise from a spiritual healing.

In a 52-page two-year study, *So Help Me God: Substance Abuse, Religion and Spirituality*, CASA finds:

"Tapping the power of religion and spirituality has enormous potential for lowering the risk of substance abuse among teens (and adults) and when combined with professional treatment, for promoting recovery."

CASA combined analysis of the National Household Survey with Teen Surveys and the General Social Survey to find that

"Teens (and adults) who consider religion important and who attend religious services weekly are far less likely to smoke, drink or use illicit drugs."

CASA research agreed that sobriety was far more likely to succeed when combined with spirituality-based 12-Step programs.

I am delighted to have my experience substantiated by research. Every year, I meet countless teens whose lives are in shambles, who are drinking, doing drugs, sexually promiscuous and/or cutting on themselves to cope with childhoods ravaged by neglect, rejection, abuse or abandonment by alcoholic mothers and fathers. Over the course of a year's communication about their problem, through calling and/or e-mail, I see incredible miracles happen as these teens turn their fears over to a Higher Power greater than themselves.

Remembering Stacey's story.

As mentioned in Chapter One, Stacey first contacted me via e-mail. At 15-years-old, she was caught up in her own serious use of marijuana, alcohol and self-mutilation. She cut on herself to release intense emotional pain, feeling trapped and at fault for all that was wrong in her family. A drug-abusing brother was now in prison; her adult sister and girlfriend visited her home often under the influence of alcohol and drugs, bringing arguments and chaotic fights with every visit; her father left the family for another relationship; and her mother had serious health issues that required Stacey to be her primary caregiver.

Stacey saw no evidence of God, but spirituality saved her sanity.

In our early e-mail exchanges, Stacey felt no connection with "God" any more. Long ago, during one of the deepest darkest nights of her childhood, she had prayed to God to let her die by morning so she would no longer have to feel terribly unloved and worthless. When she woke the next morning in the same uncomfortable circumstances, she concluded there was no God or that she was so worthless even God had stopped caring about her. With no spiritual solace, her heart became bitter, resentful, filled with self-pity and the perfect vacuum for substance abuse to fill.

I have learned not to criticize teens as they unload their sad sagas, and not to judge them as they reveal alcohol and drug abuse to me. Somewhere, sometime, somehow, someone has to listen and allow them to get out their rage, fear and pain. After months of encouragment, she began to correlate that my compassion came from the loving God that I came to know in my own recovery from life with an alcoholic/addict.

She told me how she was able to sleep for the first time in many months by imagining God holding her in a loving embrace as she closed her eyes at night, despite continuing curses from her mother. And then came the day she decided *not* to smoke dope, drink, take pills or cut on her body anymore in order to cope with her feelings. Instead she remembered the kindness our e-mails had brought her; and she began believing in a Higher Power. Better yet, she could comprehend and feel loved by a Power greater than herself because she had experienced what it is to be unconditionally loved, accepted, and her transgressions forgiven.

A few months later, she e-mailed that her mother had been especially critical. A flash of loving insight filled her mind, *"I'm worthy of more than this! God loves me."* She stopped her own negative self-criticism in its tracks. She was able to see her mother's words as an expression of her mother's own emotional fear and despair rather than a fault in herself. For the first time, she did not feel her mother's criticisms as something personal, rather as the ravings of a very unhappy woman. Stacey felt compassion and detachment. Stacey experienced a miraculous change in attitude!

We all have heard stories of how God heals. Some people believe; some doubt. Some do not even choose to listen. But I witnessed first-hand Stacey's transformation, from a path of emptiness and destruction to one of hope and self-worth. I saw the power of unconditional love, patience, kindness and courtesy. I was richly rewarded to see her spiritual awakening. I was reminded that, just as I have been blessed to be God's instrument in some tender child's life, others are being used to help guide mine! My own faith was greatly reinforced by Stacey's heart-warming transformation through faith from complete desolation to a life with hope!

Epilogue

Teens in middle school today continue to be tender, wide-eyed, childish, thoughtful, eager, moody, playful, taunting ... they are open and experiencing the entire spectrum of human emotions. Most importantly, they are hungry to be loved, and want to be appreciated for their expanding sense of individuality and self-expression. They will make a hero and role model of any adult who opens up to them honestly and lovingly as long as that adult treats them with respect. Middle school teens can be just plain irritating, but also, a whole lot of fun!

Teens in high school are a more mature mixture of the above, more critical and selective, yet charming and playful, sensitive yet more protective and suspicious. They retain enough child to be precious and are becoming adult enough to treat their opinions, dreams and losses with respect and serious consideration. They appreciate an adult who does not lie, cheat, manipulate or use them. They are loyal to their dying breath to a peer or adult they trust, who respects them, and is one they can admire, love and respect in return.

Teens are a reminder of the thrill of being alive!
Teens whose spirits have been deeply wounded are
a heartbreak and devastating loss to us all.

Notes from my journey to reinforce just what we are up against.

I am on my way to the airport, an-hour-and-a-half drive from a breadbasket community to an international airport where I will hop a plane for a typical six to nine hour journey home. I have spent two days speaking to several hundred teens in almost-exclusively white middle-class schools. So much was stirred in my heart and my mind that I write on a tablet as I drive so I will not forget, not misrepresent the reality God has prepared me to see and to share with you.

The scenery I drive by is idyllic – perfect spring day, crisp cool 65-degree sunshine. A lush carpet of green spreads across rolling farmland and the sky is a classic uninterrupted blue but for a floating plush pillow of white cloud. Life appears ever so tranquil and contented here in middle America.

As I drive toward the airport, my mind relaxes to the meditative sound of the wind around the car and the gentle vibration of highway pavement beneath the tires. I make a call on my cell phone to my message center, expecting a business inquiry or two, a "Hi, you back?" from a friend, and a "See you tonight, honey, been missing you!" invitation from my husband.

My reverie and my denial are shattered by a message from a 7th grade girl from one of the schools I spoke at just yesterday:

> "*Ms. Vanderlip, you came to my school yesterday and I need your help. Your assembly really made me think. Last night, I cut up my arm again. My Mom and Stepdad were fighting bad; and my Stepdad told me it was all my fault again. My Mom didn't say anything.*
>
> *My Stepdad's son is a drug addict. So a while ago my mom put a lock on my door to protect me. He broke into my room last week when no one else was home and molested me. I don't want to give my mom any more trouble, so I didn't tell her.*
>
> *She won't leave my Stepdad, even when he hits her. I don't know what to do. I know it's not right to cut on myself, but I get so overwhelmed and desperate. PLEASE call back. Bye.*"

Another precious 13-year-old girl has shared her heartbreaking problem, though it was but one of several dozen preteens who clamored to share equally troubling life stories with me at yesterday's schools.

More memories from the day before flood my mind:

Now I recall the 30 or more boys and girls who gathered in a circle and sat on the auditorium stage floor to talk with me about alcoholic, drug-addicted, abusive parents/stepparents, siblings and step-siblings. Every single one of them was wounded, lonely and hopeless. All had adults at home that regularly berated, criticized and degraded them. And everyone of them said straight out,

"*I feel like a loser. I feel scared and worry all the time.*"

And I can still feel the tugs at my heart as I clearly remember how several girls pulled up their sleeves to show me cutting scars on their forearms. One 8th grade girl came vividly to mind. Her eyes held the knowing look of what it was to know serious emotional pain that has taken you to the edge and back. Only 13-years-old, yet she shared without hesitation,

"I used to cut on myself, but I quit two months ago. I have a friend who also cut on herself and we both knew it wasn't right, so we decided to call each other whenever we felt like cutting. We both stopped that way. You gotta have support to quit or you can't."

She offered to be support to another girl wanting to quit. They agreed and decided on their own to exchange phone numbers. **An ad hoc peer support group was formed!** I thanked God for the amazing miracle I witnessed: a teen that has overcome a painful past eagerly offering to help a peer with her own experience, strength and hope.

When I got home last night, I checked my e-mails and found one more teen reaching out for help. "A Lost 14 Year Old", she referred to herself. I remembered her from the talking circle: a petite brunette – quiet, with a saddened, forlorn, wizened-beyond-her-years look upon her face. She had nodded "yes" to the question when I asked the group if they were growing up in a home where a parent had a drug or alcohol problem.

Her e-mail read:

"I have an 18-year-old boyfriend. We've been dating over a year."

("What's a 13-year-old girl doing with an 18-year-old boy?!" my mind raged as I read the e-mail. Then I got real and reminded myself that today's 13-year-old girls have had more sexual exposure than I had by 30. Many have already dealt with the sexual advances of drunken stepdads, half-brothers and/or mom's boyfriends by the age of 10.)

Her e-mail went on,

"We started having sex a month ago, and I wanted to know how to protect myself. Do you think my 18-year-old girlfriend can get me something without anyone contacting my parents?"

The question saddened me, as it may you. Our baby girls are women so very young; and we're not talking Afghanistan or Iraq or Third World Latin America.

I recommended:

- I think you are young to be having a sexual relationship and that being involved with an 18-year-old guy at 13 has serious potential drawbacks. You may be looking for love because you aren't feeling loved at home. You did say that one of your parents has a drinking or drug problem. Is there fighting in the house? Are you getting yelled at or ignored? These family situations can leave you lonely and feeling rejected. Do you think you are in this relationship because you feel desperate and just need to feel loved?
- You're going to grow and change a lot in how you think and feel between now and 18, and even more after you are 21. Let yourself have time to change and find out what you really want for the rest of your life. Right now, you are really involved with your boyfriend and may be very much in love.
- I do commend you for seeking contraceptives since you have become sexual with your boyfriend. That is a smart option if you continue to be sexually active with him. I do, however, encourage you to talk to your Mom about the relationship and your wanting contraceptives. You said in your e-mail that she likes your boyfriend, so talk it out with her if you think you can. See if your Mom thinks it is the right move. She is still your Mom and you have several more years at home where she can be helpful and guide you if you open up to her.

  If she isn't someone you feel safe or trust, then how about talking to the school counselor or school nurse? Find a family planning clinic and go talk to them. They will be able to give you good information. I don't know their rules on giving birth control to 13-year-olds, so go check it out. But also, learn the facts about alcoholism and how you have been affected as a child of an alcoholic.
- Learn how it impacts your relationship and choices with your boyfriend. If finding love, no matter the consequences, is your motive or if you feel like no one could ever love you, then you may be in a relationship to fill the hole inside rather than actually finding the right man to be your mate for life.

- You can build your own self-esteem by learning how to love yourself, and how to take care of yourself. It starts with learning about the disease of alcoholism and how all the neglect and abuse at home isn't your fault. It wasn't that you aren't lovable; it was about your parents having a disease."

OK. So I made another attempt to open the mind of an uninformed teen and explain how they are making choices based on loneliness and shattered self-esteem because their parents are broken. This time, a 13-year-old girl chose a boyfriend over cutting or drugs or alcohol. Maybe she would think and talk to her mom. Maybe she'll talk to her counselor.

And the boys have problems, too.

Teen boys also spoke that day at the school. A 14-year-old boy asked,

"What do you do if your parents make you take drugs with them?"

I've heard this far too many times before: Parents giving kids beer at 3 years of age; 5- to 10-year-olds forced to smoke dope with parents across the kitchen table:

"Don't be such a goody goody. Take a hit an' loosen up. Have some fun!" says pothead Mom to her pre-teen son as he attempts to refuse the pot she shoves in his face.

I urged this 10-year-old boy to talk to his counselor, get help to handle the uncomfortable situation at home and get some healthy adult guidance into his life. He agreed, thank goodness, and wrote his name on a sheet of paper for me to deliver to the counselor that afternoon.

My one day in this idyllic-appearing community was a powerful reminder: **Family ills plague teens emotionally everyday yet these serious social concerns are still terribly under discussed and, more often, kept secret in our society.**

I was also reeling from the obvious misguided sexuality of many middle school teens as recalled the middle school counselor's request to include comments on oral sex.

> *"Please make a comment about how oral sex is not good for middle school girls to be doing. They don't even think of it as sex."*

In one month alone, I had middle school counselors in three different regions of the country share the same concern.

> *"The girls are too embarrassed to talk to the boys but don't see anything wrong with giving them oral sex," two middle school counselors shared with me. "I ask them if they think it is inappropriate; and they don't see anything wrong with it. They just tell me that the boys like it and that's why they do it. How do we get it across to them that it isn't healthy, that it is dangerous? You can catch diseases."*

Young teens were already questioning their sexual preferences as well, as three 13-year-old girls came up altogether and asked,

> *"Should you be mad if your lesbian friends try to touch you and hit on you?"*

And a 12-year-old boy anxiously sought an answer to his concern,

> *"How do you know you are gay?"*

So many issues on teen minds and so little time!

There are so many issues for teens to sort through and so many teens have to figure them out for themselves. They actually are eager for adults to take their adolescent curiosity, pain, grief, fears and search for identity seriously. Will you? Are you willing to help them sort out family problems from their own self-worth? Can you listen thoughtfully instead of with a critical mind? Can you maintain your cool as they discover their sexual identity? Can you give them sufficient attention and affection so that they have the capacity to care about others rather than bully and gossip in an empty attempt to feel important? Help them understand where and when to draw boundaries, what is reasonable to expect from others, and what is unacceptable treatment, tolerance and compassion.

Since neither the cities nor farmlands, the North, South, East or West are immune to our social ills any more, the safety of our children must come from:

- Parents and parent education programs
- Adequate counseling and psychological services in the schools
- School service clubs that promote character and values (FCCLA, KEY Club, FHA, 4H, DECA, FBLA, peer helpers, SADD, MADD, Youth to Youth and other sober and drug free clubs)
- Faith-based youth programs
- Community youth centers
- Community anti-drug and alcohol coalitions
- Extracurricular activities encouraged and supported by parents: sport, hobbies, interests, musical instruments, drama, art, community service. Busy teens have no time to get in trouble!

And adults who care about our youth must take a stand and protest all forms of media that exploit the naiveté of our young: over-sexualizing at every turn; promoting violence as a praiseworthy means to an end; and aggrandizing hopelessness and inadequacy to teens in order to promote products. Let your voice be heard. Many socially-redeeming non-profits provide opportunities to easily e-mail your congressional representatives and media with your opinions on these issues.

Most importantly, we must support other parents. The community, school, and religious community cannot do it all. More empathetic and involved parenting from the get-go does dramatically reduce teen problems.

Reach out to the poor and overworked; to the single parent – mom or dad; to the abandoned parent; and to families riddled with alcoholism, drug addiction, mental health issues and the subsequent financial affliction. **Provide adults with support, education, and recovery, because parents have always been – and continue to be – the greatest influence on their teens, for good or for bad.**

And, as my dear friend and conscientious parent role model, Toni always says, "Parenting a teen is not a popularity contest."

It requires much boldness, patience and a willingness to endure a teenager's bountiful energy, roller-coaster emotions, insatiable curiosity, and gut-wrenching moments of disdain and wrath!

My prayers go with each and every one of you who cared enough to take the time to read this book. Be you a parent, grandparent, aunt or uncle, teacher, counselor, therapist, probation officer, mentor, social worker, child advocate, or basic caring adult, you will be blessed as you offer a compassionate heart, a patient spirit, and an open mind to teens! Now, go listen to a teen today and don't forget to give and receive the hugs and encouragement!

Teen Poetry

Many teens find writing poetry the best vehicle for releasing the pent up emotions that otherwise drive them to drugs and alcohol, cutting on themselves and contemplating suicide.

Here are a few poems teens have written and agreed to have me share with you. It is their hope that adults will open up their minds and hearts to the severity of emotional pain many teens are in when rejected, abused and/or neglected by the parents they so desperately need to support them.

Though their poetry can seem very dark, it is actually the release of very distressed emotions. May these poems touch your heart and encourage your love to flow to teens within your sphere.

How Can You?

By Megan McIntosh

How can you write what you feel,
When you feel nothing at all?
How can you cry, when you hurt
If you're numb to the fall?
How can you smile at the world
If the world let's you down?
How can you swim in the sea,
If you'll only drown?
How can you speak,
If you don't have a voice?
How can you choose,
If you don't have a choice?
How can you breathe,
If you've no life to live?
How can you die,
If you cannot forgive?

A Sip of Pain

By Megan McIntosh

Pain soars through my veins,
I befriend the darkness,
I embrace my death,
I see you there, I need you now,
Your glitter is my freedom,
Your sweet pain I'll sip tonight,
not too much, not just yet,
they don't understand....I love you.
Caress me beautiful pain,
fall into my veins,
set me free, don't let me be.
I am, numb to you now,
so touch me more, let me soar,
I want to be no more.
We tried this several times before, and we've
failed, but help me now
realease me from my tomb.
I am trapped in flesh and bone,
a disease that burns and breathes,
kill me now, it festers....it seethes,
I love you pain, and your gentle embrace,
I am feable and frail, so caress me again,
and we'll follw the crimson river to death,
not too soon, not just yet.

Death

By Megan McIntosh

Death is the beginning
Death is the end
Death is me
You wanna tell a friend?
Death is a riddle
Death is a cure
Death is a medicine
Do you really wanna know more?
Death is a game
Death is a way out
Death is a chance
Will you carry it out?
Death is here
Death is now
Death will come
will you take the bow?
Death is my friend
Death is my love
Death is the almighty
Is it from above?
Do you understand me?
Do you even care?
Death does
I see it in its glare
Death is everything, that we see
Death, is it a part of me?
Death is the world's strife
Death is my hate
Could it be that death is life,
Or am I too late?

A Pet Called Emotion...

By Kat

The emotions inside...
(The heart...)

It's like a pet you never wanted
And it seems like you're stuck with it for life.
You try to starve it,
But you find yourself feeding it once in awhile.
You want it to go away,
Unnoticed.
But that never happens.
The hungrier it gets, the more of a savage it becomes
It scrounges for trash to pick at
And it survives...

You try to cover it up.
You throw it in your closet.
Along with old forgotten memories,
But it breaks the closet door down.
And it lives on...

You tease and play with it
You toss a distraction across the street,
In front of a truck.
But it always manages to get out of the way.
And it still lives on...

You hate it.
You wish it would just go away.
Go, and leave you alone.
But it won't,
Because someone gave it to you.
You're its master for now and forever.
It won't run away,

It won't die,
It won't hide...

How can you get rid of this thing?
You can't.
You just have to live with it.

INDEX

To contact Susie Vanderlip for speaking engagements at your school, conference, or community:

Call: 800-707-1977 or
E-mail: Susie@legacyofhope.com

LEGACY
3128 E. Chapman Avenue #112
Orange, CA 92869

Gratitude List

Practice replacing self-pity, gossip, judgements of others and critical thoughts of yourself with an 'Attitude of Gratitude!'

Begin by listing 5 or more things you are grateful for in your day:

Gratitude List

Gratitude List

Gratitude List

____

____

____

____

____

____

____

____

____

____

____

____

____

____

____

____

____

____

____

____

____

____

Notes

Notes